HMH SCIENCE DIMENSIONS™

ASSESSMENT GUIDE

Module K

4000559759

Printed in the U.S.A.

ISBN 978-0-544-88302-4

2 3 4 5 6 7 8 9 10 0928 26 25 24 23 22 21 20 19 18
4500703412 B C D E F G

Table of Contents

Introduction

Overview of NGSS Assessment in HMH Science Dimensions™

***HMH Science Dimensions* assessment has been specially designed to help ensure that your students have the knowledge and skills necessary to achieve the Next Generation Science Standards Performance Expectations.**

HMH Science Dimensions assessment has been designed using a scaffolded approach to help you identify how your students are progressing in their ability to apply knowledge to solve problems and explain phenomena.

HMH Science Dimensions formative and summative assessment options are intended to give you maximum flexibility in evaluating what your students know and what they can do. This assessment program is based on the principle that assessment can provide a valuable learning opportunity for students.

In an ideal world, all assessment is formative. But in reality, students must periodically demonstrate mastery of science concepts and science practices in a high-stakes environment. The summative assessments provided in this Assessment Guide can help you ensure that your students are prepared to demonstrate mastery of NGSS Performance Expectations in whatever form future high-stakes assessments may take, whether print, digital, or performance-based.

All *HMH Science Dimensions* tests are available online, in print, and in an editable Word format. All quizzes, tests, and performance-based assessments in this Assessment Guide have a digital component that provides the same interaction online. You may choose to use the digital path, the print path, or a combination of the two.

This Assessment Guide is your directory to assessment in *HMH Science Dimensions*. In it you'll find copy masters for Beginning-of-Year Tests, Unit Pretests, Lesson Quizzes, Unit Tests, End-of-Module benchmark tests, and Performance-Based Assessments. At the back of this Assessment Guide you will find answers, explanations of most answers, and scoring rubrics for constructed response questions. You will also find information about the Webb's Depth of Knowledge (DOK) for each item, and the NGSS dimensions aligned to each item.

The following pages will provide you with information about the structure and philosophy behind each type of assessment included in this Assessment Guide.

Scaffolding in HMH Science Dimensions *Assessments*

HMH Science Dimensions assessments are designed to increase in difficulty and complexity. Scaffolding occurs both within tests and between tests.

Within each test, students first encounter lower DOK items to help bolster their confidence. This scaffolding should enable students to build on the knowledge and understanding they initially demonstrate as they respond to more demanding items.

Scaffolding between tests is described by the DOK progression shown in the table below. Several of the test types described below and on the following pages can be used either as formative or as summative instruments, depending on whether you use them primarily for teaching or primarily for evaluation.

DOK Progression in *HMH Science Dimensions* Assessment

Formative Assessment
Beginning-of-Year Test: DOK 1 and 2; consists of multiple choice and technology-enhanced items
Unit Pretest: DOK 1; consists of multiple choice
Lesson Quiz: mostly DOK 1 and 2; consists of multiple choice and constructed response items
Summative Assessment
Unit Test (A and B): DOK 1, 2, and 3; consists of multiple choice, technology-enhanced items, constructed response items, and interrelated item clusters
End-of-Module Test (A and B): mostly DOK 2 and 3; consists of multiple choice, technology-enhanced items, constructed response items, and interrelated item clusters
Performance-Based Assessment: DOK 2 and 3 items; hands-on performance demonstrating DOK 4; consists of open-ended activities and a summative interrelated item cluster

Skills Measurement in HMH Science Dimensions *Assessments*

The primary skills measurement used in *HMH Science Dimensions* to drive scaffolding is Depth of Knowledge (DOK). In addition, assessment items include Bloom's Traditional and Bloom's Revised process skills information.

Webb's Depth of Knowledge (DOK) for Science

DOK 1 Recall and Reproduction requires recall of information, such as a fact, definition, term, or a simple procedure, as well as performing a simple science process or procedure. DOK 1 keywords include *identify*, *name*, *list*, *label*, and *define*.

DOK 2 Skills and Concepts requires mental processing beyond simple recall. Items require students to make a connection between one concept and another, or recall and use a relationship between concepts. DOK 2 keywords include *predict*, *summarize*, *classify*, *relate*, and *graph*.

DOK 3 Strategic Thinking requires deep knowledge using reasoning, evidence, planning, or analysis of relationships among concepts. These items include tasks that require multiple mental steps to arrive at an answer. DOK 3 keywords include *compare*, *critique*, *revise*, and *explain phenomena*.

DOK 4 Extended Thinking requires high cognitive demand and is very complex. Students are required to relate ideas within or among content areas and to select or devise an approach for designing an experiment or solving a problem. The Performance-Based Assessments provide a DOK 4 level of assessment.

Bloom's Traditional

Bloom's Traditional taxonomy includes six categories of increasingly complex cognitive levels.

Knowledge requires students to recognize and recall facts and data.

Comprehension requires students to interpret, translate, summarize, or paraphrase information.

Application requires students to use information in a different context.

Analysis requires students to separate a whole into parts and show relationships among the parts.

Synthesis requires students to combine elements into a new form.

Evaluation requires students to apply rational criteria to judge or make decisions.

Bloom's Revised

Bloom's Revised taxonomy comprises six categories, some of which are equivalent to those in Bloom's Traditional taxonomy.

Remembering requires students to recall information, facts, procedures, or concepts.

Understanding requires students to explain and recognize the implications of ideas, concepts, methods, or procedures.

Applying requires students to use information or carry out a procedure in a setting similar to the example.

Analyzing requires students to use information or carry out a procedure in a different setting.

Evaluating requires students to justify a decision or a course of action.

Creating requires students to generate new ideas, products, or ways of viewing things, or reorganize elements into a new pattern.

Formative Assessment

Assessing Prior Knowledge, Addressing Misconceptions, and Informing Remediation

Beginning-of-Year Test

The Beginning-of-Year Test is made up of questions representative of the concepts found in the Performance Expectations from Grade 5. This test can help you identify areas in which students may require reteaching or additional support throughout the upcoming year.

There is one Beginning-of-Year Test for each domain, Life, Earth, and Physical Science. The Beginning-of-Year test for each domain can be found in the first module for that domain.

The Life Science Beginning-of-Year Test is found at the beginning of Module B.

The Earth Science Beginning-of-Year Test is found at the beginning of Module E.

The Physical Science Beginning-of-Year Test is found at the beginning of Module I.

Unit Pretest

Each of the units begins with a Unit Pretest that assesses prior knowledge related to the upcoming unit content. The Unit Pretest can be used to help you identify gaps in prerequisite knowledge and vocabulary, and ensure that misconceptions are identified and addressed during the course of the lessons.

Lesson Quiz

The Lesson Quizzes are designed to provide short-interval checkpoints to ensure student comprehension of lesson concepts before continuing to the next lesson. They can be used to guide reteaching and remediation.

Classroom Discussion

Discussion offers an organic opportunity to gauge how well students are absorbing the material, and to assess any misconceptions or gaps in their understanding. Students also learn from each other in this informal exchange.

Tips for Classroom Discussion

- Allow students plenty of time to reflect and formulate their answers.
- Call on students if you sense they have something to add but haven't spoken yet.
- At the same time, allow reluctant students not to speak unless they choose to.
- Encourage students to respond to each other as well as to you.

Summative Assessment

Demonstrating Mastery of NGSS Disciplinary Core Ideas, Crosscutting Concepts, and Science and Engineering Practices

Unit Tests (Test A)

The on-level Unit Tests (Test A) provide assessment of the specific dimensions of the Performance Expectations that are associated with the unit content. Unit Tests incorporate interrelated item clusters centered around one topic that offer a more robust assessment of Performance Expectations. Unit Tests also incorporate three-dimensional rubrics associated with open-ended items. These rubrics can help you determine how students are progressing toward mastery of Disciplinary Core Ideas, Crosscutting Concepts, and Science and Engineering Practices.

Unit Tests (Test B)

The modified Unit Tests (Test B) are targeted to help struggling readers and English language learners demonstrate their abilities related to the specific dimensions of the Performance Expectations that are associated with the unit content. These items have a slightly lower difficulty and reading level, but are visually identical to the on-level tests and assess the same NGSS dimensions. The digital versions of these tests include audio for added reading support.

End-of-Module Tests (Test A)

The on-level End-of-Module Tests (Test A) are designed to help you assess student ability to achieve the Performance Expectations in a format that helps to prepare students for next generation standardized assessments. These tests are primarily made up of technology-enhanced items, interrelated item clusters, and incorporate three-dimensional rubrics to help identify mastery of all three dimensions.

End-of-Module Tests (Test B)

Like the modified Unit Tests, the modified End-of-Module Tests (Test B) are targeted to help struggling readers and English language learners demonstrate their science mastery with less emphasis on reading ability. These items have a slightly lower difficulty and reading level but are visually identical to the on-level test, and assess the same NGSS dimensions. The digital versions of these tests include audio for added reading support.

Performance-Based Assessments

Performance-Based Assessments (PBAs) provide authentic hands-on assessment of the Performance Expectations. The PBAs are targeted to fully assess Performance Expectations that require a hands-on aspect for full completion. They also combine aspects of multiple Performance Expectations to give students the opportunity to make connections across content areas. The PBAs allow students to demonstrate their ability to perform Science and Engineering Practices and apply Crosscutting Concepts to solve problems, explain phenomena, and make conceptual connections across Disciplinary Core Ideas and Performance Expectations.

Interrelated Item Clusters

As specifically called for by the developers of the NGSS, *HMH Science Dimensions* incorporates interrelated sets of assessment items, or item clusters, in Unit Tests, End-of-Module Tests, and Part 2 of the Performance-Based Assessments. Very rarely can a single question address an entire Performance Expectation. In order to allow students to demonstrate understanding of Disciplinary Core Ideas, use Science and Engineering Practices, and apply Crosscutting Concepts, multiple opportunities must be provided. Clustering items around a single topic provides the opportunity to dive deeper into a concept, and allows students to demonstrate the extent of their progress toward achieving a Performance Expectation.

Three-Dimensional Rubrics

Evidence-Based Scoring on the NGSS Three Dimensions

Open-ended assessment items in *HMH Science Dimensions* Unit Tests, End-of-Module Tests, and Part 2 of Performance-Based Assessments are scored using a three-dimensional rubric that allows you to evaluate student responses on all of the NGSS dimensions aligned to the question.

These rubrics rely on an evidence-based approach to assessment that evaluates student-generated responses against specific claims and evidence of mastery.

Not all questions will be aligned to all three dimensions. Some focus on Science and Engineering Practices (SEPs) in the context of a Disciplinary Core Idea (DCI). Some focus on applying Crosscutting Concepts (CCCs) in the context of a Disciplinary Core Idea (DCI). Still others focus on evaluating student understanding of the Disciplinary Core Ideas (DCI) themselves.

The following example demonstrates a three-dimensional rubric for a question aligned to all three dimensions. The Claims section identifies the knowledge or skill the student should demonstrate related to a particular dimension. The Evidence of Mastery sections provide an explanation for an adequate student response in order for the student to receive full credit for that NGSS dimension.

DCI, SEP, CCC - 3 points	
Claims	The student is able to: 1. precisely define the design task's criteria (DCI); and 2. identify constraints that limit the design (SEP); and 3. list possible impacts of technology on people and the environment (CCC).
Evidence of Mastery of Disciplinary Core Ideas	1 point for correctly calculating the number of generators needed, providing a precise criterion **Part 2:** One point is earned for calculating the number of generators needed. To calculate the number of generators needed, students should divide 45,000 kWh/day by 50 kWh/day. This gives the student 900 wave generators that are needed to fully replace the fuel-burning power plant. The following response, or an equivalent, is acceptable. • 900 wave generators
Evidence of Mastery of Science and Engineering Practices	1 point for correctly identifying one constraint related to installing wave generators **Part 1:** One point is earned for identifying one constraint related to the use of wave generators, such as ocean depth, space around the generators, and the ability to transport the electrical energy. The following response, or an equivalent, is acceptable. • A constraint might be that the ocean has to be at least 45 meters deep in that area.
Evidence of Mastery of Crosscutting Concepts	1 point for correctly identifying possible impacts of wave generators **Part 3:** One point is earned for identifying one possible environmental impact and one possible impact to humans of using wave generators. The following response, or an equivalent, is acceptable. • One impact on humans could be that boats could run into the wave generators and be damaged. One environmental impact would be that they wouldn't have to burn fossil fuels, reducing air pollution.

Performance-Based Assessment (PBA)

HMH Science Dimensions Performance-Based Assessments (PBAs) provide students with an authentic hands-on opportunity to demonstrate science and engineering practices, to solve complex problems, and to make connections among NGSS Performance Expectations.

Each Performance-Based Assessment consists of two or three performance tasks followed by a summative Part 2 section of questions. The performance tasks include teacher support for materials and preparation, answers, sample models, and support for guiding students through open-ended performance assessment. Each task also includes observational rubrics to help you score student performance. Supplemental Teacher Materials found online provide additional tips for administering these Performance-Based Assessments.

Using Performance-Based Assessment

The key to performance-based assessment is observation. Before beginning a PBA, make a plan for observation that will allow you to observe all students as they are demonstrating skills. Review the rubric in advance so you know what to look for and are well prepared to evaluate student performance. Review the student procedure and make a note of steps in which you would expect to see students demonstrating specific skills identified in the observational rubric.

Administering PBA Tasks

Collaboration: PBA tasks are designed to allow students to interact and to work either collaboratively or independently. You can decide, based on time, materials availability, and classroom dynamics, whether you would like students to work individually or in groups. Additionally, opportunities are provided within certain PBAs for peer assessment and student feedback.

Resources: Many tasks will require student research. Consider in advance whether you will allow students to use their textbooks, library books, or Internet search access. If Internet research is required, be sure to secure time in the computer lab or allow students to bring their own devices as needed. Because these PBAs are also available digitally, you have the option to allow students to use a device such as a computer or tablet to record their progress.

Scoring the Tasks: You may choose to score student performance of the hands-on tasks using the observational rubric only, as a true performance assessment. You may also incorporate procedure and summary items into the task scores. Additionally, task procedure and summary responses can serve as notes available for students to use during the summative Part 2 portion of the PBA.

No Score: If you are unable to observe all students performing all of the rubric criteria, the "no score" option is available to avoid deducting points from students who may have performed the skill well but simply were not seen.

Accommodations: The supplemental materials include some suggestions for accommodating students with special needs. For each task you'll want to consider ways to allow all students to participate in a manner that is consistent with their abilities.

Administering PBA Part 2

Part 2 of the Performance-Based Assessment is a summative item cluster. It is intended to be completed independently. You can decide whether or not students will be allowed to use their notes from the tasks when completing Part 2. Alternately, you may choose not to assign Part 2 and score only the performance aspect of these PBAs.

PBA as Project-Based Learning

Performance-Based Assessments can also be used as a learning tool. Options for Project-Based Learning are included in the teacher support for each PBA.

Safety Symbols in PBAs

Because performance-based assessments incorporate hands-on investigations, there are safety considerations associated with them. The following safety symbols will appear in the teacher materials and student instructions for performance-based assessments when appropriate to emphasize important notes of caution. Share this information with students to help them learn what the symbols represent so that they can take the appropriate precautions.

	**Eye Protection** • Wear approved safety goggles at all times in the lab as directed. • If chemicals get into your eyes, flush your eyes immediately. • Do not wear contact lenses in the lab. • Do not look directly at the sun or any intense light source or laser.
	**Hand Safety** • Do not cut an object while holding the object in your hand. • Wear appropriate protective gloves when working with an open flame, chemicals, solutions, or wild or unknown plants. • Use a heat-resistant mitt to handle equipment that may be hot.
	**Clothing Protection** • Wear an apron or lab coat at all times in the lab. • Tie back long hair, secure loose clothing, and remove loose jewelry so that they do not knock over equipment, get caught in moving parts, or come into contact with hazardous materials or electrical connections. • Do not wear open-toed shoes, sandals, or canvas shoes in the lab. • When outside for lab, wear long sleeves, long pants, socks, and closed shoes.
	**Glassware Safety** • Inspect glassware before use; do not use chipped or cracked glassware. • Use heat-resistant glassware for heating materials or storing hot liquids. • Notify your teacher immediately if a piece of glassware or a light bulb breaks.
	**Sharp-Object Safety** • Use extreme care when handling all sharp and pointed instruments. • Cut objects on a suitable surface, always in a direction away from your body. • Be aware of sharp objects or edges on equipment or apparatus.
	**Scissors Safety** • Use care when cutting with scissors. • Do not run with scissors.
	**Chemical Safety** • If a chemical gets on your skin, on your clothing, or in your eyes, rinse it immediately (shower, faucet or eyewash fountain) and alert your teacher. • Do not clean up spilled chemicals yourself unless your teacher directs you to do so. • Do not inhale any gas or vapor unless your teacher directs you to do so. • Handle materials that emit vapors or gases in a well-ventilated area.
	Electrical Safety • Do not use equipment with frayed electrical cords or loose plugs. • Fasten electrical cords to work surfaces by using tape. • Do not use electrical equipment near water or when clothing or hands are wet. • Hold the plug housing when you plug in or unplug equipment. • Be aware that wire coils in electrical circuits may heat up rapidly.

Safety Symbols, cont.

Heating Safety

- Be aware of any source of flames, sparks, or heat (such as open flames, heating coils, or hot plates) before working with any flammable substances.
- Avoid using open flames.
- Know the location of lab fire extinguishers and fire-safety blankets.
- Know your school's fire-evacuation routes.
- If your clothing catches on fire, walk to the lab shower to put out the fire.
- Never leave a hot plate unattended while it is turned on or while it is cooling.
- Use tongs or appropriate insulated holders when handling heated objects.
- Allow all equipment to cool before storing it.

Plant Safety

- Do not eat any part of a plant or plant seed.
- When outside, do not pick any wild plants unless your teacher instructs you to do so.
- Wash your hands thoroughly after handling any part of a plant.

Animal Safety

- Handle animals only as your teacher directs.
- Treat animals carefully and respectfully.
- Wash your hands thoroughly after handling any animal.

Proper Waste Disposal

- Clean and sanitize all work surfaces and personal protective equipment after each lab period as directed by your teacher.
- Dispose of hazardous materials only as directed by your teacher.
- Dispose of sharp objects (such as broken glass) in the appropriate sharps or broken glass container as directed by your teacher.

Hygienic Care

- Keep your hands away from your face while you are working on any activity.
- Wash your hands thoroughly before you leave the lab or after any activity.
- Remove contaminated clothing immediately.

Classroom Observation

Use this checklist to help you observe Science and Engineering Practices.

Rating Scale	
3 Outstanding	1 Needs Improvement
2 Satisfactory	0 Did Not Demonstrate Skill
NS Did not have the opportunity to observe	

Teacher Directions:

This rubric allows for performance observation of 12 students. Make copies as needed. If students are working in groups, record the group name.

Group Name ___________

Names of Students

Science and Engineering Practices												
Asking Questions												
Defining Problems												
Developing Models												
Using Models												
Planning Investigations												
Carrying Out Investigations												
Analyzing Data												
Interpreting Data												
Using Mathematics and Computational Thinking												
Constructing Explanations												
Designing Solutions												
Engaging in Argument from Evidence												
Obtaining and Evaluating Information												
Communicating Information												
Total												

Portfolio Assessment

Guidelines for Student Evaluation through Portfolio Assessment

A portfolio is a showcase for student work, a place where many types of assignments, projects, reports, and data sheets can be collected. The work samples in the collection provide snapshots of the student's efforts over time, and taken together they reveal the student's growth, attitudes, and understanding. Portfolio assessment involves meeting with each student to discuss the work and to set goals for future performance. In contrast with formal assessments, portfolio assessments have these advantages:

1. They give students a voice in the assessment process.

2. They foster reflection, self-monitoring, and self-evaluation.

3. They provide a comprehensive picture of a student's progress.

Tips for Portfolio Assessment

- Make a basic plan. Decide how many work samples will be included in the portfolios and what period of time they represent.
- Explain the portfolio and its use. Describe the portfolio an artist might put together, showing his or her best or most representative work, as part of an application for school or a job. The student's portfolio is based on this model.
- Together with your class decide on the required work samples that everyone's portfolio will contain.
- Explain that the students will choose additional samples of their work to include. Have students remember how their skills and understanding have grown over the period covered by the portfolio, and review their work with this in mind. The best pieces to choose may not be the longest or neatest.
- Have students record their reasoning as they make their selections and assemble their portfolios.
- Explain to students how you will evaluate the contents of their portfolios.
- Use the portfolios for conferences, grading, and planning. Give students the option of taking their portfolios home to share.

My Science Portfolio

What Is in My Portfolio	Why I Chose It
1.	
2.	
3.	
4.	
5.	
6.	
7.	

I organized my Science Portfolio this way because ______________________________

____

____

____

____

____

Student Presentation

Guidelines for Evaluating Student Written, Oral, and Visual Presentations

The following guidelines can be used as a starting point for evaluating student presentation of alternative assessments. For each category, use only the criteria that are relevant for the particular format you are evaluating; some criteria will not apply for certain formats.

Written Work

- Matches the assignment in format (essay, journal entry, newspaper report, etc.)
- Begins with a clear statement of the topic and purpose
- Provides information that is essential to the reader's understanding
- Includes supporting details that are precise, related to the topic, and effective
- Follows a logical pattern of organization
- Uses transitions between ideas
- When appropriate, uses diagrams or other visuals
- Uses correct spelling, capitalization, and punctuation
- Uses correct grammar and usage
- Varies sentence structures
- Writes neatly and legibly

Posters and Displays

- Matches the assignment in format (brochure, poster, storyboard, etc.)
- Presents well-researched topic and quality information
- Communicates an obvious, overall message on the poster
- Uses large titles on poster, with obvious message or purpose
- Conveys important information by using images that are big and clear
- Gives more important ideas and items more space and uses larger images or text
- Uses colors for a purpose, such as to link words and images
- Uses visual cues, such as arrows, letters, or numbers, to make sequence of presentation easy to follow
- Uses artistic elements that are appropriate and add to the overall presentation
- Uses neat text
- Follows rules for correct spelling, capitalization, and punctuation of captions and labels

Oral Presentations

- Matches the assignment in format (speech, news report, etc.)
- Delivers presentation with enthusiasm for topic
- Pronounces words clearly and can easily be heard
- Presents information in a logical, interesting sequence that the audience can follow
- Uses visual aids that are relevant to content, very neat, and artistic
- Often makes eye contact with audience
- Listens carefully to questions from the audience and responds accurately
- Stands straight, facing the audience
- Uses movements appropriate to the presentation; does not fidget
- Covers the topic well in the time allowed
- Gives enough information to clarify the topic, but does not include irrelevant details

Multimedia Presentations

- Researches topic well and presents essential information
- Shows evidence of an original and inventive approach to product
- Conveys an obvious overall message in presentation
- Contains all the required media elements, such as text, graphics, sounds, videos, and animations
- Uses fonts and formatting appropriately to emphasize words; uses color appropriately to enhance the fonts
- Uses logical sequence of presentation and/or easy and understandable navigation
- Uses artistic elements that are appropriate and add to the overall presentation
- Effectively combines multimedia elements with words and ideas
- Follows rules for correct spelling, capitalization, and punctuation of written elements

Next Generation Science Standards

Standards Codes in HMH Science Dimensions *Assessment*

The following tables provide the coding system used in *HMH Science Dimensions.* This coding system allows you to track student progress on all three dimensions of the NGSS.

The original NGSS documents provide codes for the Performance Expectations and for the headings for the Disciplinary Core Ideas. These codes are reflected in the following tables of codes.

In addition, we have developed an intuitive coding system for the bulleted standards statements of the Disciplinary Core Ideas (DCI), the Science and Engineering Practices (SEP), and the Crosscutting Concepts (CCC).

These *HMH NGSS Three Dimensions* standards codes are available to download to your learning management system from Academic Benchmarks. The use of the *HMH NGSS Three Dimensions* standards codes will allow you to track student progress toward mastery of all three dimensions of the Next Generation Science Standards. They will also help you target remediation to fit each student's needs as they work toward mastery of Performance Expectations.

An important feature of this set of NGSS standards codes is that each SEP and CCC statement is represented by a single code. Across the middle school grade band, the same SEP and CCC standards appear repeatedly and are reinforced through the course of student learning. By using the *HMH NGSS Three Dimensions* codes, you can track student progress and target remediation for all three dimensions of NGSS, in addition to tracking progress toward the Performance Expectations.

Middle School Physical Science Performance Expectations

PE Title	PE codes	PE Text
Matter and Its Interactions	**MS-PS1-1**	Develop models to describe the atomic composition of simple molecules and extended structures.
Matter and Its Interactions	**MS-PS1-2**	Analyze and interpret data on the properties of substances before and after the substances interact to determine if a chemical reaction has occurred.
Matter and Its Interactions	**MS-PS1-3**	Gather and make sense of information to describe that synthetic materials come from natural resources and impact society.
Matter and Its Interactions	**MS-PS1-4**	Develop a model that predicts and describes changes in particle motion, temperature, and state of a pure substance when thermal energy is added or removed.
Matter and Its Interactions	**MS-PS1-5**	Develop and use a model to describe how the total number of atoms does not change in a chemical reaction and thus mass is conserved.
Matter and Its Interactions	**MS-PS1-6**	Undertake a design project to construct, test, and modify a device that either releases or absorbs thermal energy by chemical processes.
Motion and Stability: Forces and Interactions	**MS-PS2-1**	Apply Newton's Third Law to design a solution to a problem involving the motion of two colliding objects.
Motion and Stability: Forces and Interactions	**MS-PS2-2**	Plan an investigation to provide evidence that the change in an object's motion depends on the sum of the forces on the object and the mass of the object.
Motion and Stability: Forces and Interactions	**MS-PS2-3**	Ask questions about data to determine the factors that affect the strength of electric and magnetic forces.
Motion and Stability: Forces and Interactions	**MS-PS2-4**	Construct and present arguments using evidence to support the claim that gravitational interactions are attractive and depend on the masses of interacting objects.
Motion and Stability: Forces and Interactions	**MS-PS2-5**	Conduct an investigation and evaluate the experimental design to provide evidence that fields exist between objects exerting forces on each other even though the objects are not in contact.
Energy	**MS-PS3-1**	Construct and interpret graphical displays of data to describe the relationships of kinetic energy to the mass of an object and to the speed of an object.
Energy	**MS-PS3-2**	Develop a model to describe that when the arrangement of objects interacting at a distance changes, different amounts of potential energy are stored in the system.

Middle School Physical Science Performance Expectations, cont.

PE Title	PE codes	PE Text
Energy	**MS-PS3-3**	Apply scientific principles to design, construct, and test a device that either minimizes or maximizes thermal energy transfer.*
Energy	**MS-PS3-4**	Plan an investigation to determine the relationships among the energy transferred, the type of matter, the mass, and the change in the average kinetic energy of the particles as measured by the temperature of the sample.
Energy	**MS-PS3-5**	Construct, use, and present arguments to support the claim that when the kinetic energy of an object changes, energy is transferred to or from the object.
Waves and Their Applications in Technologies for Information Transfer	**MS-PS4-1**	Use mathematical representations to describe a simple model for waves that includes how the amplitude of a wave is related to the energy in a wave.
Waves and Their Applications in Technologies for Information Transfer	**MS-PS4-2**	Develop and use a model to describe that waves are reflected, absorbed, or transmitted through various materials.
Waves and Their Applications in Technologies for Information Transfer	**MS-PS4-3**	Integrate qualitative scientific and technical information to support the claim that digitized signals are a more reliable way to encode and transmit information than analog signals.
Engineering Design	**MS-ETS1-1**	Define the criteria and constraints of a design problem with sufficient precision to ensure a successful solution, taking into account relevant scientific principles and potential impacts on people and the natural environment that may limit possible solutions.
Engineering Design	**MS-ETS1-2**	Evaluate competing design solutions using a systematic process to determine how well they meet the criteria and constraints of the problem.
Engineering Design	**MS-ETS1-3**	Analyze data from tests to determine similarities and differences among several design solutions to identify the best characteristics of each that can be combined into a new solution to better meet the criteria for success.
Engineering Design	**MS-ETS1-4**	Develop a model to generate data for iterative testing and modification of a proposed object, tool, or process such that an optimal design can be achieved.

* The Performance Expectations marked with an asterisk integrate traditional science content with engineering.

Middle School Physical Science Disciplinary Core Ideas

DCI Title	DCI Code	DCI Text
Matter and Its Interactions	**DCI.MS-PS1.A.1**	Substances are made from different types of atoms, which combine with one another in various ways. Atoms form molecules that range in size from two to thousands of atoms. (MS-PS1-1)
Matter and Its Interactions	**DCI.MS-PS1.A.2**	Solids may be formed from molecules, or they may be extended structures with repeating subunits (e.g., crystals). (MS-PS1-1)
Matter and Its Interactions	**DCI.MS-PS1.A.3**	Each pure substance has characteristic physical and chemical properties (for any bulk quantity under given conditions) that can be used to identify it. (MS-PS1-2),(MS-PS1-3)
Matter and Its Interactions	**DCI.MS-PS1.A.4**	Gases and liquids are made of molecules or inert atoms that are moving about relative to each other. (MS-PS1-4)
Matter and Its Interactions	**DCI.MS-PS1.A.5**	In a liquid, the molecules are constantly in contact with others; in a gas, they are widely spaced except when they happen to collide. In a solid, atoms are closely spaced and may vibrate in position but do not change relative locations. (MS-PS1-4)
Matter and Its Interactions	**DCI.MS-PS1.A.6**	The changes of state that occur with variations in temperature or pressure can be described and predicted using these models of matter. (MS-PS1-4)
Matter and Its Interactions	**DCI.MS-PS1.B.1**	Substances react chemically in characteristic ways. In a chemical process, the atoms that make up the original substances are regrouped into different molecules, and these new substances have different properties from those of the reactants. (MS-PS1-2),(MS-PS1-3),(MS-PS1-5)
Matter and Its Interactions	**DCI.MS-PS1.B.2**	The total number of each type of atom is conserved, and thus the mass does not change. (MS-PS1-5)
Matter and Its Interactions	**DCI.MS-PS1.B.3**	Some chemical reactions release energy, others store energy. (MS-PS1-6)
Motion and Stability: Forces and Interactions	**DCI.MS-PS2.A.1**	For any pair of interacting objects, the force exerted by the first object on the second object is equal in strength to the force that the second object exerts on the first, but in the opposite direction (Newton's third law). (MS-PS2-1)

Middle School Physical Science Disciplinary Core Ideas, cont.

DCI Title	DCI Code	DCI Text
Motion and Stability: Forces and Interactions	**DCI.MS-PS2.A.2**	The motion of an object is determined by the sum of the forces acting on it; if the total force on the object is not zero, its motion will change. The greater the mass of the object, the greater the force needed to achieve the same change in motion. For any given object, a larger force causes a larger change in motion. (MS-PS2-2)
Motion and Stability: Forces and Interactions	**DCI.MS-PS2.A.3**	All positions of objects and the directions of forces and motions must be described in an arbitrarily chosen reference frame and arbitrarily chosen units of size. In order to share information with other people, these choices must also be shared. (MS-PS2-2)
Motion and Stability: Forces and Interactions	**DCI.MS-PS2.B.1**	Electric and magnetic (electromagnetic) forces can be attractive or repulsive, and their sizes depend on the magnitudes of the charges, currents, or magnetic strengths involved and on the distances between the interacting objects. (MS-PS2-3)
Motion and Stability: Forces and Interactions	**DCI.MS-PS2.B.2**	Gravitational forces are always attractive. There is a gravitational force between any two masses, but it is very small except when one or both of the objects have large mass—e.g., Earth and the sun. (MS-PS2-4)
Motion and Stability: Forces and Interactions	**DCI.MS-PS2.B.3**	Forces that act at a distance (electric, magnetic, and gravitational) can be explained by fields that extend through space and can be mapped by their effect on a test object (a charged object, or a ball, respectively). (MS-PS2-5)
Energy	**DCI.MS-PS3.A.1**	The term "heat" as used in everyday language refers both to thermal energy (the motion of atoms or molecules within a substance) and the transfer of that thermal energy from one object to another. In science, heat is used only for this second meaning; it refers to the energy transferred due to the temperature difference between two objects. (secondary to MSPS1- 4)
Energy	**DCI.MS-PS3.A.2**	The temperature of a system is proportional to the average internal kinetic energy and potential energy per atom or molecule (whichever is the appropriate building block for the system's material). The details of that relationship depend on the type of atom or molecule and the interactions among the atoms in the material. Temperature is not a direct measure of a system's total thermal energy. The total thermal energy (sometimes called the total internal energy) of a system depends jointly on the temperature, the total number of atoms in the system, and the state of the material. (secondary to MS-PS1-4)

Middle School Physical Science Disciplinary Core Ideas, cont.

DCI Title	DCI Code	DCI Text
Energy	**DCI.MS-PS3.A.3**	Motion energy is properly called kinetic energy; it is proportional to the mass of the moving object and grows with the square of its speed. (MS-PS3-1)
Energy	**DCI.MS-PS3.A.4**	A system of objects may also contain stored (potential) energy, depending on their relative positions. (MS-PS3-2)
Energy	**DCI.MS-PS3.A.5**	Temperature is a measure of the average kinetic energy of particles of matter. The relationship between the temperature and the total energy of a system depends on the types, states, and amounts of matter present. (MS-PS3-3),(MS-PS3-4)
Energy	**DCI.MS-PS3.B.1**	Energy is spontaneously transferred out of hotter regions or objects and into colder ones. (MS-PS3-3)
Energy	**DCI.MS-PS3.B.2**	The amount of energy transfer needed to change the temperature of a matter sample by a given amount depends on the nature of the matter, the size of the sample, and the environment. (MS-PS3-4)
Energy	**DCI.MS-PS3.B.3**	When the motion energy of an object changes, there is inevitably some other change in energy at the same time. (MS-PS3-5)
Energy	**DCI.MS-PS3.C.1**	When two objects interact, each one exerts a force on the other that can cause energy to be transferred to or from the object. (MS-PS3-2)
Energy	**DCI.MS-PS3.D.1**	The chemical reaction by which plants produce complex food molecules (sugars) requires an energy input (i.e., from sunlight) to occur. In this reaction, carbon dioxide and water combine to form carbon-based organic molecules and release oxygen. (secondary to MS-LS1-6)
Energy	**DCI.MS-PS3.D.2**	Cellular respiration in plants and animals involve chemical reactions with oxygen that release stored energy. In these processes, complex molecules containing carbon react with oxygen to produce carbon dioxide and other materials. (secondary to MS-LS1-7)
Waves and Their Applications in Technologies for Information Transfer	**DCI.MS-PS4.A.1**	A simple wave has a repeating pattern with a specific wavelength, frequency, and amplitude. (MS-PS4-1)

Middle School Physical Science Disciplinary Core Ideas, cont.

DCI Title	DCI Code	DCI Text
Waves and Their Applications in Technologies for Information Transfer	**DCI.MS-PS4.A.2**	A sound wave needs a medium through which it is transmitted. (MS-PS4-2)
Waves and Their Applications in Technologies for Information Transfer	**DCI.MS-PS4.B.1**	When light shines on an object, it is reflected, absorbed, or transmitted through the object, depending on the object's material and the frequency (color) of the light. (MS-PS4-2)
Waves and Their Applications in Technologies for Information Transfer	**DCI.MS-PS4.B.2**	The path that light travels can be traced as straight lines, except at surfaces between different transparent materials (e.g., air and water, air and glass) where the light path bends. (MS-PS4-2)
Waves and Their Applications in Technologies for Information Transfer	**DCI.MS-PS4.B.3**	A wave model of light is useful for explaining brightness, color, and the frequency-dependent bending of light at a surface between media. (MS-PS4-2)
Waves and Their Applications in Technologies for Information Transfer	**DCI.MS-PS4.B.4**	However, because light can travel through space, it cannot be a matter wave, like sound or water waves. (MS-PS4-2)
Engineering Design	**DCI.MS-ETS1.A.1**	The more precisely a design task's criteria and constraints can be defined, the more likely it is that the designed solution will be successful. Specification of constraints includes consideration of scientific principles and other relevant knowledge that are likely to limit possible solutions. (MS-ETS1-1)
Engineering Design	**DCI.MS-ETS1.B.1**	A solution needs to be tested, and then modified on the basis of the test results, in order to improve it. (MS-ETS1-4)
Engineering Design	**DCI.MS-ETS1.B.2**	There are systematic processes for evaluating solutions with respect to how well they meet the criteria and constraints of a problem. (MS-ETS1-2), (MS-ETS1-3)
Engineering Design	**DCI.MS-ETS1.B.3**	Sometimes parts of different solutions can be combined to create a solution that is better than any of its predecessors. (MS-ETS1-3)
Engineering Design	**DCI.MS-ETS1.B.4**	Models of all kinds are important for testing solutions. (MS-ETS1-4)

Middle School Physical Science Disciplinary Core Ideas, cont.

DCI Title	DCI Code	DCI Text
Engineering Design	**DCI.MS-ETS1.C.1**	Although one design may not perform the best across all tests, identifying the characteristics of the design that performed the best in each test can provide useful information for the redesign process—that is, some of those characteristics may be incorporated into the new design. (MS-ETS1-3)
Engineering Design	**DCI.MS-ETS1.C.2**	The iterative process of testing the most promising solutions and modifying what is proposed on the basis of the test results leads to greater refinement and ultimately to an optimal solution. (MS-ETS1-4)

Middle School Science and Engineering Practices

SEP Heading	SEP Code	SEP Text
Asking Questions and Defining Problems	**SEP.MS.A.1**	Ask questions to identify and/or clarify evidence and/or the premise(s) of an argument.
Asking Questions and Defining Problems	**SEP.MS.A.2**	Ask questions that can be investigated within the scope of the classroom, outdoor environment, and museums and other public facilities with available resources and, when appropriate, frame a hypothesis based on observations and scientific principles.
Asking Questions and Defining Problems	**SEP.MS.A.3**	Define a design problem that can be solved through the development of an object, tool, process or system and includes multiple criteria and constraints, including scientific knowledge that may limit possible solutions.
Developing and Using Models	**SEP.MS.B.1**	Develop a model to describe unobservable mechanisms.
Developing and Using Models	**SEP.MS.B.2**	Develop and/or use a model to generate data to test ideas about phenomena in natural or designed systems, including those representing inputs and outputs, and those at unobservable scales.
Developing and Using Models	**SEP.MS.B.3**	Develop and/or use a model to predict and/or describe phenomena.
Planning and Carrying Out Investigations	**SEP.MS.C.1**	Collect data to produce data to serve as the basis for evidence to answer scientific questions or test design solutions under a range of conditions.
Planning and Carrying Out Investigations	**SEP.MS.C.2**	Conduct an investigation and/or evaluate and/or revise the experimental design to produce data to serve as the basis for evidence that meet the goals of the investigation.
Planning and Carrying Out Investigations	**SEP.MS.C.3**	Plan an investigation individually and collaboratively, and in the design: identify independent and dependent variables and controls, what tools are needed to do the gathering, how measurements will be recorded, and how many data are needed to support a claim.
Analyzing and Interpreting Data	**SEP.MS.D.1**	Analyze and interpret data to determine similarities and differences in findings.
Analyzing and Interpreting Data	**SEP.MS.D.2**	Analyze and interpret data to provide evidence for phenomena.
Analyzing and Interpreting Data	**SEP.MS.D.3**	Construct, analyze, and/or interpret graphical displays of data and/or large data sets to identify linear and nonlinear relationships.

Middle School Science and Engineering Practices, cont.

SEP Heading	SEP Code	SEP Text
Using Mathematics and Computational Thinking	**SEP.MS.E.1**	Use mathematical representations to describe and/or support scientific conclusions and design solutions.
Constructing Explanations and Designing Solutions	**SEP.MS.F.1**	Construct an explanation that includes qualitative or quantitative relationships between variables that predict(s) and/or describe(s) phenomena.
Constructing Explanations and Designing Solutions	**SEP.MS.F.2**	Construct a scientific explanation based on valid and reliable evidence obtained from sources (including the students' own experiments) and the assumption that theories and laws that describe the natural world operate today as they did in the past and will continue to do so in the future.
Constructing Explanations and Designing Solutions	**SEP.MS.F.3**	Apply scientific ideas, principles, and/or evidence to construct, revise and/or use an explanation for real-world phenomena, examples, or events.
Constructing Explanations and Designing Solutions	**SEP.MS.F.4**	Apply scientific ideas or principles to design, construct, and/or test a design of an object, tool, process or system.
Constructing Explanations and Designing Solutions	**SEP.MS.F.5**	Undertake a design project, engaging in the design cycle, to construct and/or implement a solution that meets specific design criteria and constraints.
Engaging in Argument from Evidence	**SEP.MS.G.1**	Construct, use, and/or present an oral and written argument supported by empirical evidence and scientific reasoning to support or refute an explanation or a model for a phenomenon or a solution to a problem.
Engaging in Argument from Evidence	**SEP.MS.G.2**	Evaluate competing design solutions based on jointly developed and agreed-upon design criteria.
Obtaining, Evaluating, and Communicating Information	**SEP.MS.H.1**	Integrate qualitative and/or quantitative scientific and/or technical information in written text with that contained in media and visual displays to clarify claims and findings.
Obtaining, Evaluating, and Communicating Information	**SEP.MS.H.2**	Gather, read, and synthesize information from multiple appropriate sources and assess the credibility, accuracy, and possible bias of each publication and methods used, and describe how they are supported or not supported by evidence.
Scientific Knowledge is Based on Empirical Evidence	**SEP.NOS.MS.B.1**	Science knowledge is based upon logical and conceptual connections between evidence and explanations.

Middle School Science and Engineering Practices, cont.

SEP Heading	SEP Code	SEP Text
Scientific Knowledge is Based on Empirical Evidence	**SEP.NOS.MS.B.2**	Science disciplines share common rules of obtaining and evaluating empirical evidence.
Scientific Knowledge is Open to Revision in Light of New Evidence	**SEP.NOS.MS.C.1**	Science findings are frequently revised and/or reinterpreted based on new evidence.
Science Models, Laws, Mechanisms, and Theories Explain Natural Phenomena	**SEP.NOS.MS.D.1**	Laws are regularities or mathematical descriptions of natural phenomena.

Middle School Crosscutting Concepts

CCC heading	CCC Code	CCC Text
Patterns	**CCC.MS.A.1**	Macroscopic patterns are related to the nature of microscopic and atomic-level structure.
Patterns	**CCC.MS.A.2**	Patterns in rates of change and other numerical relationships can provide information about natural and human designed systems.
Patterns	**CCC.MS.A.3**	Patterns can be used to identify cause and effect relationships.
Patterns	**CCC.MS.A.4**	Graphs, charts, and images can be used to identify patterns in data.
Cause and Effect	**CCC.MS.B.1**	Relationships can be classified as causal or correlational, and correlation does not necessarily imply causation.
Cause and Effect	**CCC.MS.B.2**	Cause and effect relationships may be used to predict phenomena in natural or designed systems.
Cause and Effect	**CCC.MS.B.3**	Phenomena may have more than one cause, and some cause and effect relationships in systems can only be described using probability.
Scale, Proportion, and Quantity	**CCC.MS.C.1**	Time, space, and energy phenomena can be observed at various scales using models to study systems that are too large or too small.
Scale, Proportion, and Quantity	**CCC.MS.C.2**	Proportional relationships (e.g., speed as the ratio of distance traveled to time taken) among different types of quantities provide information about the magnitude of properties and processes.
Scale, Proportion, and Quantity	**CCC.MS.C.3**	Phenomena that can be observed at one scale may not be observable at another scale.
Systems and System Models	**CCC.MS.D.1**	Systems may interact with other systems; they may have sub-systems and be a part of larger complex systems.
Systems and System Models	**CCC.MS.D.2**	Models can be used to represent systems and their interactions—such as inputs, processes and outputs—and energy, matter, and information flows within systems.

Middle School Crosscutting Concepts, cont.

CCC heading	CCC Code	CCC Text
Energy and Matter	**CCC.MS.E.1**	Matter is conserved because atoms are conserved in physical and chemical processes.
Energy and Matter	**CCC.MS.E.2**	Within a natural or designed system, the transfer of energy drives the motion and/or cycling of matter.
Energy and Matter	**CCC.MS.E.3**	Energy may take different forms (e.g. energy in fields, thermal energy, energy of motion).
Energy and Matter	**CCC.MS.E.4**	The transfer of energy can be tracked as energy flows through a designed or natural system.
Structure and Function	**CCC.MS.F.1**	Complex and microscopic structures and systems can be visualized, modeled, and used to describe how their function depends on the shapes, composition, and relationships among its parts; therefore, complex natural and designed structures/systems can be analyzed to determine how they function.
Structure and Function	**CCC.MS.F.2**	Structures can be designed to serve particular functions by taking into account properties of different materials, and how materials can be shaped and used.
Stability and Change	**CCC.MS.G.1**	Explanations of stability and change in natural or designed systems can be constructed by examining the changes over time and forces at different scales, including the atomic scale.
Stability and Change	**CCC.MS.G.2**	Small changes in one part of a system might cause large changes in another part.
Stability and Change	**CCC.MS.G.3**	Stability might be disturbed either by sudden events or gradual changes that accumulate over time.
Scientific Knowledge Assumes an Order and Consistency in Natural Systems	**CCC.NOS.MS.A.1**	Science assumes that objects and events in natural systems occur in consistent patterns that are understandable through measurement and observation.
Science is a Human Endeavor	**CCC.NOS.MS.B.1**	Advances in technology influence the progress of science and science has influenced advances in technology.
Science is a Human Endeavor	**CCC.NOS.MS.B.2**	Scientists and engineers are guided by habits of mind such as intellectual honesty, tolerance of ambiguity, skepticism, and openness to new ideas.
Science Addresses Questions About the Natural and Material World.	**CCC.NOS.MS.C.1**	Scientific knowledge can describe the consequences of actions but does not necessarily prescribe the decisions that society takes.

Middle School Crosscutting Concepts, cont.

CCC heading	CCC Code	CCC Text
Interdependence of Science, Engineering, and Technology	**CCC.STSE.MS.A.1**	Engineering advances have led to important discoveries in virtually every field of science and scientific discoveries have led to the development of entire industries and engineered systems.
Influence of Engineering, Technology, and Science on Society and the Natural World	**CCC.STSE.MS.B.1**	All human activity draws on natural resources and has both short and long-term consequences, positive as well as negative, for the health of people and the natural environment.
Influence of Engineering, Technology, and Science on Society and the Natural World	**CCC.STSE.MS.B.2**	The uses of technologies and any limitations on their use are driven by individual or societal needs, desires, and values; by the findings of scientific research; and by differences in such factors as climate, natural resources, and economic conditions.
Influence of Engineering, Technology, and Science on Society and the Natural World	**CCC.STSE.MS.B.3**	Technology use varies over time and from region to region.
Influence of Engineering, Technology, and Science on Society and the Natural World	**CCC.STSE.MS.B.4**	Technologies extend the measurement, exploration, modeling, and computational capacity of scientific investigations.

Name: ______________________ Date: ______________

Unit 1
Unit Pretest

Pretest: Forces and Motion

Read each question. Circle the letter of the correct answer.

1. Which of the following is an action exerted on an object that may change the object's state of rest or motion?

A. mass

B. force

C. velocity

D. acceleration

2. Which of these units is the standard international unit of force?

A. gram

B. pound

C. newton

D. kilogram

3. A moving car backs into a parked car in a parking lot. Why would the bumpers on both cars be dented?

A. The parked car was made of weaker material than the car that was moving.

B. The car that was moving was made of weaker material than the parked car.

C. When one car bumps into the other car, they collide with equal and opposite force.

D. The bumpers of both cars would not have become dented as a result of this minor collision.

4. The same force is applied separately to two objects, A and B. B has twice the mass of A. What happens?

A. B's acceleration is half that of A.

B. B's acceleration is twice that of A.

C. B's acceleration is one-fourth that of A.

D. B's acceleration is four times that of A.

5. Which of these forces is being applied by the boy shown here?

A. gravitational force

B. fundamental force

C. contact force

D. field force

6. A metal ball sits motionless on a flat surface. Which of these would make the ball move?

A. The force of gravity becomes less.

B. The force of gravity becomes greater.

C. Two equal horizontal opposing forces act upon the ball.

D. Two unequal horizontal opposing forces act upon the ball.

7. There are four objects: A, B, C, and D. The distance between any two objects is the same.

Their masses are:

A = 2B

B = 1/4C

D = 3/4C

Which of the diagrams correctly ranks the interactions between these objects, in terms of their gravitational attractive forces, from strongest to weakest?

A. A–B, B–C, C–D, D–A

B. C–D, D–A, A–B, B–D

C. B–C, C–D, D–A, A–B

D. C–D, D–A, A–B, B–C

8. An index card is placed across the top of a drinking glass. A coin is then placed on top of the index card. A student quickly flicks the card sideways off the glass. Which of these explains why the coin falls into the glass rather than moving to the side with the index card?

A. Newton's first law of motion

B. Newton's second law of motion

C. Newton's third law of motion

D. Newton's law of universal gravitation

9. The picture shows an object resting on a balance.

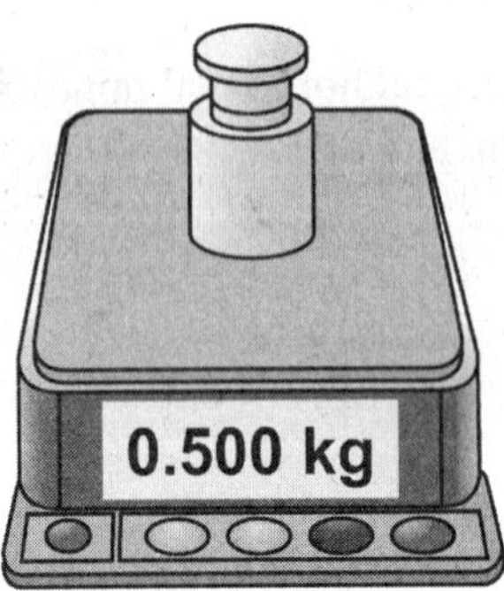

The weight of an object is given by $F = mg$, where $g = 9.8\ m/s^2$. With what force does the object push down on the balance?

A. 9.3 kg·m/s² **C.** 4.90 kg·m/s²

B. 9.8 kg·m/s² **D.** 0.500 kg·m/s²

10. Objects labeled A, B, and C all have the same distance from each other. The gravitational attraction between objects A and B is less than the attraction between objects B and C. The attraction between objects A and C is less than the attraction between the other two sets of objects. What is the relationship between the masses of objects A, B, and C?

A. The mass of object A equals the mass of object C.

B. The mass of object A equals the mass of object B.

C. The mass of A is less than C, which is less than B.

D. The mass of C is greater than B, which is greater than A.

11. What change could cause an apple hanging from a tree branch to fall?

A. loss of gravity

B. loss of a sideways force on the left

C. loss of a sideways force on the right

D. loss of the upwards force opposing gravity

12. Which force diagram shows an unbalanced force that will result in a change in the direction of an object's motion?

A. 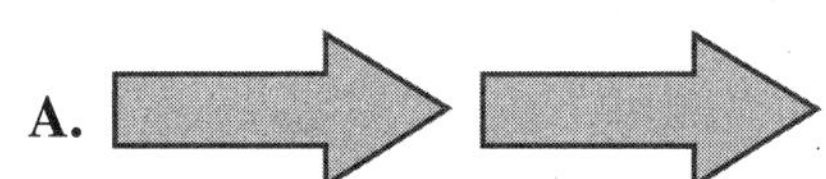

C. 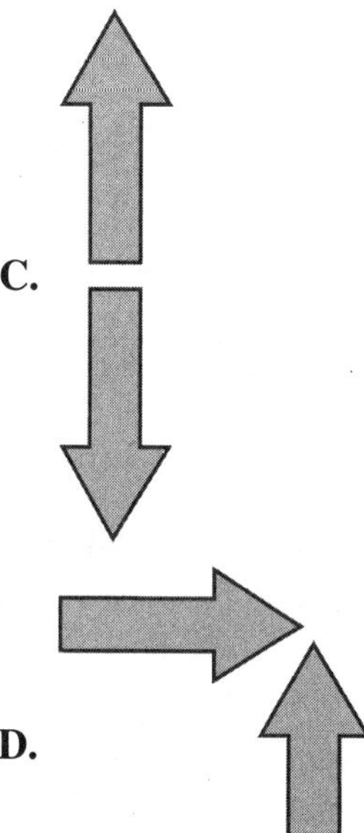

D.

B. 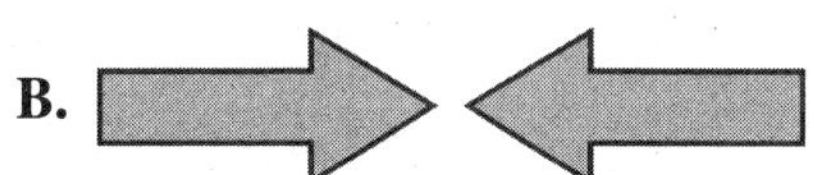

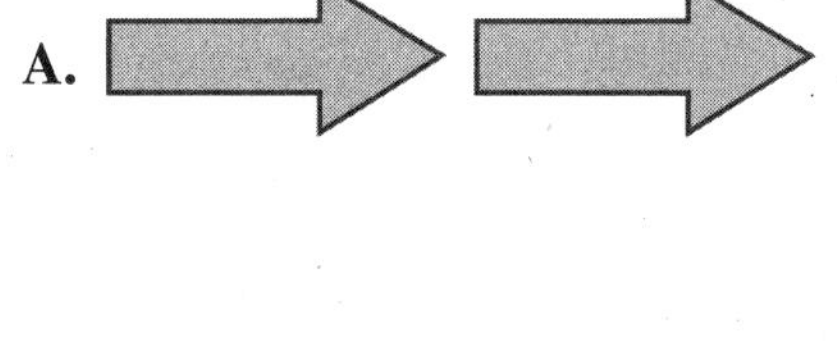

13. Between which of these objects will the gravitational force be the smallest, if the objects are the same distance apart?

A. a marble and a baseball

B. a marble and a bowling ball

C. a baseball and a bowling ball

D. a bowling ball and a basketball

14. A skydiver jumps out of a plane. She falls downward at a very fast speed. When she opens her parachute, she slows down. What force pulled the skydiver to the ground?

A. friction

B. gravity

C. air resistance

D. parachute pull

15. A tennis ball hits a wall. Which of these statements is true?

A. The tennis ball's force is unopposed by the wall.

B. The tennis ball's speed doubles when it hits the wall.

C. The wall exerts a force in the same direction as the tennis ball's force.

D. The wall exerts a force in the opposite direction to the tennis ball's force.

Quiz: Introduction to Forces

Read each question. Circle the letter of the correct answer.

1. What is gravity?

   A. a contact force

   B. a frictional force

   C. a magnetic force

   D. a noncontact force

2. Which of these is considered a contact force?

   A. the force between two magnets

   B. the gravitational pull of a planet

   C. the friction between an object and air

   D. the force between two charged particles

3. A box has two forces acting on it. One force is 100 N upward. Another force is 50 N downward. What is the net force on the box?

   A. 50 N upward

   B. 100 N upward

   C. 50 N downward

   D. 100 N downward

4. Melanie watched the path a baseball followed after a pitcher threw it. She noticed that the ball traveled horizontally away from the pitcher as well as downward toward the ground. What force caused the ball to accelerate in the downward direction when it was thrown?

   A. applied force

   B. air resistance

   C. electrical force

   D. gravitational force

5. Why are some forces considered to be noncontact forces?

   A. Objects must be far apart in order to exert a force.

   B. Objects do not have to touch each other to experience a force.

   C. Objects push each other apart to increase the distance between them.

   D. Objects must be large in size in order to exert a force that is strong enough to notice.

6. Why is the friction force considered to be a contact force?

   A. Friction affects only solid objects.

   B. Friction always acts in the same direction.

   C. Friction is produced when objects slide past one another.

   D. Friction acts in a direction opposite to the direction of an object's motion.

7. Why is the magnetic force considered to be a noncontact force?

   A. Magnets must be far apart in order to exert a force.

   B. Magnets do not have to touch each other to experience a force.

   C. Magnets push each other apart to increase the distance between them.

   D. Magnets must be large in size in order to exert a force that is strong enough to notice.

Name: ____________________ Date: ____________________

Unit 1 Lesson 1
Lesson Quiz

Read each statement. Write your answer on the lines.

8. A bird flies at 12.5 meters per second. The wind speed is 4.5 meters per second.

What is the speed of the bird when it flies with the wind?

____

____

What is the speed of the bird when it flies against the wind?

____

____

____

9. Marek is trying to push a box of sports equipment across the floor. The arrow on the box is a vector showing the force Marek exerts.

Describe all the forces acting on the box.

____

____

Explain what needs to happen for the box to start moving.

____

____

____

10. The diagram shows the forces acting on a box.

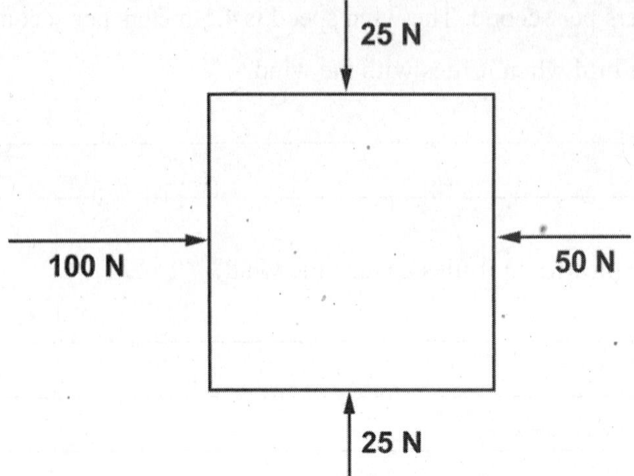

Explain how to calculate the net force in any direction on the box.

____

____

Determine the net force upward or downward.

____

____

Determine the net force to the right or left.

____

____

Predict how the box will move.

____

____

Quiz: Gravity and Friction

Read each question. Circle the letter of the correct answer.

1. Which of these describes the gravitational force from a planet?

A. large and pulls objects toward itself

B. small and pulls objects toward itself

C. large and pushes objects away from itself

D. small and pushes objects away from itself

2. Which pair of objects has the largest gravitational force?

A. marble and car

B. marble and baseball

C. car and bowling ball

D. There is no gravitational force between any of these pairs of objects.

3. Sean is moving heavy furniture by sliding it across the floor. He puts a blanket underneath the furniture. Why did this help him?

A. The blanket protects the side of the furniture from bumping against the wall.

B. The blanket reduces the gravitational force between the furniture and the floor.

C. The friction is larger between the blanket and the floor than between the furniture and the floor.

D. The friction is smaller between the blanket and the floor than between the furniture and the floor.

4. Two basketballs are sitting 1 m apart and are not moving. Which best explains why the gravitational force does not cause them to move?

A. No gravitational force exists between the two objects because they are not touching.

B. The gravitational force between the two objects is weak because they are 1 m apart.

C. No gravitational force exists between the two objects because their masses are small.

D. The gravitational force between the two objects is weak because their masses are small.

5. If someone drops a cup, it falls to the ground. Why doesn't the gravitational force between the person's hand and the cup keep the cup from falling?

A. The cup does not experience any gravitational force because it is not a planet.

B. The gravitational force between the hand and the cup is so strong that it pushes the cup down.

C. There is no gravitational force between the hand and the cup, so Earth's gravitational force pulls the cup down.

D. There is a gravitational force between the hand and the cup, but Earth's gravity is stronger, so Earth's gravity pulls the cup down.

6. In which situation is it better to have low friction?

   A. a skydiver uses a parachute

   B. a student walks down a hallway

   C. a ladder leans against the wall

   D. a hockey puck slides toward the goal

7. Planets A and B are both the same size, but planet B has three times the mass of planet A. How does the weight of an object compare on the two planets?

   A. The weight of an object is the same on both planets.

   B. The weight of an object is three times larger on planet A.

   C. The weight of an object is three times larger on planet B.

   D. The weight of an object will depend on more factors than just the weight and size of the planet.

Read each statement. Write your answer on the lines.

8. A spaceship is moving in a straight line on its way to a planet. The pilot sees that the planet is ahead and to the left. She claims that she does not need to use the engines to push the ship toward the planet. Explain why the pilot is correct or incorrect.

   ___

   ___

   ___

   ___

   ___

9. A carpenter uses sandpaper on a piece of wood. Before, the wood felt rough. After, the wood felt smooth.

   Did the friction between the hand and the wood increase or decrease after using the sandpaper?

   ___

   ___

   Describe what the sandpaper did to the wood to make it smoother.

   ___

   ___

   ___

10. Two objects, A and B, are 10 m apart. Objects C and D are 20 m apart. The gravitational attraction between objects C and D is greater than the attraction between objects A and B. Explain the reason for the difference in gravitational attraction.

____

____

____

____

____

Quiz: Newton's Laws of Motion

Read each question. Circle the letter of the correct answer.

1. Jessica is comparing two balls. One ball has a mass of 1 kg, and the other has a mass of 2 kg. She pushes each with a force of 100 N. How do the accelerations of the two balls compare?

   A. The 1 kg ball accelerates the same as the 2 kg ball.

   B. The 1 kg ball accelerates half as much as the 2 kg ball.

   C. The 1 kg ball accelerates twice as much as the 2 kg ball.

   D. The 1 kg ball accelerates four times as much as the 2 kg ball.

2. A fisherman steps off a boat, which is in the water, onto a dock. What happens?

   A. The boat and dock do not move.

   B. The boat moves toward the dock.

   C. The boat moves away from the dock.

   D. The dock moves away from the boat.

3. Look at the diagram of forces acting on an object.

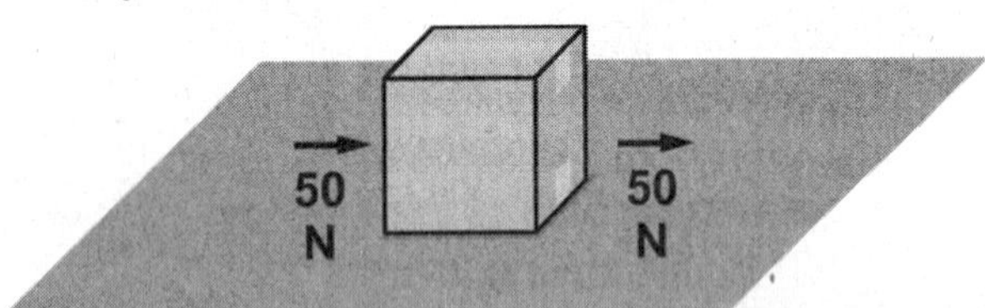

   The picture shows a push and a pull acting on a box of books sitting on the floor. What is the net force toward the right on the box?

   A. 0 N

   B. 50 N

   C. 100 N

   D. 2,500 N

4. When two objects having different masses collide, they move away from each other at different speeds. Which is true of the forces exerted at the moment of impact?

   A. The forces exerted when they collide are equal and opposing.

   B. The forces exerted when they collide are unequal and opposing.

   C. The forces exerted when they collide are equal and in the same direction.

   D. The forces exerted when they collide are unequal and in the same direction.

5. An airplane is traveling at a speed of 200 m/s relative to the Earth. A person walks toward the front of the plane at a speed of 1 m/s. How fast is that person traveling in reference to the other people on the airplane?

   A. 0 m/s

   B. 1 m/s

   C. 200 m/s

   D. 201 m/s

6. Two equal forces act in opposite directions on object A. Two unequal forces act in opposite directions on object B. If these are the only forces acting on objects A and B, which of these conclusions is true?

   A. Only object A will accelerate.

   B. Only object B will accelerate.

   C. Both object A and object B will accelerate.

   D. Neither object A nor object B will accelerate.

7. The diagram shows the forces acting on a running shoe.

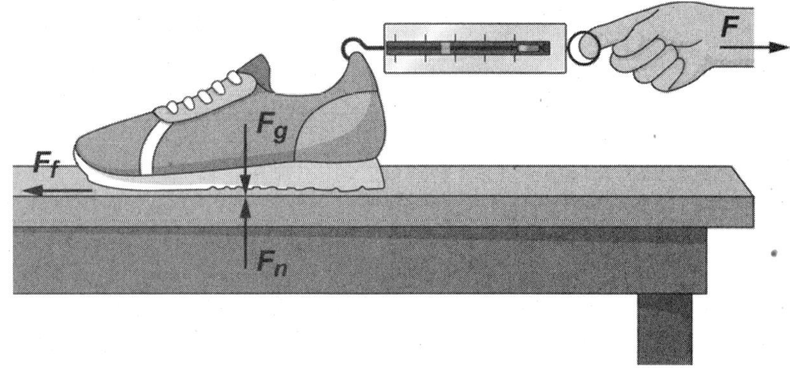

As force F is applied, the shoe does not move. Which statement describes the forces?

A. The net force is acting to the left.

B. The net force is moving to the right.

C. The net force is acting in an upward direction.

D. The net force is zero, and all the forces are balanced.

Read each statement. Write your answer on the lines.

8. A 1 kg object accelerates at a rate of 5 m/s^2. Calculate the net force on the object and explain how its motion is changing.

______

______

______

______

______

9. Describe the forces that are acting on a person who is standing still on a sidewalk, and identify whether the forces are balanced or unbalanced. Describe how the forces would change if the person started walking.

______

______

______

______

______

10. Two ice skaters on ice push away from each other. What will be the effect of the forces of their pushing each other if their masses are different?

___

___

___

___

___

Name: ______________________ Date: ______________________

Unit 1 Lesson 4
Lesson Quiz

Quiz: Engineer It • Collisions between Objects

Read each question. Circle the letter of the correct answer.

1. During a baseball game, a hitter strikes the ball with a bat. When this happens, the ball and the bat exert a force on each other. Why does the ball accelerate away from the bat more than the bat accelerates away from the ball?

   A. The ball has less mass, so it exerts less force on the bat.

   B. The ball has greater velocity before the collision, so the force affects the ball more than it affects the bat.

   C. The ball has less mass, so the equal force on the ball and the bat causes greater acceleration of the ball.

   D. The bat exerts more force than the ball because the batter is exerting a force on the bat as it hits the ball.

2. One marble is moving and collides with a stationary marble. Which of these statements is true?

   A. Each marble exerts a force on the other, and the two forces are equal and in opposite directions.

   B. Each marble exerts a force on the other, and the two forces are the same in magnitude and direction.

   C. Each marble exerts a force on the other, and the two forces are proportional to the masses of the marbles.

   D. The moving marble exerts a force on the stationary marble, but the stationary marble does not exert a force on the moving marble.

3. A soccer player kicks a ball. The player's foot exerts a force on the ball. The ball exerts a force on the foot. Why don't the forces cancel out to result in a net force of zero?

   A. The ball moves before the forces can cancel out.

   B. The forces become unbalanced due to air resistance.

   C. The force on the ball is greater than the force on the foot.

   D. The forces are exerted on different objects, and neither force is zero.

4. The front of a car is designed to crumple during a crash. What is the purpose of this?

   A. to decrease the mass of the car, decreasing the force of the collision

   B. to increase the amount of time it takes for the collision to occur, decreasing the force of the collision

   C. to increase the amount of time it takes for the collision to occur, decreasing the acceleration of the car

   D. to decrease the amount of time it takes for the collision to occur, increasing the acceleration of the car

5. A golfer has a choice of several golf clubs with different masses that he can use to hit a golf ball. He can swing all the clubs at the same speed. If he wants to hit the golf ball as far as possible, which club should he choose?

   A. the club with the greatest mass because it will have a greater acceleration

   B. the club with the smallest mass because it will have a greater acceleration

   C. the club with the greatest mass because it will provide the largest force to the golf ball

   D. the club with the smallest mass because it will provide the largest force to the golf ball

Read each statement. Write your answer on the lines.

6. A worker at a delivery company is packing a fragile object in a box. He needs to choose a material to go into the box to keep the object from breaking. Identify one property that the material must have in order to solve the design problem and explain why it must have this property.

____

____

____

____

____

7. In many sports, players wear helmets. A manufacturer is testing the performance of its helmets by pelting stationary helmets with balls. Describe the motion of both objects before and after the collision and explain how a helmet helps protect a player's head.

____

____

____

____

____

8. Two bumper cars move toward each other and collide. In what situation would they have the same acceleration during the collision?

Directions: Read the passage, then answer the questions that follow.

Newton's Third Law

Ben has two carts with masses of 100 g and 200 g. He pushes the smaller cart toward the larger cart and they collide. The smaller cart rebounds back in the direction it came from. He measures the force on the smaller cart from the larger cart to be 5 N.

9. What was the magnitude of the acceleration of the smaller cart?

Circle the letter of the correct answer.

A. 20 m/s^2

B. 50 m/s^2

C. 200 m/s^2

D. 500 m/s^2

10. What force does the smaller cart exert on the larger cart?

Circle the letter of the correct answer.

A. 2.50 N

B. 5 N

C. 10 N

D. 15 N

Name: ______________________ Date: ______________________

Unit Test: Forces and Motion

Read each question. Circle the letter of the correct answer.

1. What is a force?

A. a pull exerted on an object

B. a measure of how heavy an object is

C. a push or a pull exerted on an object

D. a change in the direction of motion of an object

2. Sasha pulls a block across the floor at a constant speed. Why doesn't the motion of the block change even though Sasha is pulling on it?

A. Sasha's force on the block is balanced by the friction force.

B. Sasha's force on the block is balanced by the gravitational force.

C. If Sasha was not pulling on the block, there would be no forces on the block, and it would speed up.

D. If Sasha was not pulling on the block, there would be no forces on the block, and it would stop moving.

3. When a comet enters the solar system, it curves toward the sun. Which statement describes why the sun does not move when a comet is nearby?

A. There is no force exerted on the sun from the comet.

B. There is no force exerted on the sun unless the sun and comet collide.

C. The force on the sun from the comet is smaller than the force on the comet from the sun because the comet's speed is too great.

D. The force on the sun from the comet is equal to the force on the comet from the sun but does not cause the sun to move because the sun is too massive.

4. The weights of four objects with different masses have been calculated to show how much each object would weigh on four different planets.

Based on the table, which object would have the largest mass and highest weight on Earth?

A. object A

B. object B

C. object C

D. object D

Weights of Four Objects on Four Planets

	Object A	Object B	Object C	Object D
Planet 1		10 N	1 N	20 N
Planet 2	10 N		0.2 N	4 N
Planet 3	100 N	20 N		40 N
Planet 4	5 N	1 N	0.1 N	

5. Rebecca is practicing her aim by throwing a ball at a target.

The ball exerts a force on the target, causing the target to fall over. But when this happens, the ball bounces backward. Why does the ball bounce backward?

A. The target exerts a larger force on the ball because the ball is very bouncy.

B. The ball exerts a larger force on the target, causing the target to have a larger change of motion than the ball.

C. The target exerts the same size force on the ball, so when the target moves in one direction, the ball moves in the opposite direction.

D. The ball exerts a smaller force on the target because the ball is smaller than the target, so the target causes the ball to bounce backward.

6. The diagram shows four blocks suspended on identical dynameters, a tool that is used for measuring the weights of objects.

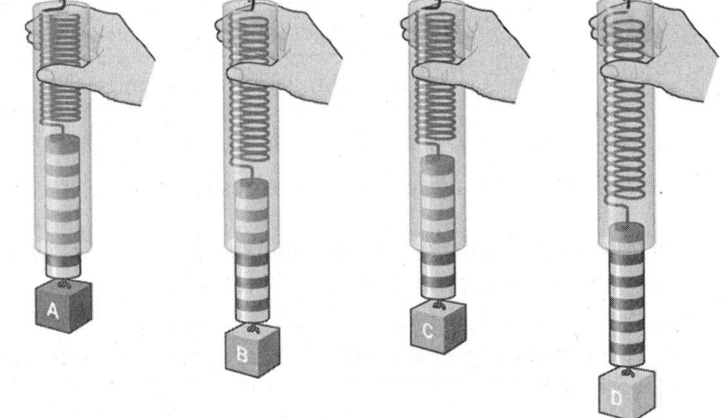

Which object has the largest weight?

A. object A

B. object B

C. object C

D. object D

7. Two cars travel on a straight road from point A to point B. Both cars accelerate to their maximum speed and then continue at that speed for the rest of the distance. Car 1 accelerates from rest to 20 m/s over 30 s. It reaches point B in 35 s. Car 2 accelerates from rest to 20 m/s over 20 s. It reaches point B in 30 s. Which car uses a larger acceleration to reach its maximum speed, and which car has a larger average speed?

A. Car 1 has both a larger acceleration and a larger average speed.

B. Car 2 has both a larger acceleration and a larger average speed.

C. Car 1 has a larger acceleration, but Car 2 has a larger average speed.

D. Car 2 has a larger acceleration, but Car 1 has a larger average speed.

Name: ______________________ Date: ______________________

Unit 1
Unit Test A

Read each question. Follow the instructions to answer the questions.

8. Chini is sliding blocks of different materials down a steel ramp. All of the blocks have similar sizes and masses. The table shows the coefficient of friction for several materials when sliding on steel. The larger the coefficient of friction, the greater the force of friction. In which order would the blocks reach the bottom of the ramp?

Number the materials from 1 to 5 with 1 as the material that will slide down the ramp the fastest and 5 as the material that will slide down the ramp the slowest.

__________ aluminum

__________ chromium

__________ glass

__________ steel

__________ titanium vanadium alloy

Material	Coefficient of friction
aluminum	0.25
chromium	0.21
glass	0.12
steel	0.23
titanium vanadium alloy	0.31

9. Write an X in the correct box for each statement to show whether each force is a contact force or a noncontact force.

Forces	Contact	Noncontact
A. gravity		
B. friction		
C. air resistance		
D. magnetic force		
E. pushing with your hands		

10. The arrows in the force diagrams represent the various forces acting on a box. The box starts out at rest.

Which diagrams match the descriptions? Write the letters of the diagrams in the correct boxes. Some boxes may contain more than one letter.

Starts moving to the left	Starts moving to the right	Stays at rest

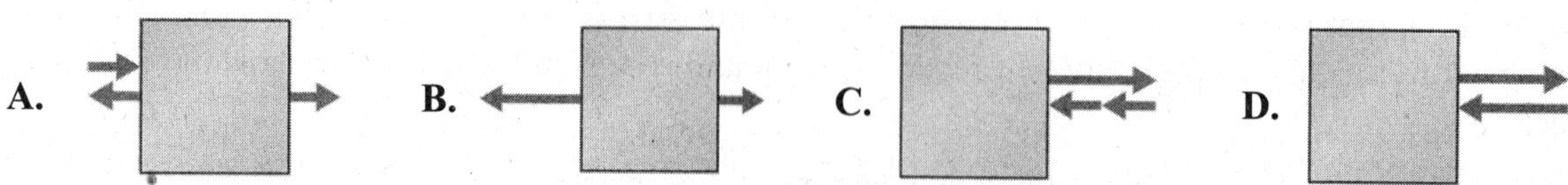

11. The diagram shows two massive objects and several points in between them.

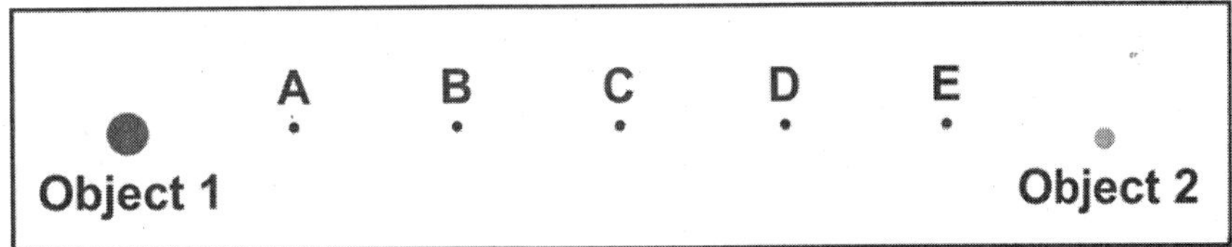

The table shows the gravitational forces from each of the two objects on a smaller 10 kg object placed at each of the points labeled A through E.

Gravitational Force on a 10 kg Object

Position	Force due to Object 1 (10^6 N)	Force due to Object 2 (10^6 N)
A	62	0.15
B	31	0.19
C	21	0.25
D	16	0.38
E	12	0.76

Henry claims that there must be a point in between points A and E where the total gravitational force is zero. Use evidence from the diagram and the table to support or refute Henry's claim.

Write the letters of the words in the boxes to correctly complete the sentences.

As the 10 kg object moves away from Object 1, the gravitational force from **1.**__________ gets larger, and the gravitational force from **2.**__________ gets smaller. At all of the points, the gravitational force from Object 1 is greater than the gravitational force from Object 2. Therefore, Henry is **3.**__________.

1. and **2.**	**3.**
A. Object 1	**E.** correct
B. Object 2	**F.** incorrect
C. both objects	
D. neither object	

12. Bill wants to do an investigation to compare the inertia of different balls. He plans to use a fan to exert a force on the balls. He will roll a ball past a fan to see how much the ball's movement changes. Bill will use several balls with different masses and use the same fan settings for each test. What are the components of his investigation?

Write the letter of the pictures or phrases that match each component of the investigation in the box next to the component. Some letters will not be used.

investigation setup	
dependent variable	
independent variable	

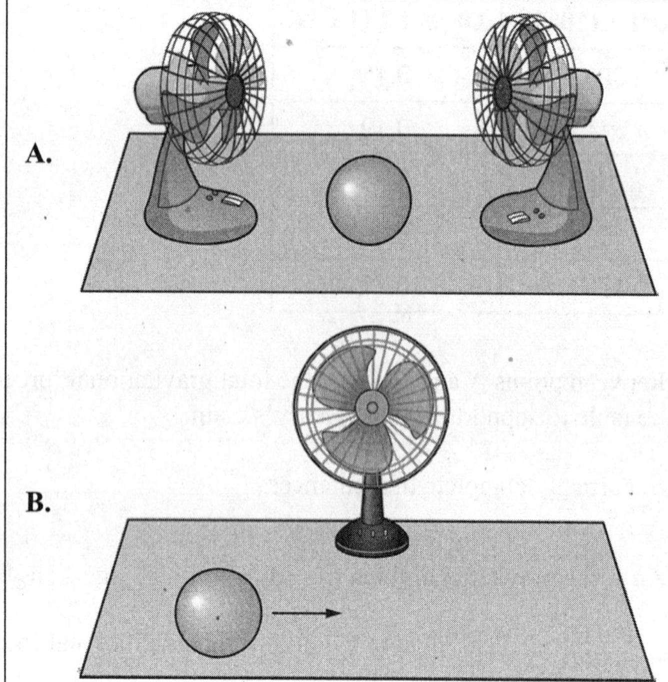

C. mass of the ball

D. color of the ball

E. mass of the fan or fans

F. speed of the fan or fans

G. direction of motion of the ball

H. direction of the fan or fans

13. An engineer is trying to improve the design of tent stakes, which are used to hold a tent in place on the ground. He is considering designing tent stakes that are larger than the ones currently available.

Write one letter in each blank to correctly complete the paragraph.

If the stakes are larger, then they will be **1.** __________, but they will require **2.** __________ to push the stake into the ground. If someone uses a heavy mallet to hit the stake, it will move the stake **3.** __________ than using a light hammer swung at the same speed. This is because the force exerted by the mallet is equal to the **4.** __________ multiplied by the acceleration.

1.	**2.**	**3.**	**4.**
A. ineffective	**D.** less force	**F.** less	**H.** size
B. less secure	**E.** more force	**G.** more	**I.** mass
C. more secure			**J.** speed

Read each statement. Write your answer on the lines.

14. At the start of a hockey game, the referee drops the puck between two players from opposing teams. Each player wants to push the puck in the opposite direction. For several seconds the puck does not move even though both players are pushing on it with their hockey sticks.

Identify the forces acting on the puck.

____

____

Explain why the puck does not move.

____

____

____

____

Describe how one of the players could get the puck to move in a direction she wants.

____

____

____

____

15. Christian is riding his bicycle. He finds that he can accelerate from rest at 0.44 m/s^2 for 5 s to reach a speed of 2.2 m/s. The total mass of Christian and his bicycle is 54 kg. Later, he straps some cargo onto the back of his bicycle. The mass of the cargo is 12 kg.

Calculate the force that Christian can exert on his bicycle before picking up the cargo and exerts the same force on his bicycle.

Calculate the acceleration of the bicycle when Christian adds the cargo and exerts the same force on his bicycle.

Identify how Christian could reach the same speed on his bicycle when he is carrying the cargo and explain your answer.

16. A competitive downhill skier has little control over the environmental conditions of the ski slope. But she can choose her equipment and practice her technique to help control her speed.

Identify the forces that are acting on the skier as she moves down the ski slope and describe how they result in her motion.

Describe one way the skier can change her equipment to increase her maximum speed.

Describe how the skier can use her body position to increase or decrease her velocity as she is skiing.

Directions: Read the passage, then answer the questions that follow.

Spaceship Shielding

A meteoroid is a small piece of rock in outer space. There are many meteoroids in space, and it is impossible for a spaceship to avoid all of them. Instead, the astronauts and equipment inside a spaceship are protected by shielding on the outside of the spaceship. The engineers that design spaceships need to take into account many factors to choose the right materials to use. The heavier a spaceship is, the more difficult and expensive it is to launch off of Earth and into space. Also, the spaceship must be able to survive the launch into space, which involves a lot of air resistance before it leaves the atmosphere of Earth. Once it gets into space, the shielding material must be able to protect the spaceship from meteoroids that collide with it.

To test new materials to help shield a spaceship from meteoroids, scientists built a device that can be used to launch rocks at a test sample. They are able to remove the air from the room where the sample is to model the environment in space. The picture shows an example of two samples after they were hit with a rock using the device.

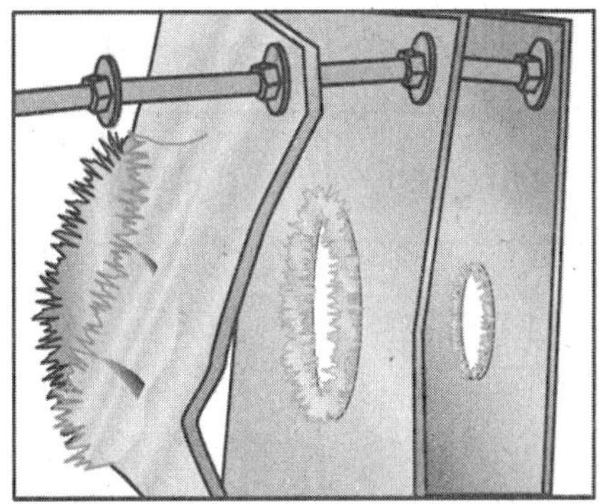

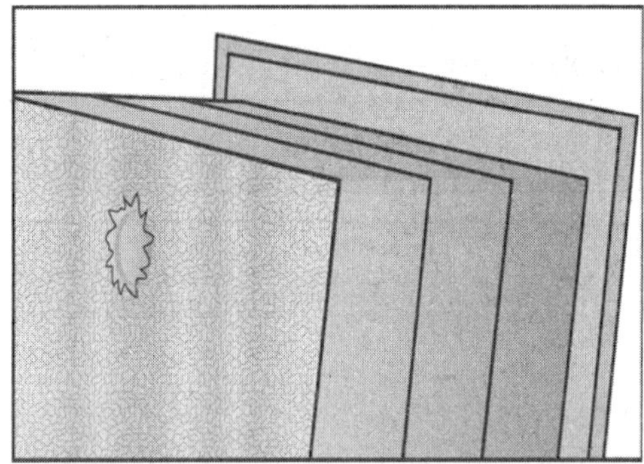

The first sample was made of multiple layers of steel. When the rock hit the first layer, it left a hole in that layer and the rock shattered into many pieces. The pieces continued to collide with the following layers, causing the holes to get larger as the rock pieces moved deeper into the shielding. The second sample was made out of a thick layer of foam covered with a thin layer of metal. The metal layer caused the rock to break apart, but then the foam absorbed the impact.

17. What are the criteria and/or constraints engineers must consider when designing shielding for spaceships?

Circle the letters of the three correct criteria and/or constraints.

A. must be light

B. must be hard

C. must be heavy

D. must be inexpensive

E. must be heat resistant

F. must absorb impacts

G. must be able to be made very thin

18. A group of engineers is designing a space station that will orbit a planet. They want to build windows so that the astronauts who stay on the space station can see outside. If there is a cloud of meteoroids that comes nearby, the astronauts will be able to lower shielding on the windows to give them extra protection. However, the windows should still be able to protect them from different-sized meteoroids that hit one at a time. The engineers decided on the criteria for the material for the windows as shown.

- protects against a meteoroid collision
- transparent or mostly transparent

The testing results of three materials are shown in the chart.

	Material 1	Material 2	Material 3
Transparency	completely transparent	mostly transparent	mostly transparent
Weight for one pane	24 kg	24 kg	33 kg
Hit with a small meteoroid	not damaged	not damaged	not damaged
Hit with a large meteoroid	damaged	not damaged	damaged
Hit with a shower of small meteoroids	damaged	damaged	not damaged

The engineers decided to use Material 2. Did they make the right decision?

Circle the letter of the correct answer.

A. no, because Material 2 is not completely transparent

B. no, because Material 2 cannot protect from meteoroid showers

C. yes, because Material 2 is the lightest material that still protects against small meteoroids

D. yes, because only Material 2 protects from different-sized meteoroids and is mostly transparent

19. The picture shows a spaceship and a meteoroid before, during, and after a collision in space. The arrows in the *Before* picture show the velocities of the spaceship and the meteoroid before the collision. Since the spaceship is moving faster, it has a longer arrow. The spaceship is more massive than the meteoroid.

- Draw arrows to show the directions of the forces of the spaceship and the meteoroid on the *During* collision picture.
- Draw arrows to show the directions of the velocities for the spaceship and the meteoroid on the *After* collision picture.

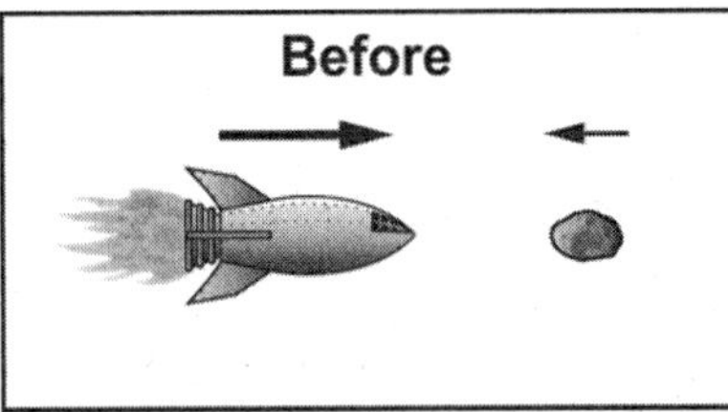

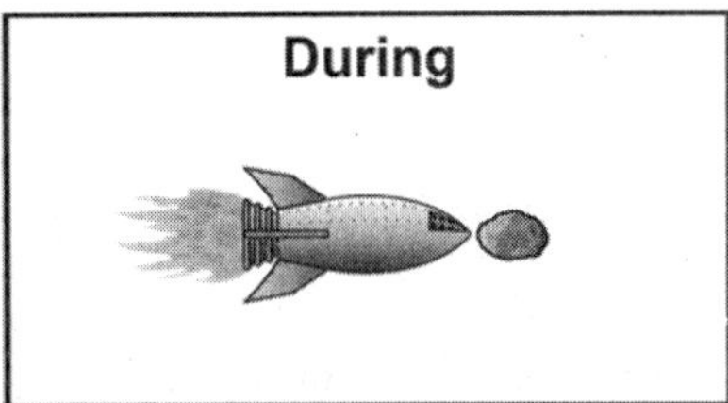

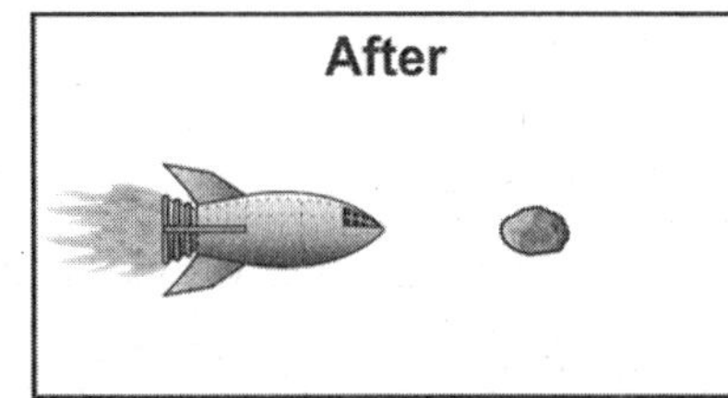

20. A student wants to set up a demonstration to show how Newton's second and third laws of motion apply to collisions between a meteoroid and a stationary spaceship in space. The student has a model spaceship, a lab stand, baseballs, cotton balls, marbles, and string.

Write your answer on the lines.

Identify which materials the student should use in the demonstration. Explain why the student should choose these materials.

____

____

____

____

Explain how the demonstration shows Newton's second and third laws.

____

____

____

____

Unit Test: Forces and Motion

Read each question. Circle the letter of the correct answer.

1. What is a force?

A. a pull exerted on an object

B. a push or a pull exerted on an object

C. a change in the direction of motion of an object

2. Sasha pulls a block across the floor at a constant speed. Why doesn't the motion of the block change even though Sasha is pulling on it?

A. Sasha's force on the block is balanced by the friction force.

B. Sasha's force on the block is balanced by the gravitational force.

C. If Sasha was not pulling on the block, there would be no forces on the block, and it would stop moving.

3. When a comet enters the solar system, it curves toward the sun. Which statement describes why the sun does not move when a comet is nearby?

A. There is no force exerted on the sun unless the sun and comet collide.

B. The force on the sun from the comet is smaller than the force on the comet from the sun because the comet's speed is too great.

C. The force on the sun from the comet is equal to the force on the comet from the sun but does not cause the sun to move because the sun is too massive.

4. The weights of four objects with different masses have been calculated to show how much each object would weigh on four different planets.

Based on the table, which object would have the largest mass and highest weight on Earth?

A. object A

B. object B

C. object C

D. object D

Weights of Four Objects on Four Planets

	Object A	Object B	Object C	Object D
Planet 1		10 N	1 N	20 N
Planet 2	10 N		0.2 N	4 N
Planet 3	100 N	20 N		40 N
Planet 4	5 N	1 N	0.1 N	

5. Rebecca is practicing her aim by throwing a ball at a target.

The ball exerts a force on the target, causing the target to fall over. But when this happens, the ball bounces backward. Why does the ball bounce backward?

A. The ball exerts a larger force on the target, causing the target to have a larger change of motion than the ball.

B. The target exerts the same size force on the ball, so when the target moves in one direction, the ball moves in the opposite direction.

C. The ball exerts a smaller force on the target because the ball is smaller than the target, so the target causes the ball to bounce backward.

6. The diagram shows four blocks suspended on identical dynameters, a tool that is used for measuring the weights of objects.

Which object has the largest weight?

A. object A

B. object B

C. object C

D. object D

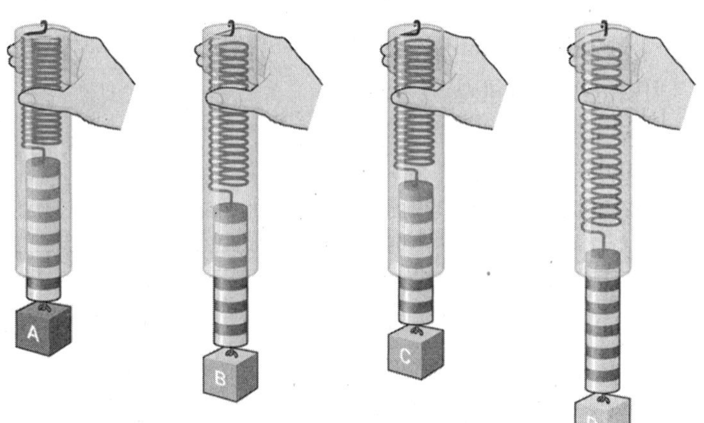

7. Two cars travel on a straight road from point A to point B. Both cars accelerate to their maximum speed and then continue at that speed for the rest of the distance. Car 1 accelerates from rest to 20 m/s over 30 s. It reaches point B in 35 s. Car 2 accelerates from rest to 20 m/s over 20 s. It reaches point B in 30 s. Which car uses a larger acceleration to reach its maximum speed, and which car has a larger average speed?

A. Car 1 has both a larger acceleration and a larger average speed.

B. Car 2 has both a larger acceleration and a larger average speed.

C. Car 2 has a larger acceleration, but Car 1 has a larger average speed.

Read each question. Follow the instructions to answer the questions.

8. Chini is sliding blocks of different materials down a steel ramp. All of the blocks have similar sizes and masses. The table shows the coefficient of friction for several materials when sliding on steel. The larger the coefficient of friction, the greater the force of friction. In which order would the blocks reach the bottom of the ramp?

Number the materials from 1 to 5 with 1 as the material that will slide down the ramp the fastest and 5 as the material that will slide down the ramp the slowest.

Material	Coefficient of friction
aluminum	0.25
chromium	0.21
glass	0.12
steel	0.23
titanium vanadium alloy	0.31

_________ aluminum

_________ chromium

_________ glass

_________ steel

_________ titanium vanadium alloy

9. Write an X in the correct box for each statement to show whether each force is a contact force or a noncontact force.

Forces	Contact	Noncontact
A. gravity		
B. air resistance		
C. magnetic force		
D. pushing with your hands		

10. The arrows in the force diagrams represent the various forces acting on a box. The box starts out at rest.

Which diagrams match the descriptions? Write the letters of the diagrams in the correct boxes.

Starts moving to the left	Starts moving to the right	Stays at rest

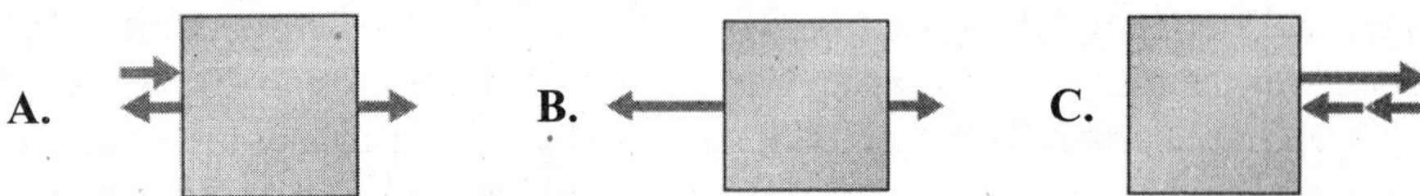

11. The diagram shows two massive objects and several points in between them.

A B C D E

Object 1 Object 2

The table shows the gravitational forces from each of the two objects on a smaller 10 kg object placed at each of the points labeled A through E.

Gravitational Force on a 10 kg Object

Position	Force due to Object 1 (10^6 N)	Force due to Object 2 (10^6 N)
A	62	0.15
B	31	0.19
C	21	0.25
D	16	0.38
E	12	0.76

Henry claims that there must be a point in between points A and E where the total gravitational force is zero. Use evidence from the diagram and the table to support or refute Henry's claim.

Write the letters of the words in the boxes to correctly complete the sentences.

As the 10 kg object moves away from Object 1, the gravitational force from **1.**__________ gets larger, and the gravitational force from **2.**__________ gets smaller. At all of the points, the gravitational force from Object 1 is greater than the gravitational force from Object 2. Therefore, Henry is **3.**__________.

1. and **2.**	**3.**
A. Object 1	**C.** correct
B. Object 2	**D.** incorrect

12. Bill wants to do an investigation to compare the inertia of different balls. He plans to use a fan to exert a force on the balls. He will roll a ball past a fan to see how much the ball's movement changes. Bill will use several balls with different masses and use the same fan settings for each test. What are the components of his investigation?

Write the letter of the pictures or phrases that match each component of the investigation into the box next to the component. Some letters will not be used.

investigation setup	
dependent variable	
independent variable	

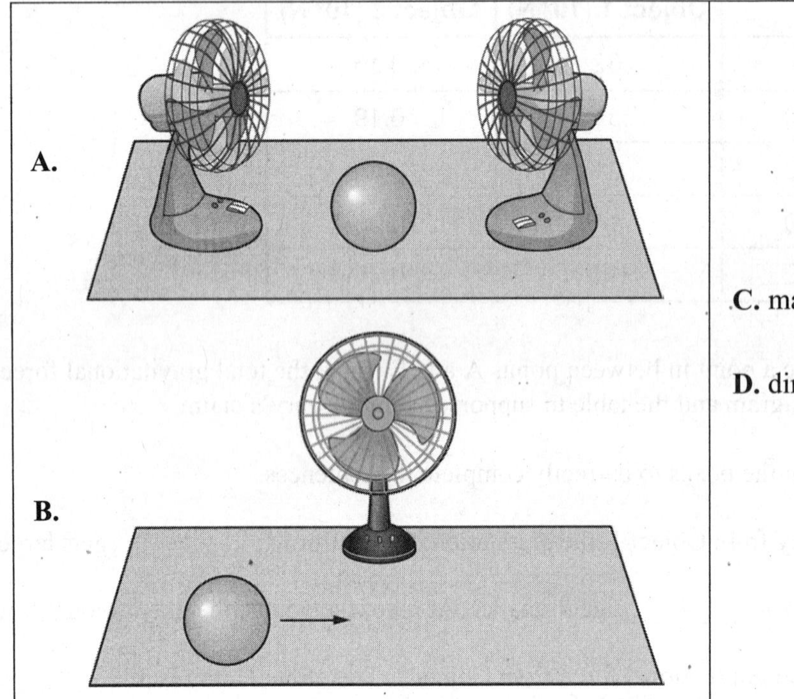

C. mass of the ball

D. direction of motion of the ball

13. An engineer is trying to improve the design of tent stakes, which are used to hold a tent in place on the ground. He is considering designing tent stakes that are larger than the ones currently available.

Write one letter in each blank to correctly complete the paragraph.

If the stakes are larger, then they will be **1.** __________, but they will require **2.** __________ to push the stake into the ground. If someone uses a heavy mallet to hit the stake, it will move the stake more than using a light hammer swung at the same speed. This is because the force exerted by the mallet or the hammer is equal to the **3.** __________ multiplied by the acceleration.

1.	**2.**	**3.**
A. less secure	**C.** less force	**E.** size
B. more secure	**D.** more force	**F.** mass

Read each statement. Write your answer on the lines.

14. At the start of a hockey game, the referee drops the puck between two players from opposing teams. Each player wants to push the puck in the opposite direction. For several seconds the puck does not move even though both players are pushing on it with their hockey sticks.

Identify the forces acting on the puck.

____

____

Explain why the puck does not move.

____

____

____

____

15. Christian is riding his bicycle. He finds that he can accelerate from rest at 0.44 m/s^2 for 5 s to reach a speed of 2.2 m/s. The total mass of Christian and his bicycle is 54 kg. Later, he straps some cargo onto the back of his bicycle. The mass of the cargo is 12 kg.

Calculate the force that Christian can exert on his bicycle before picking up the cargo.

Identify how Christian could reach the same speed on his bicycle when he is carrying the cargo and explain your answer.

16. A competitive downhill skier has little control over the environmental conditions of the ski slope. But she can choose her equipment and practice her technique to help control her speed.

Identify the forces that are acting on the skier as she moves down the ski slope and describe how they result in her motion.

Describe one way the skier can change her equipment to increase her maximum speed.

Directions: Read the passage, then answer the questions that follow.

Spaceship Shielding

A meteoroid is a small piece of rock in outer space. There are many meteoroids in space, and it is impossible for a spaceship to avoid all of them. Instead, the astronauts and equipment inside a spaceship are protected by shielding on the outside of the spaceship. The engineers that design spaceships need to take into account many factors to choose the right materials to use. The heavier a spaceship is, the more difficult and expensive it is to launch off of Earth and into space. Also, the spaceship must be able to survive the launch into space, which involves a lot of air resistance before it leaves the atmosphere of Earth. Once it gets into space, the shielding material must be able to protect the spaceship from meteoroids that collide with it.

To test new materials to help shield a spaceship from meteoroids, scientists built a device that can be used to launch rocks at a test sample. They are able to remove the air from the room where the sample is to model the environment in space. The picture shows an example of two samples after they were hit with a rock using the device.

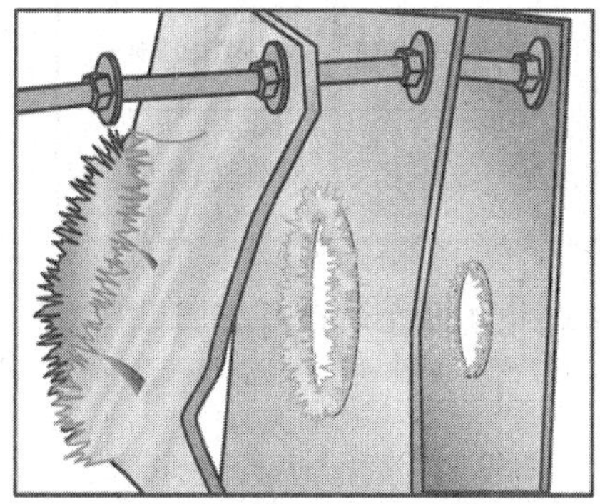

The first sample was made of multiple layers of steel. When the rock hit the first layer, it left a hole in that layer and the rock shattered into many pieces. The pieces continued to collide with the following layers, causing the holes to get larger as the rock pieces moved deeper into the shielding. The second sample was made out of a thick layer of foam covered with a thin layer of metal. The metal layer caused the rock to break apart, but then the foam absorbed the impact.

17. What are the criteria and/or constraints engineers must consider when designing shielding for spaceships?

Circle the letters of the three correct criteria and/or constraints.

A. must be light
B. must be hard
C. must be inexpensive
D. must be heat resistant
E. must absorb impacts
F. must be able to be made very thin

18. A group of engineers is designing a space station that will orbit a planet. They want to build windows so that the astronauts who stay on the space station can see outside. If there is a cloud of meteoroids that comes nearby, the astronauts will be able to lower shielding on the windows to give them extra protection. However, the windows should still be able to protect them from different-sized meteoroids that hit one at a time. The engineers decided on the criteria for the material for the windows as shown.

- protects against a meteoroid collision
- transparent or mostly transparent

The testing results of three materials are shown in the chart.

	Material 1	**Material 2**	**Material 3**
Transparency	completely transparent	mostly transparent	mostly transparent
Weight for one pane	24 kg	24 kg	33 kg
Hit with a small meteoroid	not damaged	not damaged	not damaged
Hit with a large meteoroid	damaged	not damaged	damaged
Hit with a shower of small meteoroids	damaged	damaged	not damaged

The engineers decided to use Material 2. Did they make the right decision?

Circle the letter of the correct answer.

A. no, because Material 2 is not completely transparent

B. yes, because Material 2 is the lightest material that still protects against small meteoroids

C. yes, because only Material 2 protects from different-sized meteoroids and is also mostly transparent

19. The picture shows a spaceship and a meteoroid before, during, and after a collision in space. The arrows in the *Before* picture show the velocities of the spaceship and the meteoroid before the collision. Since the spaceship is moving faster, it has a longer arrow. The spaceship is more massive than the meteoroid.

- Draw two arrows to show the directions of the forces of the spaceship and the meteoroid on the *During* collision picture.
- Draw two arrows to show the directions of the velocities for the spaceship and the meteoroid on the *After* collision picture.

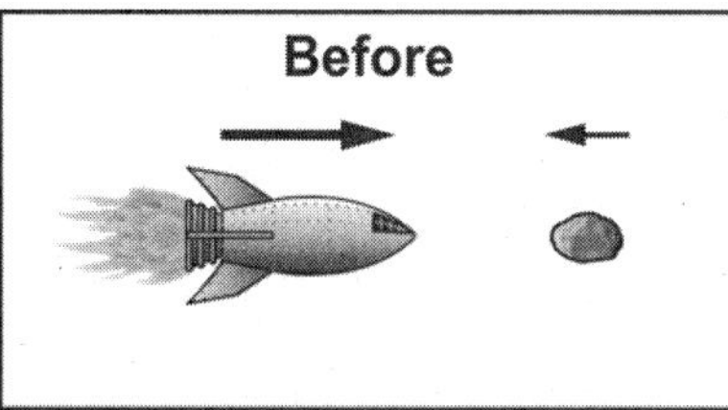

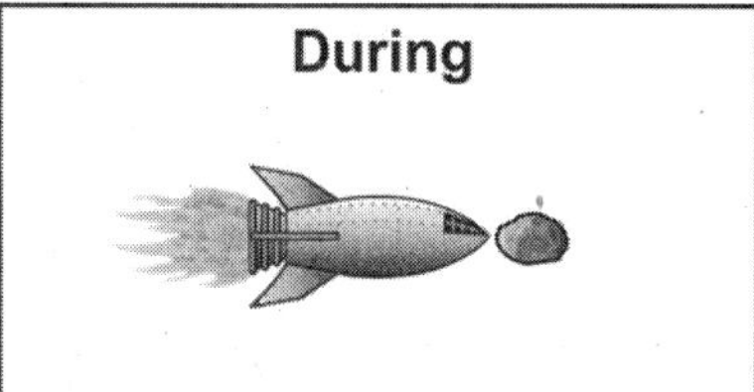

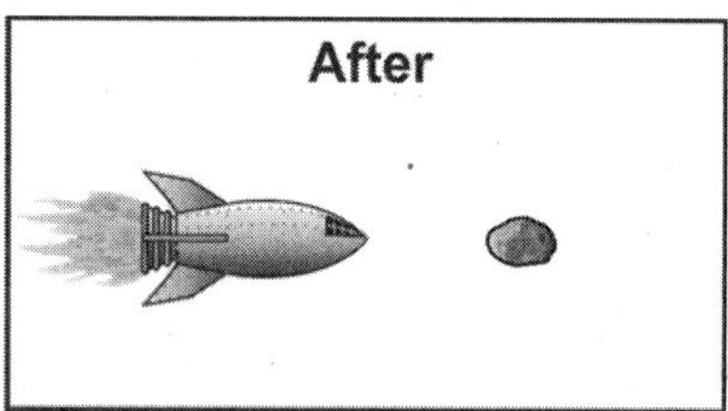

20. A student wants to set up a demonstration to show how Newton's second and third laws of motion apply to collisions between a meteoroid and a stationary spaceship in space. The student has a model spaceship, a lab stand, baseballs, cotton balls, marbles, and string.

Write your answer on the lines.

Identify which materials the student should use in the demonstration. Explain why the student should choose these materials.

Explain how the demonstration shows Newton's second and third laws.

Name: ______________________ Date: ______________________

Unit 2
Unit Pretest

Pretest: Electric and Magnetic Forces

Read each question. Circle the letter of the correct answer.

1. Which object would be attracted by a magnet?

A. an iron nail

B. a latex balloon

C. a piece of paper

D. an aluminum paper clip

2. An object is most likely to become electrically charged by gaining or losing which type of particles?

A. neutral particles

B. positive particles

C. negative particles

D. none of the above

3. The end of one bar magnet is placed near the end of another bar magnet. The two ends seem to push each other apart. Which of these statements is true?

A. The two ends are like poles.

B. The two ends are unlike poles.

C. There are like charges on the two ends.

D. There are unlike charges on the two ends.

4. Which of these is a ferromagnetic material?

A. aluminum

B. copper

C. diamond

D. iron

5. Sometimes the north and south poles of atoms in a material will line up. What is the term for the region where this occurs?

A. domain

B. ferromagnetic

C. magnetic field

D. magnetic pole

6. Where is the magnitude of force around this object the greatest?

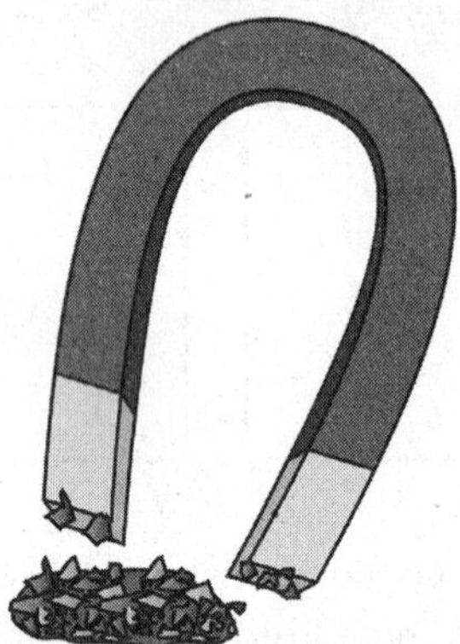

A. The magnitude is greatest close to the poles.

B. The magnitude is greatest far from the poles.

C. The magnitude is equal at all points on the field.

D. The magnitude is greatest halfway between poles.

7. What would be the effect of bringing a negatively-charged metal ball near an iron bar?

A. The bar would become negatively charged and repel the metal ball.

B. The bar would become positively charged and attract the metal ball.

C. A magnetic north pole would be generated on the bar, and it would repel the metal ball.

D. A magnetic south pole would be generated on the bar, and it would attract the metal ball.

8. The interaction between electric energy and magnetism has been an important topic in 20th-century science. Which term describes this interaction?

A. electromagnetism

B. ferromagnetic

C. magnetic field

D. static electricity

9. Why are certain materials, such as copper and aluminum, not magnetic?
   A. The individual atoms that make up the materials do not have magnetic fields.
   B. The individual atoms that make up the materials align themselves into domains.
   C. The magnetic fields of the individual atoms that make up the materials cancel each other out.
   D. The magnetic fields of the individual atoms that make up the materials are highly unstable and easily lost.

10. All charged objects create an electric field around them. What two factors determine the strength of two electric fields upon the charged objects creating them?
   A. how charged the object creating the field is and the mass of the two charged objects
   B. how charged the object creating the field is and the distance between the two charged objects
   C. how charged the object creating the field is and whether the objects are positively or negatively charged
   D. how charged the object creating the field is and the density of the two charged objects

11. Joe has an idea to cut a bar magnet in half so that he can have one magnet with a north pole and one magnet with a south pole. What is wrong with this idea?
   A. It is impossible to cut a magnet in half.
   B. It is impossible to create an extremely small magnet.
   C. It is impossible to create a magnet with only one magnetic pole.
   D. It is impossible to separate two opposite magnetic poles once they are in contact with each other.

12. Which of these best describes electric charge?
   A. a force that causes objects to heat up
   B. a high-voltage material that can cause damage to objects
   C. a fundamental property that causes electric and magnetic interactions
   D. a particle that moves freely through matter and causes static electricity to build up on objects

13. Which of these is an example of a force that acts at a distance?
   A. An airplane experiences friction as it moves through air.
   B. A book experiences a normal force as it rests on a table.
   C. A soccer ball experiences a force as it is kicked across a field.
   D. A magnet is pushed away when it is brought near the end of another magnet.

14. Daniel has a long piece of copper wire. He shapes the wire into a coil. What could Daniel do to create an electric current in the wire?
   A. shake the wire very quickly
   B. submerge the wire into a pan of hot water
   C. move a bar magnet in and out of the wire coil
   D. connect the two free ends of the wire so that they form a closed path

15. Which of these best describes how a powerful electromagnet could be used in a junkyard?
   A. It could move heavy objects made of iron.
   B. It could convert electrical energy into mechanical energy.
   C. It could light up the area so workers can see at night.
   D. It could provide a voltage source for old electronic equipment.

Name: ______________________ Date: ______________________

Unit 2 Lesson 1
Lesson Quiz

Quiz: Magnetic Forces

Read each question. Circle the letter of the correct answer.

1. The attractive force between two magnets increases. Which statement explains why this would happen?

A. The like poles of the magnets are pointed at each other and move farther apart.

B. The like poles of the magnets are pointed at each other and move closer together.

C. The unlike poles of the magnets are pointed at each other and move farther apart.

D. The unlike poles of the magnets are pointed at each other and move closer together.

2. Kim has two bar magnets. First, she places them beside one another, as shown in Picture A. Then, she moves one of the bar magnets so they are placed as shown in Picture B. How did the magnetic force change?

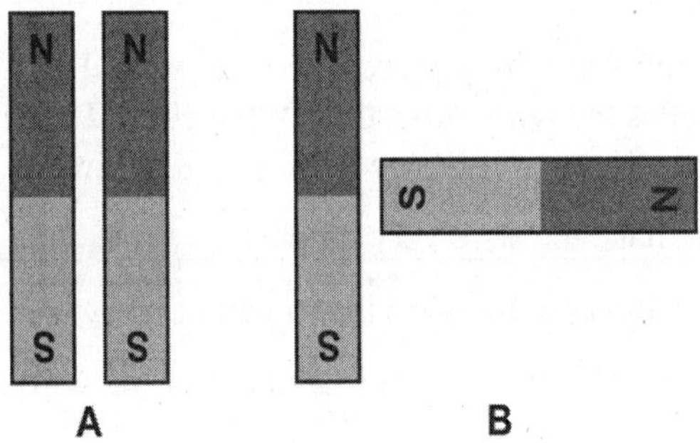

A. The bars go from attracting each other to repelling each other.

B. The bars go from repelling each other to attracting each other.

C. The bars go from repelling each other to the second bar rotating.

D. The bars go from attracting each other to the second bar rotating.

3. Which of these determines whether or not a material is magnetic?

A. the density of the material

B. the weight of the material on Earth

C. the alignment of atoms in the material

D. the number of elements that make up the material

4. Candice claims that all magnets have two magnetic poles. Which of these observations would best support her claim?

A. Iron is attracted to a magnet but not to other pieces of iron.

B. When a bar magnet is cut in half, each half has a north pole and a south pole.

C. The north pole of a compass needle is attracted to the south pole of a bar magnet.

D. The strength of the magnetic force from a bar magnet decreases as the magnet is pulled away from another object.

5. Angela tries to pick up a copper penny using a bar magnet, but the penny does not move. Next, she tries to pick up an iron nail using the bar magnet, and the nail lifts up toward the magnet. Which of the following best describes a ferromagnetic material like iron?

A. Ferromagnetic materials conduct electricity easily.

B. Ferromagnetic materials produce their own magnetic force.

C. Ferromagnetic materials are nonmetals that produce magnetic forces.

D. Ferromagnetic materials have magnetic domains that align with a magnetic field.

6. A magician wants to use magnets to create a new illusion for her show. She plans to hide strong magnets in her shoes and inside a special rug on the stage. When she tests the illusion, she finds that her shoes stick to the rug. What will happen if she flips the poles of the magnets in each of her shoes?

   A. Her shoes will float above the rug.

   B. Her shoes will still be stuck to the rug.

   C. Her shoes will no longer be affected by the rug.

   D. Her shoes will stick to each other instead of to the rug.

7. Why can some objects be magnetized by rubbing one pole of an existing magnet in one direction along the object?

   A. The motion of the existing magnet against the object aligns the magnetic domains of the object.

   B. The motion of the existing magnet against the object scrambles, or unaligns, the magnetic domains of the object.

   C. The motion of the existing magnet against the object generates an electric current that transforms the object into an electromagnet.

   D. The motion of the existing magnet against the object wears away the object's surface, exposing the naturally occurring magnets underneath.

Read each statement. Write your answer on the lines.

8. A student finds three unmarked bar magnets in a lab. She wants to know how strong each of the magnets is. She also has a set of paper clips. Explain how she could use the paper clips to determine the strength of each magnet.

____

____

____

____

____

9. Ajit has a bar magnet, a copper rod, an iron rod, and a steel rod. First, he moves the magnet toward the middle of the copper rod. Next, he moves the magnet toward the middle of the iron rod. Finally, he moves the magnet toward the middle of the steel rod. In each step of his investigation, he writes down his observations.

Describe the goal of Ajit's investigation.

____

____

Identify one way Ajit can improve his investigation.

____

____

____

10. Use the diagram to answer the question.

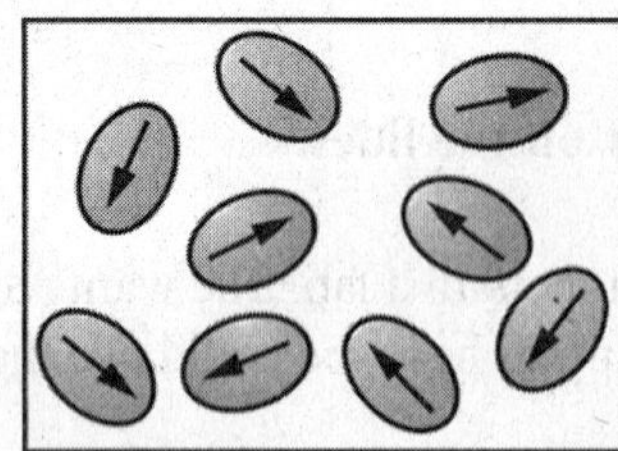

The image models the alignment of magnetic domains in a material.

Explain how a model of the material would look if it became magnetized.

____

____

Explain why the domains in your model would create a magnetic material while the domains in the first model do not.

____

____

____

Quiz: Electric Forces

Read each question. Circle the letter of the correct answer.

1. A repelling force occurs between two charged objects when the charges are of _______________.

   A. like signs

   B. unlike signs

   C. equal magnitude

   D. unequal magnitude

2. When Bethany walks across a carpet, her socks pick up many electric charges. Later in the day, these charges are no longer present on her socks. What most likely happened to the charges?

   A. The charges disappeared.

   B. The charges switched signs.

   C. The charges transferred to another object.

   D. The charges broke apart into smaller particles.

3. During a lightning storm, the bottom of a cloud gains a strong negative electric charge. Which of these describes the charge at the top of a tall metal pole directly under the cloud?

   A. The top of the pole would have no charge.

   B. The top of the pole would have a positive charge.

   C. The top of the pole would have a negative charge.

   D. The charge of the pole would not be affected by the charge of the cloud.

4. This image shows two circular objects. Each object has an electric charge, as shown.

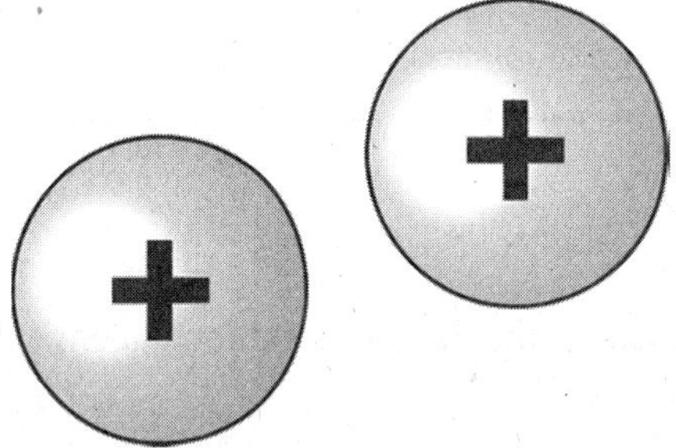

   Which statement describes the force that is exerted on the objects due to their electric charge?

   A. There is a force pushing both objects to the left.

   B. There is a force pulling the objects toward each other.

   C. There is a force pushing the objects away from each other.

   D. There is no force on the objects due to their electric charge.

Name: ______________________ Date: ______________________

Unit 2 Lesson 2

Lesson Quiz

5. The diagram shows two pairs of charged objects. Objects A and B are interacting with each other, and objects C and D are interacting with each other.

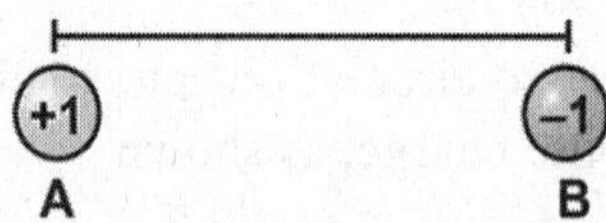

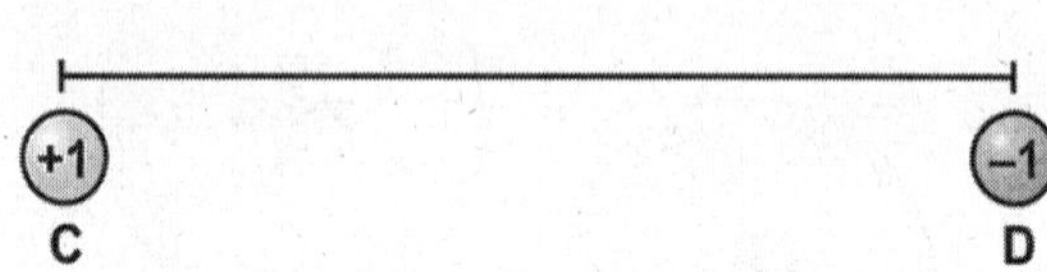

Based on the diagrams, which statement is true?

A. There are no electric forces because the charges in each pair of objects cancel.

B. The electric force between A and B is smaller than the electric force between C and D.

C. The electric force between A and B is greater than the electric force between C and D.

D. The electric force between A and B is identical in magnitude to the electric force between C and D.

6. What happens when a rubber rod is rubbed with a piece of fur, giving the rod a negative charge?

A. Negative charges are moved from the rod to the fur.

B. Negative charges are moved from the fur to the rod.

C. Negative charges are added to the rod, and the fur remains neutral.

D. Positive charges are removed from the rod, and the fur remains neutral.

7. The distance between a positively charged object and a negatively charged object increases. If everything else remains constant, what happens to the electric force between the objects?

Choose the correct answer.

A. The electric force decreases.

B. The electric force increases.

C. The electric force remains constant.

D. There is not enough information to answer this question.

Read each statement. Write your answer on the lines.

8. A balloon is held near a person's hair, and the hair is not affected. The same balloon is rubbed on a piece of carpeting, and the balloon now attracts hair. Define electric charge and describe how it relates to this situation.

____

____

____

____

____

9. Describe how a neutral material becomes attracted to a negatively charged object brought near it.

10. A glass rod is rubbed briefly with silk and the rod becomes able to attract and lift a number of small pieces of paper. If the rod is rubbed with silk for a longer period of time, explain what will happen and why.

Quiz: Fields

Read each question. Circle the letter of the correct answer.

1. A small bar magnet is shown. A compass is placed beside the magnet so that the center of the compass is next to the center of the magnet. Which of these is true?

A. The north pole of the compass needle points at the magnet's south pole.

B. The south pole of the compass needle points at the magnet's north pole.

C. The north pole of the compass points in the same direction as the magnet's south pole.

D. The north pole of the compass needle points in the same direction as the magnet's north pole.

2. Two aluminum balls are 5 cm apart. One is negatively charged, and the other is positively charged. A small magnet is placed between the two balls but is not touching either of them. The aluminum balls remain stationary. Which statement describes the electric and magnetic fields?

A. There is a magnetic field due to the magnet and no electric field.

B. There is a magnetic field between the two balls and no electric field.

C. There is an electric field between the two balls and no magnetic field.

D. There is an electric field between the two balls and a magnetic field due to the magnet.

3. The diagram shows the magnetic field surrounding a magnet.

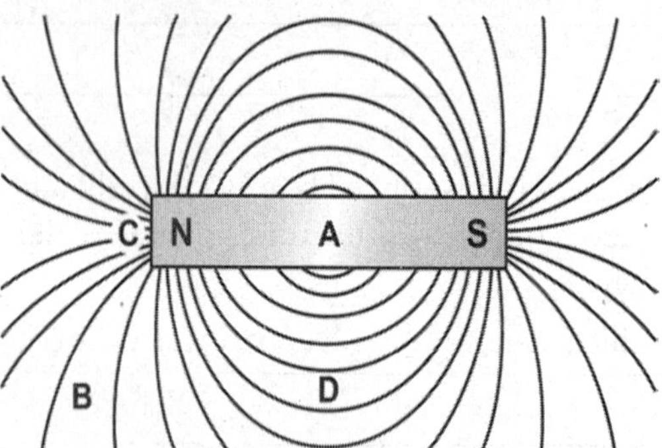

Where is the magnetic force the strongest?

A. position A

B. position B

C. position C

D. position D

4. A positively charged pith ball is hanging from a string. A negatively charged rod is then held a short distance away. How will the pith ball be affected?

A. It will not be affected because only the rod has an electrical field.

B. The fields on the pith ball and the rod will interact, causing an attractive force.

C. The fields on the pith ball and the rod will interact, causing a repulsive force.

D. It will not be affected because the pith ball and the rod are not touching.

5. Which of these best describes a magnetic field?

   A. a measure of the length of a magnet

   B. the force that pushes two magnets away from each other

   C. an invisible region that surrounds the north pole of a magnet

   D. a region around a magnet in which magnetic forces can be measured

6. Stephan claims that Earth has both a gravitational field and a magnetic field. Which statement best supports his claim?

   A. Any object will fall to the ground.

   B. A bar magnet will fall to the ground.

   C. Any object will fall to the ground, and a compass can be used for navigation.

   D. A compass points in the direction of both the magnetic and gravitational fields.

7. A student is brushing her hair. As the hairbrush is brought near her head, the hair seems to reach toward the hairbrush. Which of the following is the best explanation?

   A. Two electric fields are interacting.

   B. Two magnetic fields are interacting.

   C. Two gravitational fields are interacting.

   D. Two electromagnetic fields are interacting.

Read each statement. Write your answer on the lines.

8. A student is conducting a scientific investigation using iron filings to show the magnetic field of magnets. She examines the magnet surrounded by filings, as shown in the diagram.

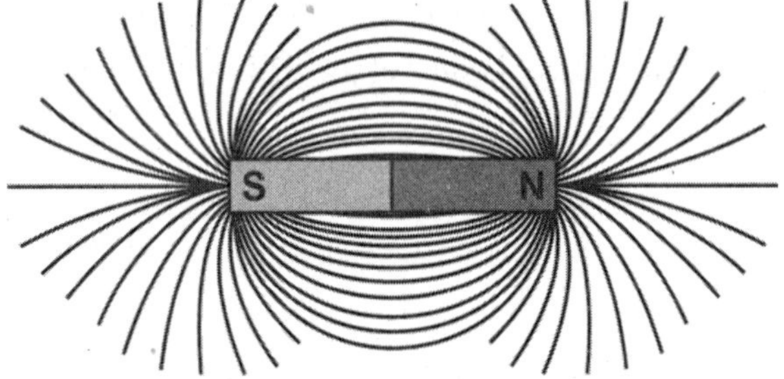

   What is the scientific question she is investigating?

   ____

   ____

   ____

   ____

   ____

9. Two charged balls are 10 cm apart. One is positively charged, and the other is negatively charged. Describe the electric field lines and any forces that would exist between the two balls.

____

____

Explain how the electric field and/or force would change if both balls had positive charge.

____

____

____

10. The model shows the magnetic field lines of object A. The first diagram represents the magnetic field of object A before object B is moved into place. The second diagram represents the magnetic field of object A when object B is held in place next to object A.

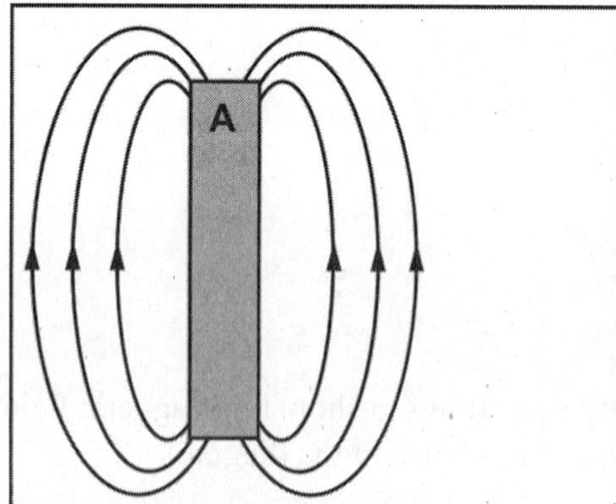

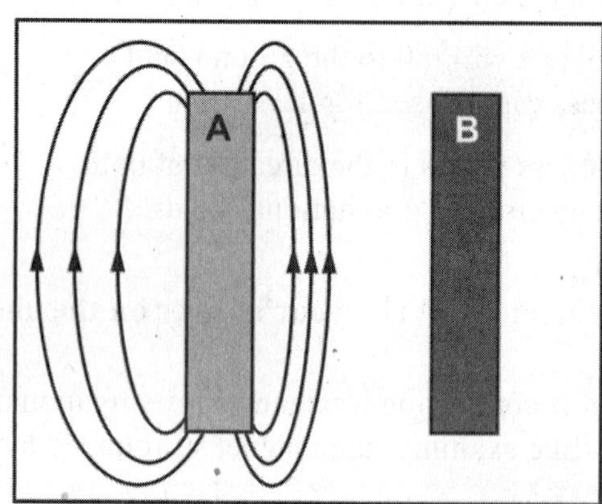

Use the magnetic field lines to determine whether object B is a magnet, a piece of iron, or a bar of nonmagnetic material. Explain your answer.

____

____

Describe the movement of object B when it is released. Explain your answer.

____

____

____

Quiz: Electromagnetism

Read each question. Circle the letter of the correct answer.

1. Which of these is the best definition of electromagnetism?

   A. the use of electrical energy to produce magnets

   B. the use of magnets to generate electric current

   C. the interaction between electric and magnetic forces

   D. the appearance in nature of objects that have both electric and magnetic fields

2. An electromagnet is made by wrapping many turns of wire around an iron bar and causing a current to flow through the wire. How would increasing the electrical current affect the electromagnet?

   A. It would make the poles of the magnet weaker.

   B. It would make the poles of the magnet stronger.

   C. It would decrease the flow of electricity in the iron bar.

   D. It would increase the flow of electricity in the iron bar.

3. Which of these correctly describes electric current?

   A. the amount of electric charge on an object

   B. the rate at which electric charges pass a given point

   C. the buildup of electric charge on the surface of an object

   D. the amount of energy it takes to move a unit of electric charge between two points

4. Which statement describes how electromagnetism can be used to generate electricity in a power plant?

   A. Moving a magnet in a coil of wire produces visible light.

   B. Magnets convert electric energy into mechanical energy.

   C. Magnets detect the presence of electric currents in nature.

   D. Moving a magnet in a coil of wire generates an electric current.

5. Two parallel wires have electrical current running through them in opposite directions. Which statement describes the force between the two wires?

   A. There are no electric or magnetic forces on the wires.

   B. There is a magnetic force pulling the wires toward one another.

   C. There is an electric force pulling the wires toward one another.

   D. There is a magnetic force pushing the wires away from one another.

6. Olga wants to test if the battery shown in the diagram still produces an electric current. She wraps a wire around a compass and connects each end to the battery as shown in the diagram.

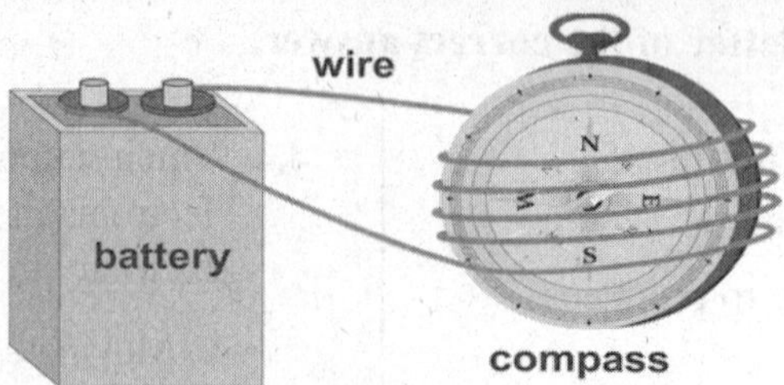

She claims that this device has properties similar to an electromagnet. Which of these statements best defends this claim?

A. When electric charges flow through the wire, the voltage of the battery increases.

B. When electric charges flow through the wire, the compass becomes demagnetized.

C. When electric charges flow through the wire, the compass becomes electrically charged.

D. When electric charges flow through the wire, they produce a magnetic field through the coil of wire.

7. Juan wants to make a motor using simple materials. He wraps copper wire around a small piece of cork and uses a pin to secure the cork to an axle balanced between two bar magnets, as shown in the diagram. Two brushes made of springy copper wire just touch two metal pins in the cork that are used to hold the ends of the copper wire in place.

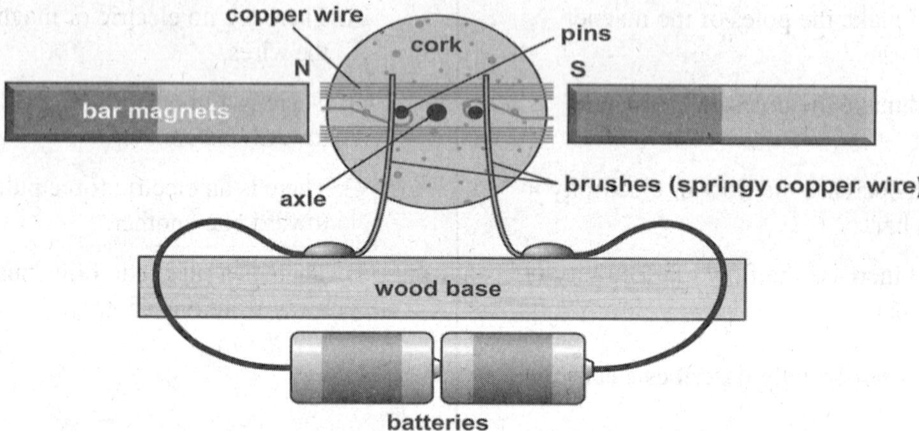

When he connects the copper wire to the batteries, he expects to see the cork spin. Why does Juan expect to see the cork spin?

A. The magnetic field produced by the current flow in the coil of wire changes the poles of the bar magnets.

B. Electric charges produced by the current flow are pushed into the bar magnets, causing the cork to move in the opposite direction.

C. The cork moves so the electric field produced by the current flow in the coil of wire aligns with the magnetic field of the bar magnets.

D. The cork moves so the magnetic field produced by the current flow in the coil of wire aligns with the magnetic field of the bar magnets.

Name: ____________________ Date: ____________________

Unit 2 Lesson 4

Lesson Quiz

Read each statement. Write your answer on the lines.

8. Pamela created an electromagnet by wrapping a copper wire around an iron nail. When she connected the wire ends to a battery, she was able to lift 4 paper clips with her electromagnet. She decided that she wanted to modify the electromagnet so that it would lift 7 paper clips. She modified the electromagnet by removing the iron nail and replacing it with an aluminum nail. However, when she modified the electromagnet, it would not lift any paper clips.

Explain why Pamela's modification caused the electromagnet to lose its magnetic properties.

____

____

Explain how Pamela could modify the electromagnet so that it will lift 7 paper clips.

____

____

____

9. A wind turbine is a machine that spins when the wind blows. The turbine blades are attached to a magnet. When the blades spin, the magnet also spins. Around the magnet, there is a coil of copper wire.

Explain what happens in the coil of copper wire when the magnet starts to spin.

____

____

Identify the name of this process.

____

____

A person wants to modify the machine so that the magnet remains stationary.

Explain how the person could modify the design of the machine so that it still produces the same effect. Explain why this modification will produce the same effect as the original design.

____

____

____

____

____

10. Idra wraps a wire around a plastic tube and connects the ends of the wires to a device that measures electric current. When she slides a bar magnet through the tube, north pole first, she sees that a small amount of electric current is produced in the wire. She slides three more bar magnets through the tube north pole first, and a small amount of electric current is produced in the wire each time.

Predict how the current will change if Idra slides the bar magnets through the tube south pole first.

____

____

Using the same materials, describe one other way Idra could change the current produced in the wire and predict how the current will change.

____

____

____

Name: ______________________ Date: ______________________

Unit Test: Electric and Magnetic Forces

Read each question. Circle the letter of the correct answer.

1. Jesse tests three magnets by observing how many paper clips he can attach to the north pole in a single chain. He finds that Magnet A holds six paper clips, Magnet B holds five paper clips, and Magnet C holds two paper clips. He warms Magnets A and C in the oven for a few minutes and repeats his procedure. This time, Magnet A holds only four paper clips, Magnet B still holds five paper clips, and Magnet C cannot hold any paper clips. Which statement explains Jesse's observations?

   A. Warming a magnet unaligned some of the magnetic domains.

   B. The forces produced by a magnet naturally become weaker over time.

   C. Warming a magnet causes the distance of its magnetic force to decrease.

   D. The poles of the magnet become reversed when warmed and cause it to repel the paper clips.

2. The picture shows two magnets interacting with uncharged iron filings.

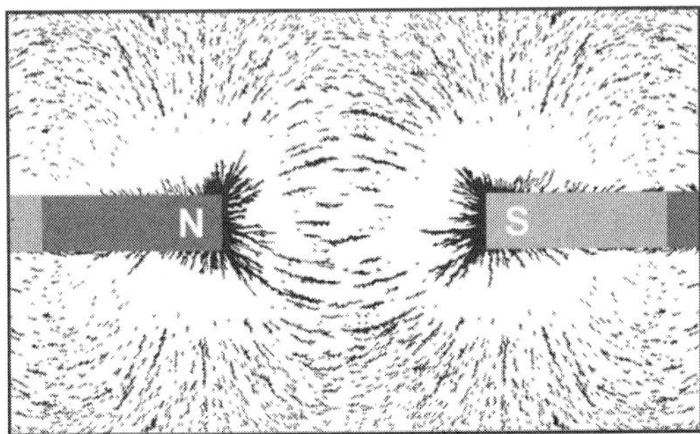

   What relationship is shown in the picture?

   A. Electric force between like ends is attractive.

   B. Magnetic force between like ends is attractive.

   C. Electric force between opposite ends is attractive.

   D. Magnetic force between opposite ends is attractive.

3. Kim has a loop of wire and a magnet. Which of these will create the largest electric current in the loop?

   A. Wrap the wire tightly around the magnet.

   B. Place the magnet in the center of the wire.

   C. Move the magnet quickly through the loop.

   D. Spin the loop of wire slowly above the magnet.

4. The diagram shows a balloon that was rubbed with a piece of cloth.

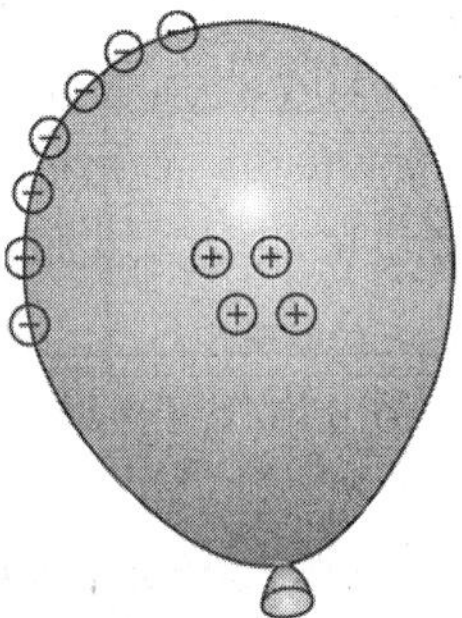

   Which statement describes the charges shown?

   A. Negative charges from the cloth were transferred to the balloon.

   B. Balloons always have more negative charges than positive charges.

   C. Negative charges appeared when the cloth was rubbed on the balloon.

   D. Some of the positive charges on the balloon disappeared when it was rubbed by the cloth.

5. Rohit is using a compass to investigate magnetic forces. Which of these will cause the compass to change direction?

   A. plastic paper clips

   B. a wooden doorknob

   C. the wire he is using to charge a cell phone

   D. the wire going from the wall to an unlit lamp

6. Sachdev finds two metal bars and decides that since they are stuck together, at least one of metal bars must be a magnet. Sachdev pulls the bars apart and uses a marker to label each end of the bars. She lays bar CD on the table and then ties a string around bar AB and hangs end A above end D, as shown in the diagram.

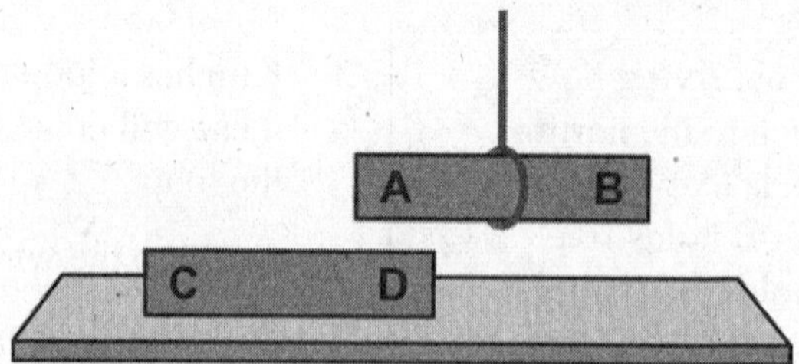

Sachdev finds that the end marked A tips downward until it is touching the end marked D. Which test allows Sachdev to draw a conclusion about the magnetic properties of each metal bar?

A. She hangs A directly above C and sees that the two ends attract. She concludes that both bar AB and bar CD always produce magnetic fields.

B. She hangs B directly above C and sees that the two ends attract. She concludes that both bar AB and bar CD always produce magnetic fields.

C. She hangs B directly above C and sees that the two ends attract. She concludes that bar CD always produces a magnetic field, but bar AB only temporarily produces a magnetic field.

D. She hangs A above the center of bar CD and finds that A is only weakly attracted to CD. She concludes that bar CD always produces a magnetic field, but bar AB only temporarily produces a magnetic field.

Read each question. Follow the instructions to answer the questions.

7. A bar magnet is placed flat on a table. A smaller bar magnet is held vertically just above the first one, with the south pole close to the first magnet and the north pole farther away. The diagram shows the larger bar magnet.

Draw a circle on the locations where the smaller magnet would encounter the strongest magnetic forces.

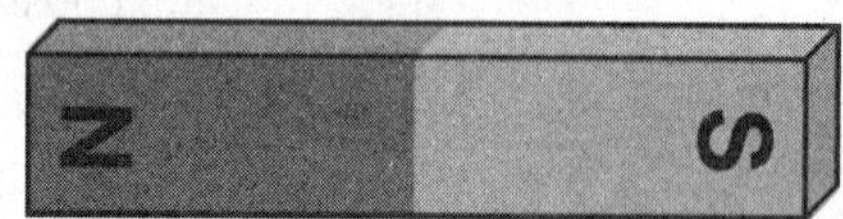

8. Several pairs of charged objects are held at different distances, and the force between each pair is measured. Each object has the same amount of charge, q, but it can be positive or negative.

Number the descriptions from 1 to 4 with 1 as the smallest force and 4 as the largest force.

__________ $+q$ and $+q$ at a distance of 2.0 cm

__________ $+q$ and $+q$ at a distance of 4.0 cm

__________ $+q$ and $-q$ at a distance of 1.0 cm

__________ $+q$ and $-q$ at a distance of 3.0 cm

9. Two magnets are shown in the diagram. Magnet A is glued to the table, and Magnet B is free to move.

Draw a circle around the sentence that explains Magnet B's motion.

There is a magnetic field around Magnet A, and a magnetic field around Magnet B. These magnetic fields extend in all directions around the magnets but cancel each other out. The magnetic field around Magnet A exerts a force on Magnet B, so Magnet B moves downward and to the right.

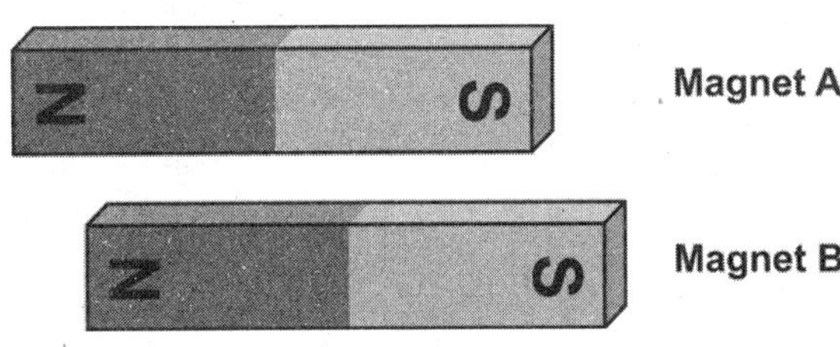

10. The diagram shows a device called a capacitor. In a capacitor, metal plates are separated by an insulating material that keeps charges from transferring between the plates. By running current through the wires, the two parallel metal plates within the capacitor become oppositely charged. Note that only the top metal plate is shown in the diagram.

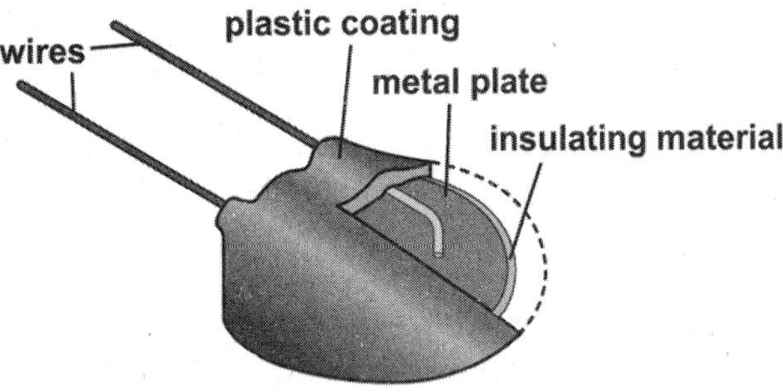

Write a letter of each element in the correct position in the table to show how each change affects the strength of the electric force between the plates.

Increase strength	Decrease strength	No change in strength

A. Reverse the wires to switch the charges on the plates.

B. Increase the thickness of the insulating material.

C. Increase the thickness of the plastic coating.

D. Decrease the current in the wires.

E. Decrease the length of the wires.

Name: ______________________ Date: ______________________

11. Diagram 1 shows ferromagnetic material in close range with a nonmagnetic material. Diagram 2 shows ferromagnetic material in close range with a magnetic material. Diagram 3 shows a magnet that has been cut in half to show how the two halves interact. Arrangements of magnetic domains are in the boxes.

Write the letters of the magnetic domain arrangements in the empty boxes for diagrams 1, 2, and 3.Some letters may be used more than once or not at all.

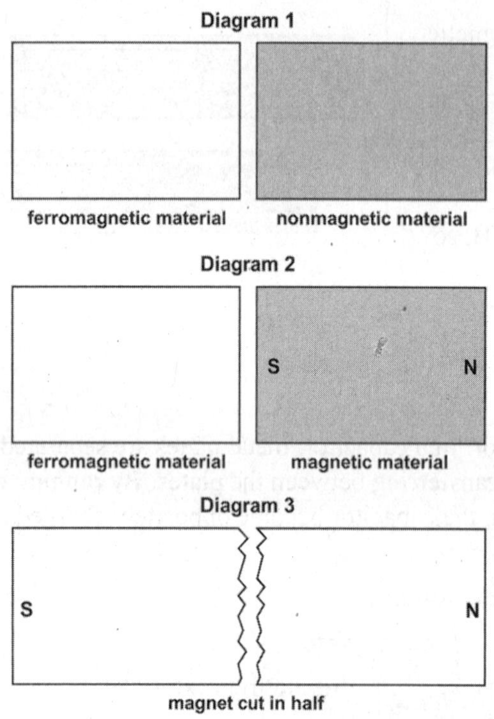

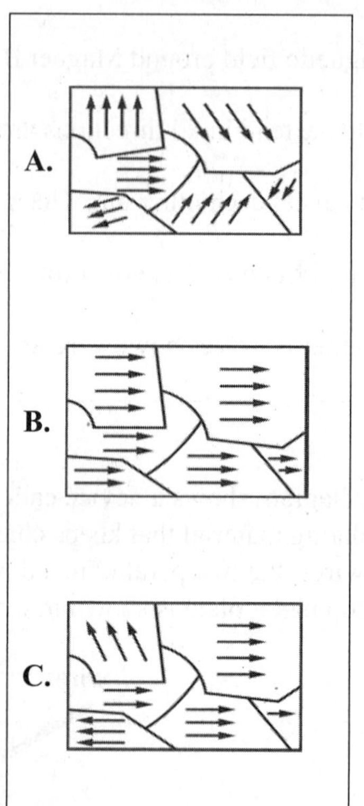

12. Gundeep tapes a bar magnet to the wall. He tapes a second bar magnet to a small aluminum lab car and moves the car into place near the wall as shown in the diagram. When he releases the car, it begins to move slowly away from the wall. He would like to run his experiment again to test other situations.

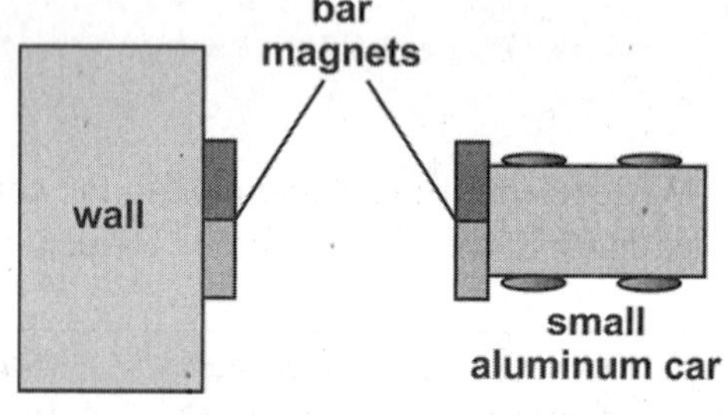

Write the letter of the phrase that describes how the car would move in the box next to the change Gundeep could make in the experiment that would cause that movement. Some letters may be used more than once or not at all.

He positions the car closer to the wall.	
He replaces the bar magnet on the wall with a stronger magnet in the same orientation.	
He positions the car closer to the wall and reverses the orientation of the magnet on the car.	
He positions the car farther from the wall and reverses the orientation of the magnet on the wall.	

A. does not move
B. moves more slowly toward wall
C. moves more quickly toward wall
D. moves more slowly away from wall
E. moves more quickly away from wall

13. Four pairs of objects are brought close to one another. The diagram shows the pairs of objects and the positive and negative charges they contain.

Draw a plus sign in the middle of each positively charged object in the image.

Draw arrows beneath each object in the image representing the movement of the object when released. If the object does not move, do not draw anything below the object. Assume that charges are free to move within an object.

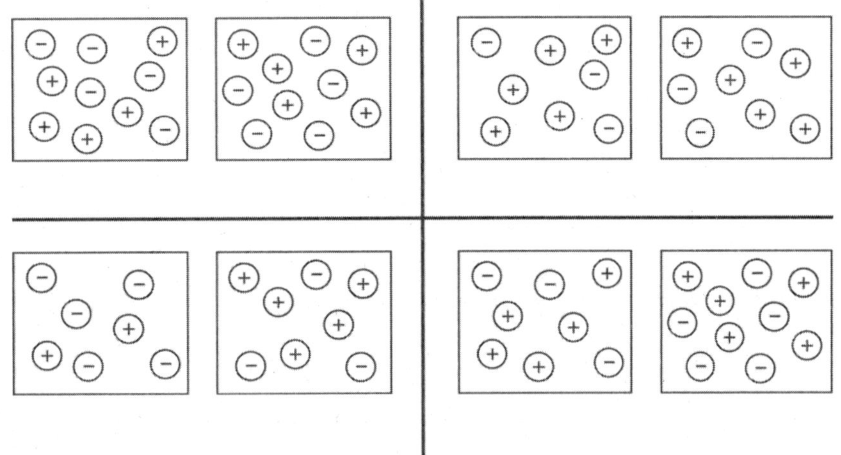

14. Karin has a tray with sand and iron shavings mixed together. She wants to use the iron shavings to study magnetic fields. She decides to design a device that will separate the iron shavings from the sand and later release them into a separate container.

Karin looked around her home and found these items:

box	batteries	insulated wire
cup	iron bolts	refrigerator magnets
glue	paper clips	
tape	wire cutters	

Several possible design criteria for Karin's device are listed in the table.

Write an X in the correct box to show whether each statement is a criterion that can be satisfied by an electromagnet or a permanent magnet or is not a criterion for Karin's device. Some statements may have more than X.

Statement	Electromagnet	Permanent magnet	Not a criterion for Karin's device
A. attracts iron but not sand			
B. can scoop up the iron and sand mixture			
C. can release iron shavings after they are collected			
D. can be constructed from or found among the items in Karin's home			

Read each statement. Write your answer on the lines.

15. Mia finds that when she places a needle near a magnet, the needle rotates to point toward the south pole of the magnet. Mia claims this provides evidence that there is a magnetic field that affects both objects.

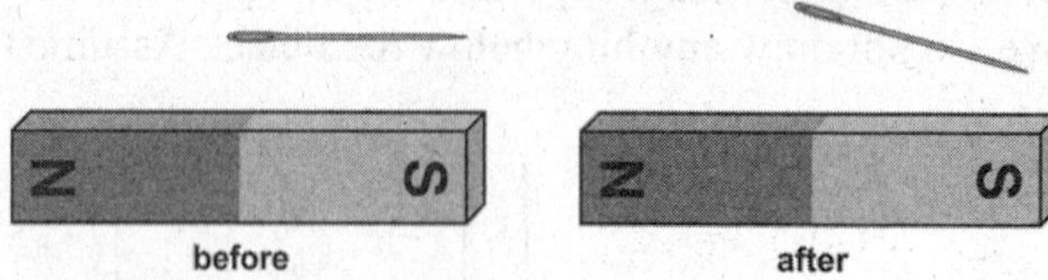

Explain why the needle rotated when Mia placed it near the magnet.

____

____

Explain why the motion of the needle does or does not provide evidence to support Mia's claim.

____

____

____

16. The model shows two planets that will attract a spacecraft from a distance.

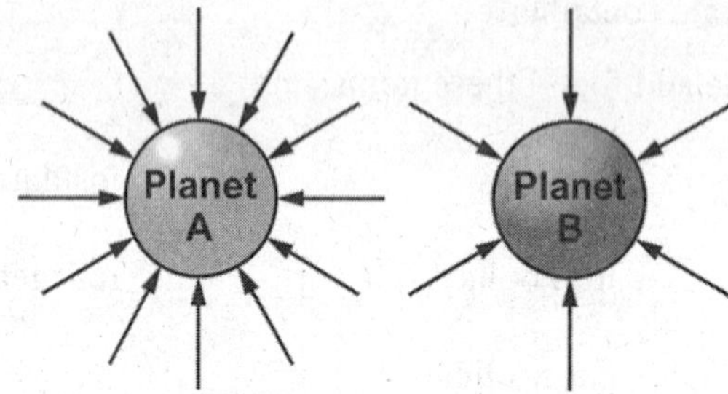

Explain what the arrows around the planets represent.

____

____

Using the model, describe how Planet A and Planet B differ.

____

____

____

Describe how the path of a spacecraft flying by each of the two planets would be affected.

____

____

____

17. This incomplete model shows three electrically charged objects that are interacting with each other.

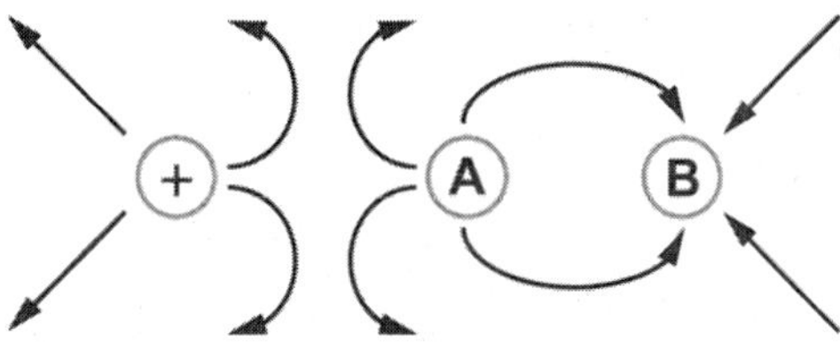

Explain what the arrows around the objects represent.

Use the model to determine the charges of objects A and B.

Describe how the model would change if the charge of object A is doubled.

Directions: Read the passage, then answer the questions that follow.

Strength of Magnetic Forces

Leisha is conducting an investigation about the strength of the forces between an electromagnet and other magnetic objects. She constructs an electromagnet from a battery, a nail, and coils of wire, as shown in the diagram. Leisha hangs a piece of iron from a string and brings it near the sharp end of the nail. She repeats her process with a bar magnet. Leisha's initial observations are shown in the table.

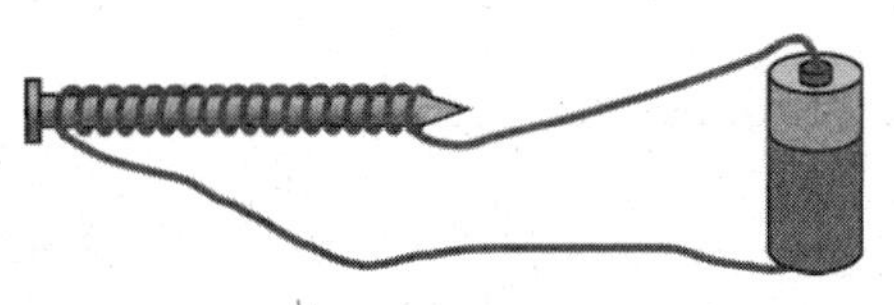

Type of object	Distance from nail	Motion of object	Speed of object
Iron	6 cm	moved toward nail	slow
Bar magnet	6 cm	north pole turned toward nail	slow
Iron	3 cm	moved toward nail	fast
Bar magnet	3 cm	north pole turned toward nail	fast

18. Based on her experiments, what hypothesis is Leisha testing?

Circle the letter of the correct answer.

A. An electromagnet exerts stronger forces on iron than on other metals.

B. An electromagnet produces stronger magnetic forces closer to the magnet.

C. An electromagnet produces both repulsive and attractive magnetic forces.

D. An electromagnet's south pole produces stronger magnetic forces than its north pole.

19. Leisha brings an electromagnet toward a piece of iron and observes that the piece of iron starts to move when the electromagnet is 6 cm away. She plans to add another 25 coils of wire to the electromagnet. Which statement explains what will happen when she brings her modified electromagnet near the piece of iron?

Circle the letter of the correct answer.

A. The strength of the magnetic force will change, so the iron will start to move when the electromagnet is less than 6 cm away.

B. The strength of the magnetic force will change, so the iron will start to move when the electromagnet is more than 6 cm away.

C. The strength of the magnetic force will change, but the iron will still start to move when the electromagnet is exactly 6 cm away.

D. The strength of the magnetic force will not change, so the iron will still start to move when the electromagnet is exactly 6 cm away.

20. Leisha thought of three ways she could change her experimental procedure:

1. Observe the direction the bar magnet moves when she brings it near the end of the nail.
2. Observe how many paper clips she can attach to the end of the nail.
3. Connect each wire to the opposite end of the battery as before.

She wants to know how changing the direction of electric current in an electromagnet affects the magnetic force.

Write your answer on the lines.

Identify which of these modifications Leisha should use in her new experiment.

____

____

Explain how each modification you selected will help her meet the goals of her investigation.

____

____

____

____

Name: ______________________ Date: ______________________

Unit 2
Unit Test B

Unit Test: Electric and Magnetic Forces

Read each question. Circle the letter of the correct answer.

1. Three magnets are tested by attaching paper clips to the north pole. Magnet A holds six paper clips, Magnet B holds five paper clips, and Magnet C holds two paper clips. Magnets A and C are warmed in the oven and then retested. Now, Magnet A holds only four paper clips, Magnet B still holds five paper clips, and Magnet C cannot hold any paper clips. Which statement explains the changes?

A. Warming a magnet unaligned some of the magnetic domains.

B. The forces produced by a magnet naturally become weaker over time.

C. Warming a magnet causes the distance of its magnetic force to decrease.

2. The picture shows iron filings around magnets.

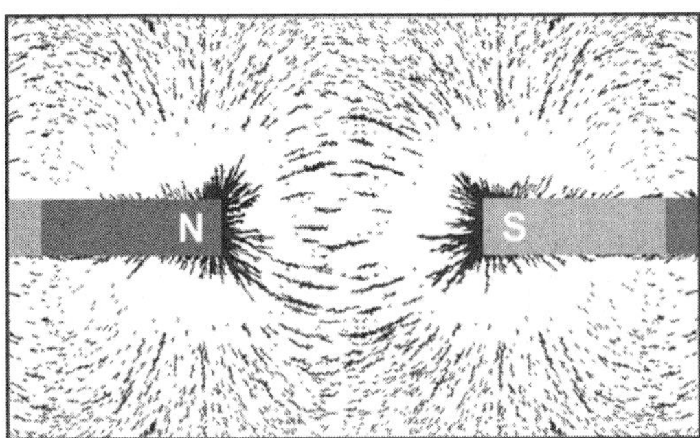

What relationship is shown in the picture?

A. Electric force between like ends is attractive.

B. Electric force between opposite ends is attractive.

C. Magnetic force between opposite ends is attractive.

3. Kim has a loop of wire and a magnet. Which of these will create the largest electric current in the loop?

A. Wrap the wire tightly around the magnet.

B. Place the magnet in the center of the wire.

C. Move the magnet quickly through the loop.

4. The diagram shows a balloon that was rubbed with cloth.

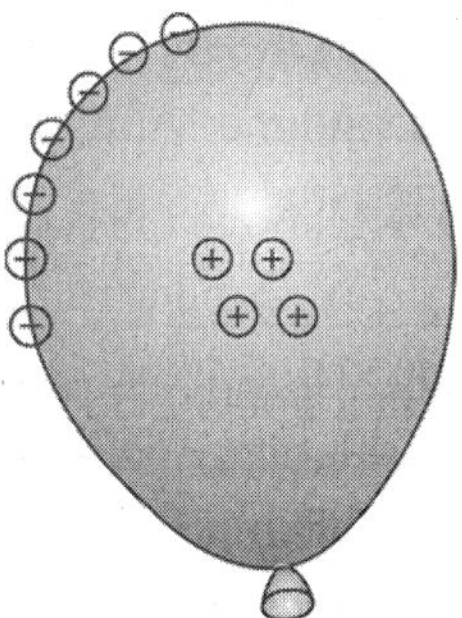

Which statement describes the charges shown?

A. Negative charges from the cloth were transferred to the balloon.

B. Some positive charges moved from the balloon to the cloth.

C. Some of the positive charges on the balloon disappeared when it was rubbed by the cloth.

5. A compass is used to study magnetic forces. Which of these will cause the compass to change direction?

A. plastic paper clips

B. the wire he is using to charge a cell phone

C. the wire going from the wall to an unlit lamp

6. Sachdev finds two metal bars. She decides one of metal bars must be a magnet since they are stuck together. She pulls the bars apart, and places bar CD on a table. She then ties a string around bar AB. She hangs end A above end D, as shown in the diagram.

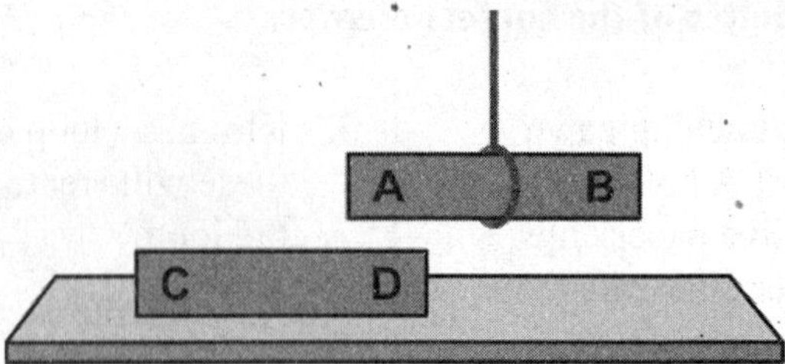

Sachdev finds that the end marked A tips downward until it is touching the end marked D.

Which other test allows Sachdev to make a conclusion about the magnetic properties of each metal bar?

A. She hangs B directly above C and sees that the two ends attract. She concludes that both bar AB and bar CD always produce magnetic fields.

B. She hangs B directly above C and sees that the two ends attract. She concludes that bar CD always produces a magnetic field, but bar AB only temporarily produces a magnetic field.

C. She hangs A above the center of bar CD and finds that A does not attract to CD. She concludes that bar CD always produces a magnetic field, but bar AB only temporarily produces a magnetic field.

Read each question. Follow the instructions to answer the questions.

7. The diagram shows a bar magnet.

Draw a circle on the locations where the south pole of another magnet would encounter the strongest magnetic forces.

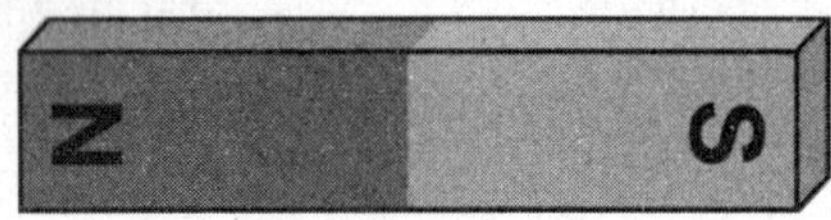

8. Two charged objects are held at different distances, and the force between the pair is measured at each distance. Both objects have the same amount of charge, q.

Number the descriptions from 1 to 3 with 1 as the smallest force and 3 as the largest force.

__________ $+q$ and $+q$ at a distance of 2.0 cm

__________ $+q$ and $-q$ at a distance of 1.0 cm

__________ $+q$ and $-q$ at a distance of 3.0 cm

9. Two magnets are shown in the diagram. Magnet A is glued to the table, and Magnet B is free to move. Draw a circle around the sentence that explains Magnet B's motion.

There is a magnetic field around Magnet A, and a magnetic field around Magnet B. These magnetic fields extend in all directions around the magnets but cancel each other out. The magnetic field around Magnet A exerts a force on Magnet B, so Magnet B moves.

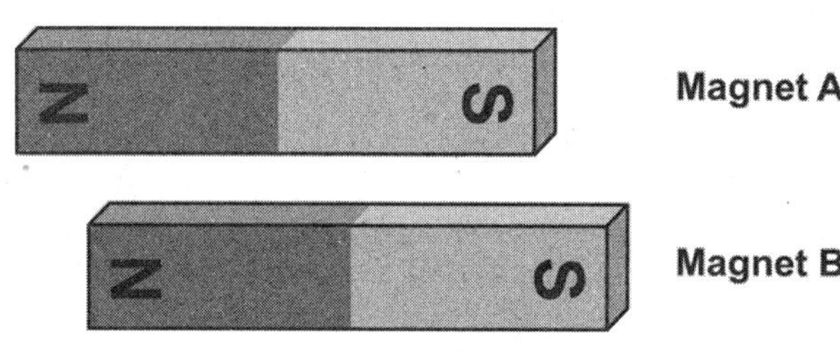

10. This is a picture of a capacitor. In a capacitor, metal plates are separated by an insulating material that keeps charges from transferring between the plates.

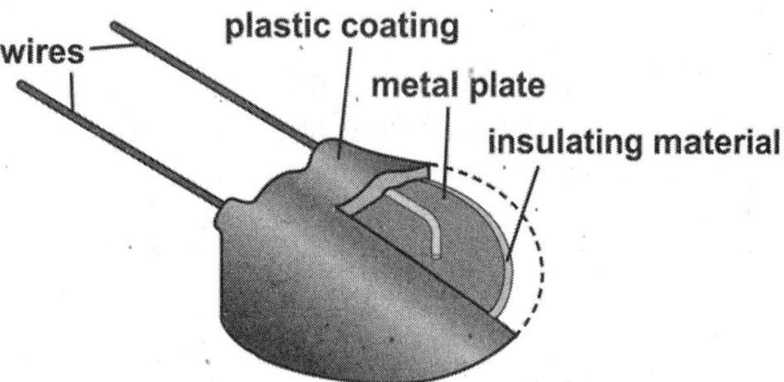

By running electric current through the wires, the two metal plates in the capacitor become charged. Another metal plate is under the insulating material.

Write a letter of each element in the correct position in the table to show how each change affects the strength of the electric force between the plates.

Decrease strength	No change in strength

A. Reverse the wires to switch the charges on the plates.

B. Increase the thickness of the insulating material.

C. Increase the thickness of the plastic coating.

Name: ______________________________ Date: ______________________

11. The diagram shows a magnet that has been cut in half to show how the two halves interact.

Write the letters of the magnetic domain arrangements in the boxes for the cut magnet.

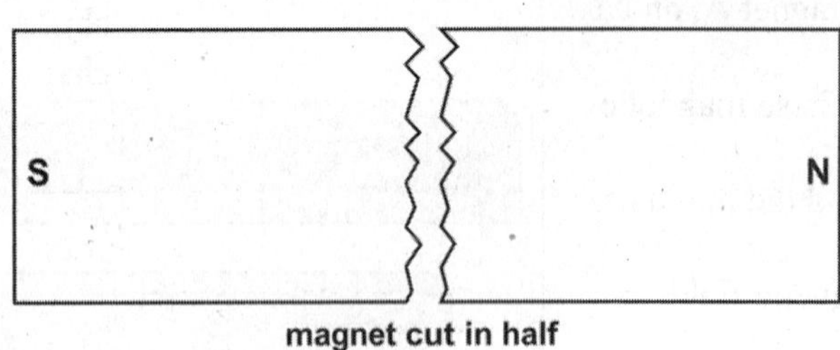

magnet cut in half

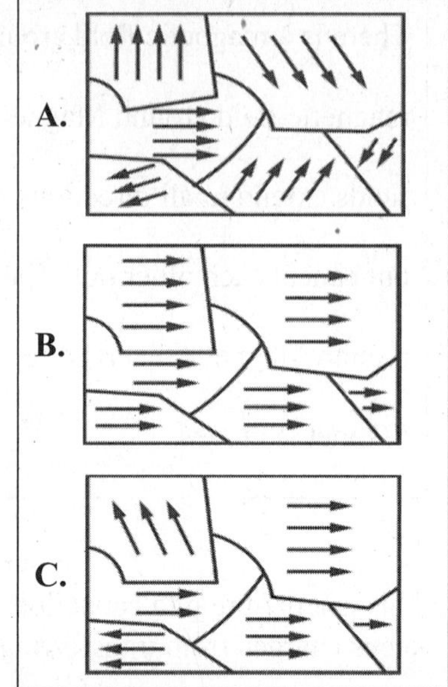

12. Gundeep tapes a bar magnet to the wall. He tapes a second bar magnet to a small aluminum lab car and moves the car into place near the wall as shown in the diagram. When he releases the car, it begins to move slowly away from the wall. He would like to run his experiment again to test other situations.

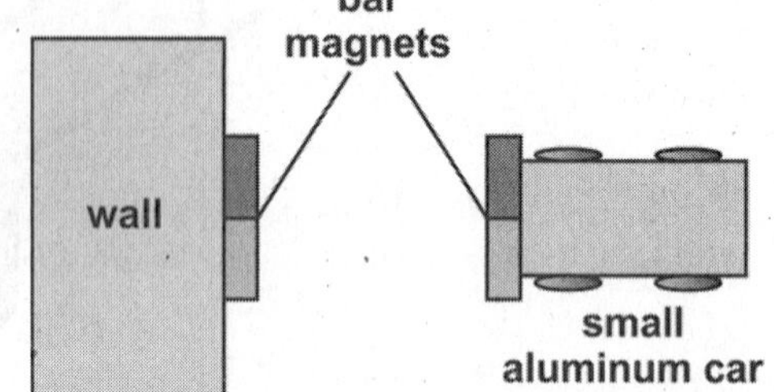

Write the letter of the phrase that describes how the car would move in the box next to the change Gundeep could make in the experiment that would cause that movement. Some letters may be used more than once or not at all.

He positions the car closer to the wall.	
He replaces the bar magnet on the wall with a stronger magnet in the same orientation.	
He positions the car closer to the wall and reverses the orientation of the magnet on the car.	
He positions the car farther from the wall and reverses the orientation of the magnet on the wall.	

A. does not move

B. moves more slowly toward wall

C. moves more quickly toward wall

D. moves more slowly away from wall

E. moves more quickly away from wall

13. Four pairs of objects are brought close to one another. The diagram shows the pairs of objects and the positive and negative charges they contain.

Draw a plus sign in the middle of each positively charged object in the image.

Draw arrows beneath each object in the image representing the movement of the object when released. If the object does not move, do not draw anything below the object. Assume that charges are free to move within an object.

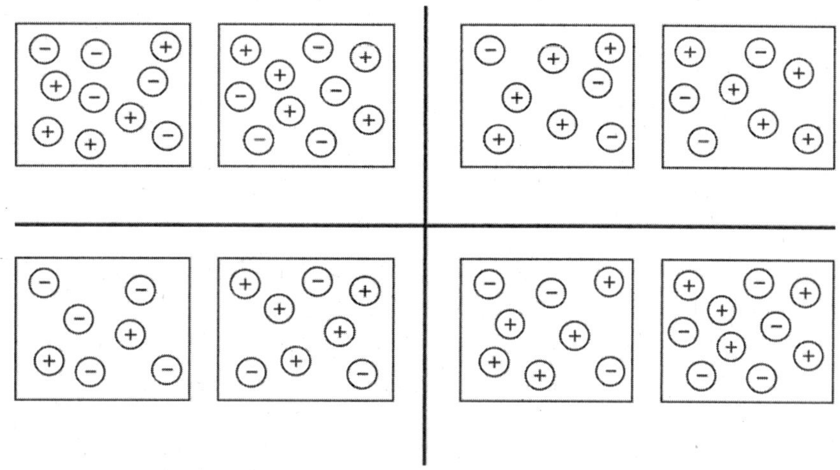

14. Karin wants to remove iron shavings from a pile of sand. Karin has refrigerator magnets. She also has batteries, insulated wire, iron bolts, and tape.

Write an X in the correct box to show whether each statement is true of an electromagnet, a permanent magnet, or both. Some statements may have more than one X.

Statement	Electromagnet	Permanent magnet
A. attracts iron but not sand		
B. can release iron shavings after they are collected		
C. can be constructed from or found among the items in Karin's home		

Read each statement. Write your answer on the lines.

15. Mia finds that when she places a needle near a magnet, the needle rotates to point toward the south pole of the magnet. Mia claims this provides evidence that there is a magnetic field that affects both objects. Explain why the needle rotated when Mia placed it near the magnet.

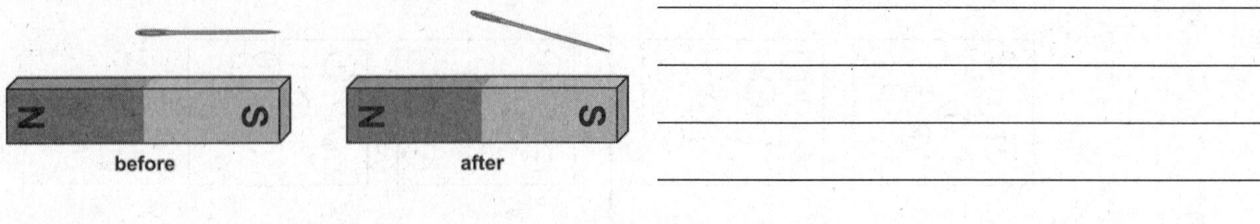

16. The model shows two planets that will attract a spacecraft from a distance. Explain what the arrows around the planets represent.

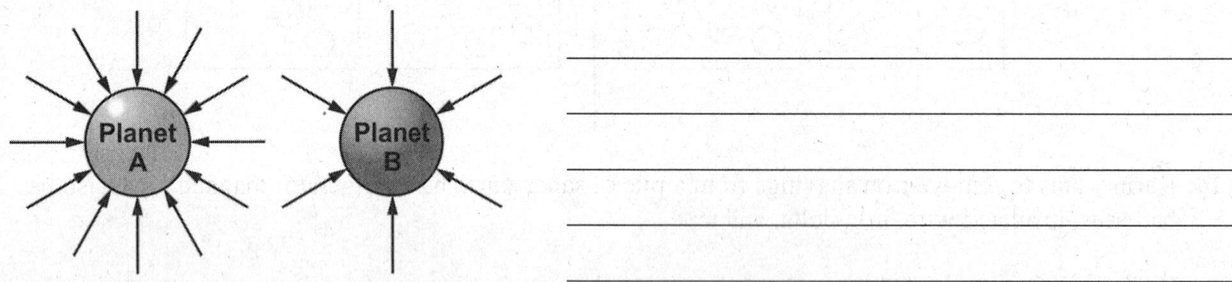

Using the model, describe how Planet A and Planet B differ.

17. This incomplete model shows three electrically charged objects that are interacting with each other. Explain what the arrows around the objects represent.

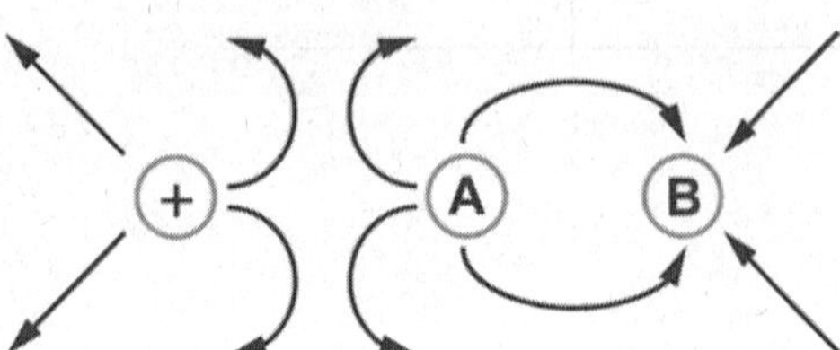

Use the model to determine the charges of objects A and B.

Directions: Read the passage, then answer the questions that follow.

Strength of Magnetic Forces

Leisha is conducting an investigation about the strength of the forces between an electromagnet and other magnetic objects. She constructs an electromagnet from a battery, a nail, and coils of wire, as shown in the diagram. Leisha hangs a piece of iron from a string and brings it near the sharp end of the nail. She repeats her process with a bar magnet. Leisha's initial observations are shown in the table.

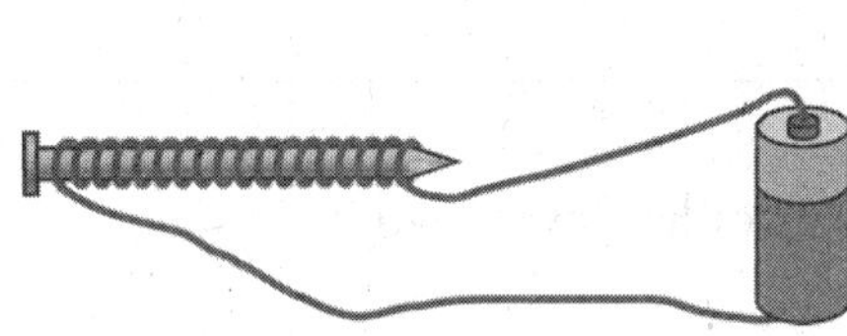

Type of object	Distance from nail	Motion of object	Speed of object
Iron	6 cm	moved toward nail	slow
Bar magnet	6 cm	north pole turned toward nail	slow
Iron	3 cm	moved toward nail	fast
Bar magnet	3 cm	north pole turned toward nail	fast

18. Based on her experiments, what hypothesis is Leisha testing?

Circle the letter of the correct answer.

A. An electromagnet exerts stronger forces on iron than on other metals.

B. An electromagnet produces stronger magnetic forces closer to the magnet.

C. An electromagnet's south pole produces stronger magnetic forces than its north pole.

19. Leisha brings an electromagnet toward a piece of iron and observes that the piece of iron starts to move when the electromagnet is 6 cm away. She plans to add another 25 coils of wire to the electromagnet. Which statement explains what will happen when she brings her modified electromagnet near the piece of iron?

Circle the letter of the correct answer.

A. The strength of the magnetic force will change, so the iron will start to move when the electromagnet is less than 6 cm away.

B. The strength of the magnetic force will change, so the iron will start to move when the electromagnet is more than 6 cm away.

C. The strength of the magnetic force will change, but the iron will still start to move when the electromagnet is exactly 6 cm away.

20. Leisha thought of three ways she could change her experimental procedure:

1. Observe the direction the bar magnet moves when she brings it near the end of the nail.
2. Observe how many paper clips she can attach to the end of the nail.
3. Connect each wire to the opposite end of the battery as before.

She wants to know how changing the direction of electric current in an electromagnet affects the magnetic force.

Write your answer on the lines.

Identify which of these modifications Leisha should use in her new experiment.

____

____

Explain how each modification you selected will help her meet the goals of her investigation.

____

____

____

____

Rubber Band Energy

Task 1: Potential Investigation

The student builds a model to represent potential energy in a system with a ruler, rubber bands, and a row of dominoes and investigates changes in amount of energy transferred.

Time Rating:

1 = less time; 4 = more time
Teacher Prep: 1
Student Prep: 1
Student Cleanup: 1
Time on Task: 45 min

Materials:

For each group

- dominoes (6)
- masking tape
- rubber band sets (3 sets of 5-6, different sizes)
- ruler (12 in. or 30 cm)
- scale (to weigh rubber bands)
- table (flat, not slanted)

For each student

- pencil
- safety goggles

Performance Expectations and 3D Learning:

MS-PS3-2 Develop a model to describe that when the arrangement of objects interacting at a distance changes, different amounts of potential energy are stored in the system.

Additional:
SEP.MS.D.3 Analyzing and Interpreting Data
CCC.MS.C.2 Scale, Proportion, and Quantity

Safety:

- Instruct students to use materials only as directed.
- Instruct students to wash their hands thoroughly after the investigation.

Tip Preparation Quick Tips:

- Consider in advance how to group students. Also consider options for adjusting materials or providing tips to students who require modification or additional assistance.
- Consider sorting the sets of rubber bands for each group using three separate containers, one for each size.
- Be sure that one of the rubber band sizes is standard type, size 14.In addition, consider using a size smaller than 14 and a size larger than 14 for the other two sets.
- Determine the number of dominoes to use by conducting a test on the tables in the classroom.
- Organize and group materials in advance to allow for a smooth transition. Select a central location in the classroom or cafeteria for the scale.
- A digital scale is preferred for more precise measurements, but a balance scale may be used as well. If needed, several rubber bands may be weighed at once and then the total mass divided by the total number of rubber bands on the scale.

Options for Project-Based Learning:

- Students can research potential energy in a system containing a rubber band while working through the concepts of their lessons.
- Students can perform additional trials using other variations in the interaction between the rubber band and the dominoes.

Task 1 – Procedure Answers:

1. Answers may vary but should explain the mechanics of how a slingshot works (by pulling the rubber band back to charge it and then releasing it as a projectile to strike another object).

2. Answers may vary but hypothesis should describe a variable (rubber band mass or the distance pulled) that will work with a 12-inch ruler. For example, "If the rubber band is pulled back more, it will transfer more energy." (The ruler size is a constant, not a variable.)
3. Answers will vary but should identify that dominoes on a slanted surface would be affected by gravity, and may slide or tip over.
8. ***Data Table 1***: Data will vary but should show that the number of dominoes increases as the ruler length increases. Some students may decide to test their rubber bands in a sequential order (from short to long, or long to short) while others will record their data without any order.
9. Answers will vary but should indicate that the longest ruler length pushed the most dominoes off the table.
10. Graphs will vary but should be similar to the one shown The x-axis should be labeled with the recorded lengths and units for each trial from *Data Table 1* and should be in order from left to right, smallest to largest length.

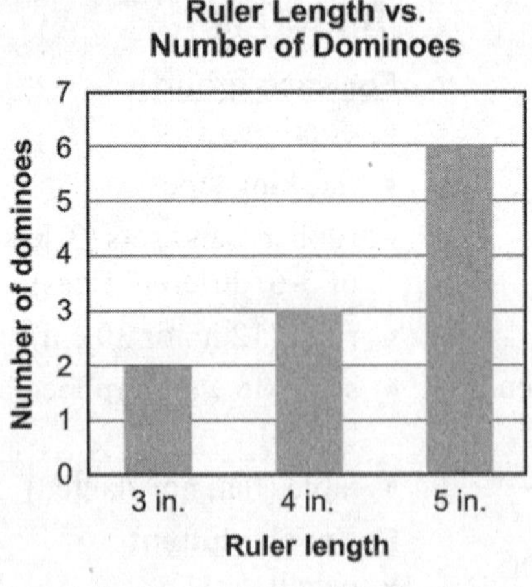

11. ***Data Table 2***: Data will vary but should show that the number of dominoes increases as the rubber band mass increases. The order of the data may be sequential or random.
12. Answers will vary but should indicate that the most massive (heaviest) rubber bands pushed the most dominoes off the table.
13. Graphs will vary but should be similar to the one shown. The x-axis should be labeled with the recorded masses and units for each trial from *Data Table 2* and should be in order from left to right, smallest to largest mass.

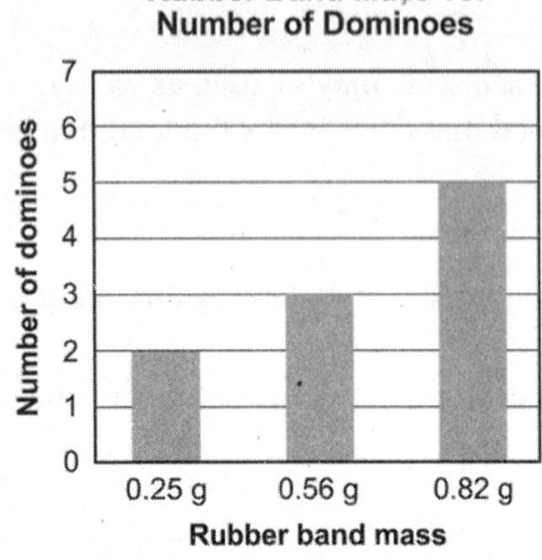

14. Answers will vary but should indicate that the trial that pushed the most dominoes off the table is either the trial with the longest length or the largest mass. It is possible that the trials with the longest length and the largest mass pushed the same number of dominoes off the table, resulting in two correct answers.

Task 1 – Summary Answers

1. Answers will vary but should explain that pulling back the rubber band stored potential energy.
2. Answers will vary but should explain that the potential energy stored in the stretched rubber band was converted to kinetic energy and then transferred to the dominoes upon impact.
3. Answers will vary but should explain that they changed either the ruler length or the mass of the rubber band, which changed the amount of potential energy in the model.
4. Answers will vary but should observe that more dominoes fell off the table for longer ruler lengths or for more massive (heavier) rubber bands.
5. Answers will vary but should explain that as the amount of potential energy stored in the system increases, the number of dominoes pushed off the table increases as well. Evidence of this is that in the first graph, the rubber band that was pulled back the farthest pushed the most dominoes off the table. Also, in the second graph, the rubber band with the most mass pushed the most dominoes off the table.

Task 1 Performance Rubric

Rating Scale

3 Outstanding	1 Needs Improvement
2 Satisfactory	0 Did Not Demonstrate Skill
NS Did not have the opportunity to observe	

Teacher Directions:
This rubric allows for performance observation of 10 students. Make copies as needed. If students are working in groups, record the group name.

Group Name ___________

Names of Students

Skills										
DCI.MS-PS3.A.4 Forces and Motion The student determines which rubber band tests contained the most stored energy, resulting in the largest transfer of energy to the dominoes.										
DCI.MS-PS3.C.1 Relationship Between Energy and Forces The student describes the interaction of the rubber band and the dominoes as a push that results in the transfer of energy.										
SEP.MS.B.3 Developing and Using Models The student uses a rubber band/ruler set-up as a model to describe energy transfer from the rubber band to the dominoes.										
CCC.MS.D.2 Systems and System Models The student explains that when objects in a system—in this case the rubber bands—change, the amount of energy in the system may also change.										
Additional SEP.MS.D.3 Analyzing and Interpreting Data The student constructs and interprets bar graphs to identify relationships between energy stored in the rubber band and number of dominoes pushed off the table.										
Additional CCC.MS.C.2 Scale, Proportion, and Quantity The student describes the relationships between ruler length and number of dominoes and between rubber band mass and number of dominoes.										

Group Name ___________

Names of Students

Skills (continued)										
Overall Achievement of Performance Expectation The student develops a model with a ruler, rubber bands, and a row of dominoes that demonstrates the change in potential energy stored and the change in the amount of energy transferred when the ruler length and mass of the rubber band are varied.										
Total										

Name: ______________________________ Date: ______________________________

Performance-Based Assessment

Rubber Band Energy

Task 1: Potential Investigation

In this task, you will build a model with a ruler, rubber bands, and a row of dominoes. You will use this model to investigate changes in energy transfer during a collision.

OBJECTIVE

Investigate changes in potential energy in a system.

SAFETY

MATERIALS

For each group

- dominoes (6)
- masking tape
- rubber band sets
- ruler (12 in. or 30 cm)
- scale (to weigh rubber bands)
- table (flat, not slanted)

For each student

- pencil
- safety goggles

PROCEDURE

Ask a question.

1. How does a slingshot transfer energy?

____

____

____

____

Write a hypothesis.

2. If you build a slingshot with a ruler and a rubber band and fire it at a row of dominoes, how can you change the amount of energy that is transferred?

____

____

____

Build a model.

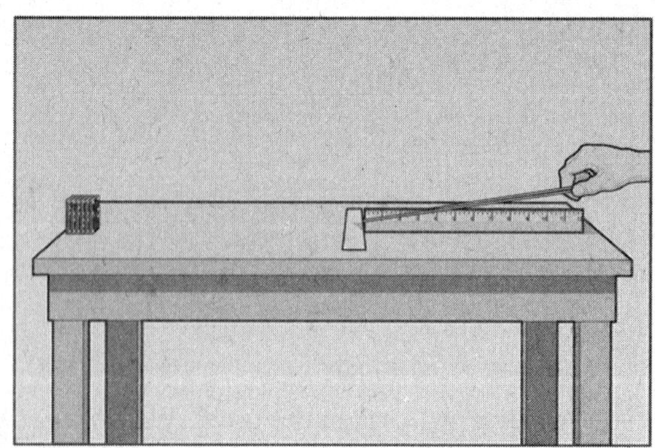

3. Stand the dominoes on their ends and arrange them so they are touching each other with no spaces between them to create a "block" of dominoes. Place the block right on the edge of one side of the table as in the image above. Why do you think the table used for this model needs to be flat and not slanted like some student desks?

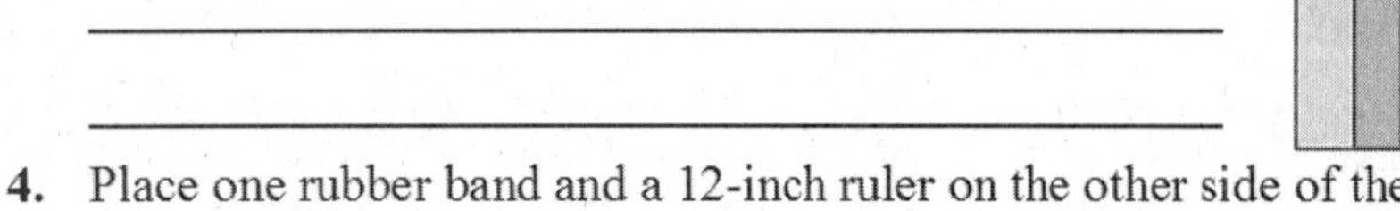

4. Place one rubber band and a 12-inch ruler on the other side of the table. Turn the ruler so the lowest number faces the dominoes. Make a starting line with masking tape to remind you where to place the ruler.

   CAUTION: Put on your safety goggles. Ask any students on the other side of the table to move away.

Test a hypothesis.

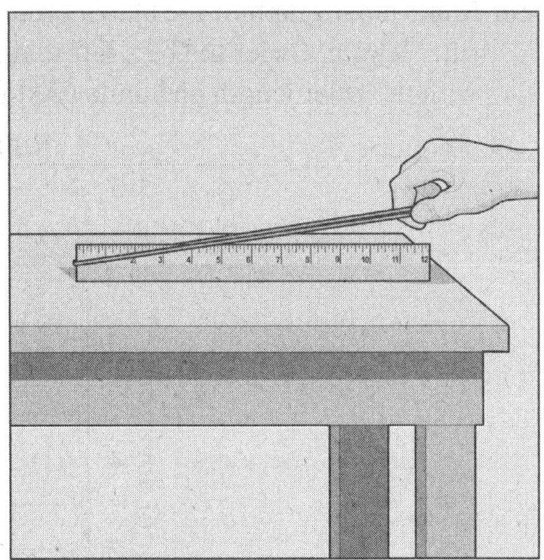

5. Stand the ruler up on the edge of the masking tape starting line. Place a rubber band in the center of the ruler edge with the lowest number.

6. Hold the ruler steady as you pull the other side of the rubber band back. Look at the number under your finger where you stopped pulling.

   CAUTION: Make sure that the ruler is still pointing at the row of dominoes and that no one is standing in the path of the rubber band.

7. Aiming at the center of the block of dominoes, let go of the rubber band while holding the ruler in place. It may take a couple of practice trials to get the rubber band to hit the dominoes in the right place.

Record your data.

8. Gather data for ruler length and number of dominoes pushed off the table for three trials.

   a. Write down how far back on the ruler you pulled the rubber band in *Data Table 1*. This variable will be called the "ruler length." Then record the number of dominoes the rubber band pushed off the table in *Data Table 1*.

   b. Line up the row of dominoes at the edge of the table again and repeat the test two more times using the same rubber band and hitting the dominoes in the same place each time. Place the rubber band in the center of the ruler edge and pull the rubber band back to a different ruler length each time. Use the same units for all trials, either inches or centimeters.

   c. Record the ruler length and number of dominoes for trials 2 and 3 in *Data Table 1*.

Data Table 1: Different Ruler Lengths

Trial	Ruler length	Number of dominoes
1		
2		
3		

Draw a conclusion.

9. Analyze the data in the table. Which ruler length pushed the most dominoes off the table?

____

____

____

10. Make a bar graph of the data in your table. Use your pencil to draw a bar to the correct height for each ruler length. Order the bars left to right from smallest to largest length. Replace the words on the *x*-axis with the ruler length and units used for each trial in *Data Table 1.*

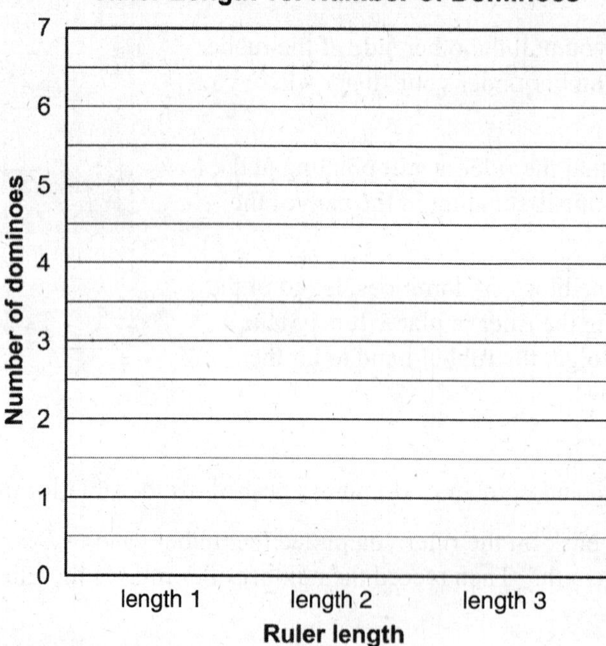

Test another hypothesis.

11. Gather data for rubber band mass and number of dominoes pushed off the table for three trials.

a. Record the mass of each rubber band in *Data Table 2*. Use the same units for each mass measurement.

b. Choose a ruler length from *Data Table 1*. One by one, pull each rubber band in the set back to the chosen length and shoot at the dominoes.

c. Line up the row of dominoes at the edge of the table again and repeat the test with each rubber band. Record the number of dominoes pushed off the table in each trial in *Data Table 2*.

Data Table 2: Different Rubber Bands

Trial	Rubber band mass	Number of dominoes
1		
2		
3		

Draw a conclusion.

12. Compare the data in the second table. Which rubber band mass pushed the most dominoes off the table?

____

____

13. Make a bar graph of the data in your table. Use your pencil to draw a bar to the correct height for each rubber band mass. Order the bars left to right from smallest to largest mass. Replace the words on the *x*-axis with the rubber band mass and units measured for each trial in *Data Table 2*.

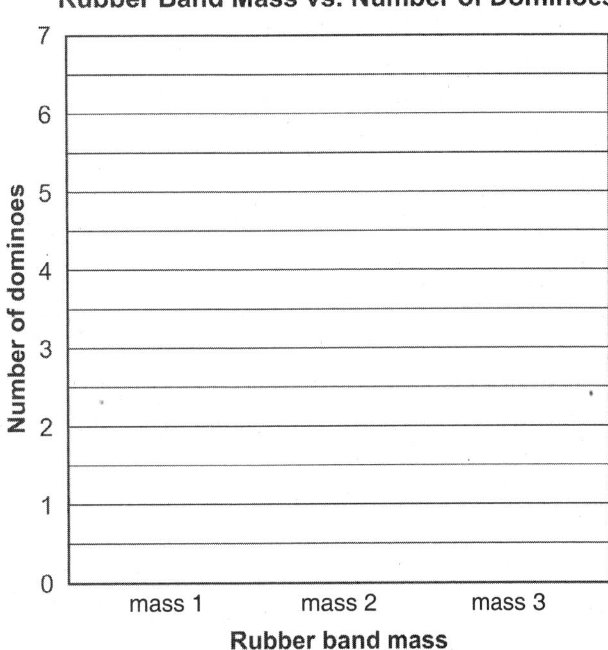

14. Now, compare the data from both graphs. Which rubber band trial transferred the most energy to the dominoes?

____

____

____

____

TASK SUMMARY

1. What kind of energy did you produce by pulling back the rubber band?

____

____

2. What happened when you released the rubber band after pulling it?

____

____

____

3. What did you change when you investigated the energy transfer two different ways?

4. What, if anything, can you conclude about the effect of the ruler length and the mass of the rubber band on the number of dominoes that can be pushed off the table?

5. How does the amount of potential energy stored in the system relate to the number of dominoes pushed off the table? Support your answer with evidence from both of the graphs you made.

Rubber Band Energy

Task 2: Interactive Forces

The student builds a model of an interactive force pair with a rubber band, recycled materials, and a row of dominoes to investigate changes in interactive force pairs during a collision.

Performance Expectations and 3D Learning:

MS-PS2-1 Apply Newton's Third Law to design a solution to a problem involving the motion of two colliding objects.

Additional:
DCI.MS-PS3.A.3 Definitions of Energy
DCI.MS-PS3.A.4 Definitions of Energy

Safety:

- Instruct students to wear goggles.
- Instruct students to use materials only as directed.
- Instruct students to wash their hands thoroughly after the investigation.

Tip Preparation Quick Tips:

- The intent of this task is for students to design and test a car powered by rubber bands that will be used to collide with dominoes.
- Determine ahead of time how many rubber bands students will need to make a chain the length of the paper towel tube. Add rubber bands to the sets for each group if needed.
- Size 14 (standard) rubber bands work best to power the car. Guide students to switch to this size rubber band if they are having a hard time getting the car to move.
- Begin collecting paper towel tubes (one for each group) and a variety of round jar and plastic container lids (for wheel-tracing guides) ahead of time.
- Vary the size of the piece of cardboard given to each group if necessary depending on the sizes of lids being used to trace the wheels.
- Mark places for students to punch holes on paper towel tube to insert axles ahead of time to make sure the holes are even.
- If there are not enough single-hole punches for each group to have their own, consider punching holes ahead of time or having groups share any that are available.
- Become familiar with the materials and procedure prior to assigning task to the students. Prepare and test a sample car using available materials and modify materials lists and student directions as needed. Clay, hot glue, tape, or whatever you have available may need to be used to keep the wheels from spinning around the axles. Wrapping rubber bands around the back wheels can create traction to help the car move more easily as well.

Time Rating:

1 = less time; 4 = more time
Teacher Prep: 2
Student Prep: 3
Student Cleanup: 1
Time on Task: 2 class periods (1 to design and build, 1 to test and gather data)

Materials:

For each group

- cardboard (1 piece, 10 in. x 10 in.)
- dominoes (6)
- duct tape (1, small piece)
- hole punch (single-hole)
- lids (round, various sizes)
- masking tape (for starting and finishing lines)
- paper clips (6, jumbo)
- paper towel tube
- pencils (2, round, unsharpened)
- rubber band sets (3 sets of 5-6, different sizes)
- scale
- scissors
- table or floor (long, flat)
- washers (5, metal)

For each student

- pencil
- safety goggles

- Organize and group materials in advance to allow for a smooth transition. Select a central location in the classroom or cafeteria for the scale.
- A digital scale is preferred for more precise measurements, but a balance scale may be used as well.
- Arrange to use the cafeteria floor or tables (or a secluded hallway) for the racetrack on the crash testing day.
- Consider options for adjusting materials or providing tips to students who require modification or additional assistance, particularly while designing and building the car.

Options for Project-Based Learning:

- Students can research and build a model of an interactive force pair and use their model to demonstrate the relationships of kinetic energy to the mass and the speed of two colliding objects while working through the concepts of their lessons.
- Students may build a rubber band car using materials available at home. They may also test a variety of variables, such as changing the body of the car and using different materials for the wheels (CDs, bottle lids, etc.).

Task 2 – Procedure Answers:

2. Drawings will vary but should be similar to the one shown and should show the paper towel tube as the body of the car with cardboard circles as wheels attached to the tube using the pencils as axles.

13. ***Data Table 1:*** Data will vary but should be reasonable and show that the number of dominoes increases as the number of wheel turns increases.
14. ***Data Table 2:*** Data will vary but should be reasonable and show that the number of dominoes increases as the mass of the car increases.

Task 2 – Summary Answers

1. Answers will vary but should indicate that the medium sized rubber band worked best because it is stretchy or thin enough to wind around the rear axle easily but still can store more potential energy than the smallest rubber band.
2. Answers will vary but should explain that the number of dominoes pushed off the table or past the finish line changed due to change in the amount of energy in the system when the number of wheel turns and mass were varied.
3. Answers will vary but should explain that the data shows that the number of dominoes pushed off the table or past the finish line increased as the number of wheel turns and car mass increased. This means that the energy of the system increases when the number of wheel turns (and therefore speed) and car mass are increased.
4. Answers will vary, but drawing should be a force diagram. An arrow or arrows from the car point down to show weight. An arrow or arrows from the track point up to show a reactive force. The two forces are balanced. Refer to *Task 2* of the *Supplemental Teacher Materials* for an example of a force diagram.

5. Answers will vary, but drawing should be a force diagram and should show force arrows pointing toward each other—the car pushes the dominoes, and the dominoes push the car. Refer to *Task 2* of the *Supplemental Teacher Materials* for an example of a force diagram.
6. Answers will vary but should explain that the rubber band car and the dominoes acted as a force pair in each trial because they always exhibited action and reaction forces. They exerted equal and opposite forces when they collided.

Print and distribute or write Task 2 Problem on board. Enlarge as needed.

Task 2 Problem

How does the energy of the system change when speed and mass change?

Use the given materials to develop a car that is powered by rubber bands, has four wheels and a body, and transfers the most energy possible to the block of dominoes.

Task 2 Performance Rubric

Rating Scale

3 Outstanding	1 Needs Improvement
2 Satisfactory	0 Did Not Demonstrate Skill
NS Did not have the opportunity to observe	

Teacher Directions:

This rubric allows for performance observation of 10 students. Make copies as needed. If students are working in groups, record the group name.

Group Name ___________

Names of Students

Skills										
DCI.MS-PS2.A.1 Forces and Motion The student draws a sketch of the rubber band car and explains how the rubber band car and the dominoes act as a force pair in each trial..										
SEP.MS.F.4 Constructing Explanations and Designing Solutions The student designs and builds a rubber band car to collide with a row of dominoes on a racetrack.										
CCC.MS.D.2 Systems and System Models The student draws arrows representing forces on a diagram of the rubber band car and the dominoes on a racetrack before and after the collision.										
Additional DCI.MS-PS3.A.3 Definitions of Energy The student analyzes the motion of the rubber band car and describes the relationship between energy and speed and between energy and mass.										
Additional DCI.MS-PS3.A.4 Definitions of Energy The student uses the relationship between stored potential energy and amount of energy transferred to explain which rubber band works best to power the car.										
Overall Achievement of Performance Expectation The student designs and builds a device to demonstrate the relationships of kinetic energy to the speed and kinetic energy to mass of two colliding objects..										
Total										

Rubber Band Energy

Task 2: Interactive Forces

In this task, you will build a model of an interactive force pair with a rubber band, recycled materials, and a row of dominoes. You will use this model to investigate changes in interactive force pairs during a collision.

OBJECTIVE

Investigate changes in interactive force pair speed and mass.

PROCEDURE

Design a model.

1. Read and discuss the *Task 2 Problem* presented by your teacher with your group.
2. Design a model of a rubber band–powered car that can be used to test the problem. You will use the materials given to you by your teacher. A chain of rubber bands will power the car. Note that the size of the wheels in your test car may vary. Discuss with your group and draw your design.

Build your model and set up the track.

3. Use the lids in the desired size or sizes to trace circles on the cardboard. Cut out all four wheels.
4. Have your teacher help you poke holes in the middle of the wheels and attach them to the body of the car using the pencils as axles.
5. Look at the data you collected about the different types of rubber bands in *Task 1*. Determine which rubber band will work the best to power the car and transfer the most energy while colliding with the dominoes.

SAFETY

MATERIALS

For each group

- cardboard (1 piece)
- dominoes (6)
- duct tape (1, small piece)
- hole punch (single-hole)
- lids (round, various sizes)
- masking tape (for starting and finishing lines)
- paper clips (6, jumbo)
- paper towel tube
- pencils (2, round, unsharpened)
- rubber bands sets
- scale
- scissors
- table or floor
- washers (5, metal)

For each student

- pencil
- safety goggles

6. Place a single row of rubber bands, end to end, along the length of the paper towel tube. Then, make the rubber band chain to power your car.

   a. Place one rubber band halfway across the top of another one.
   b. Pull one side of the bottom rubber band through the middle of the top one and back through the middle of the bottom one.
   c. Pull the end of each rubber band in the opposite direction. This will make a knot in the middle.
   d. Repeat the rubber band knot steps, placing the bands already in a chain on top and the new rubber band on bottom. Make a chain using all the rubber bands you lined up. This will ensure that the chain reaches the entire length of the paper towel tube.

Step 1

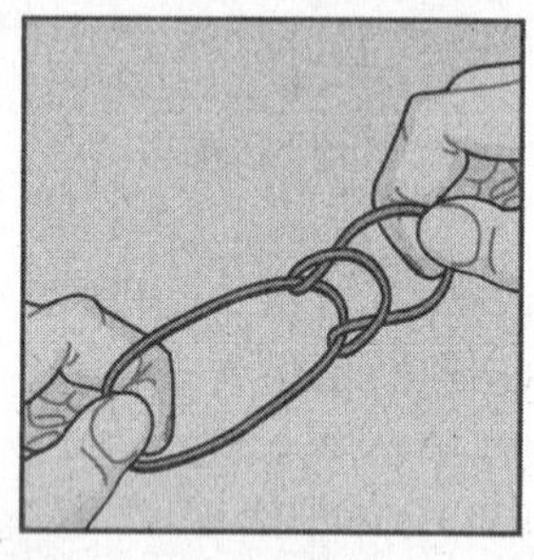
Step 2

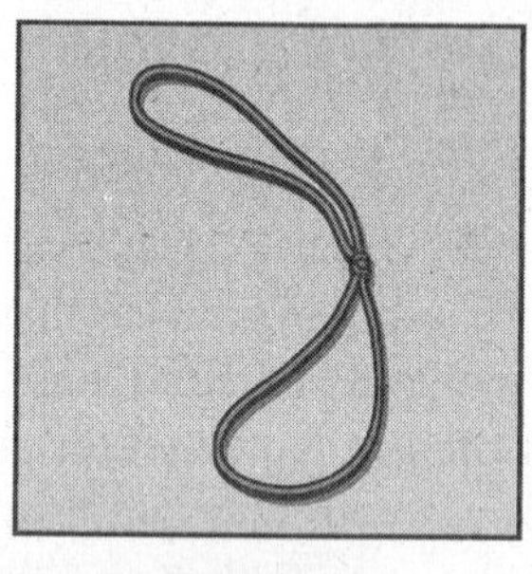
Step 3

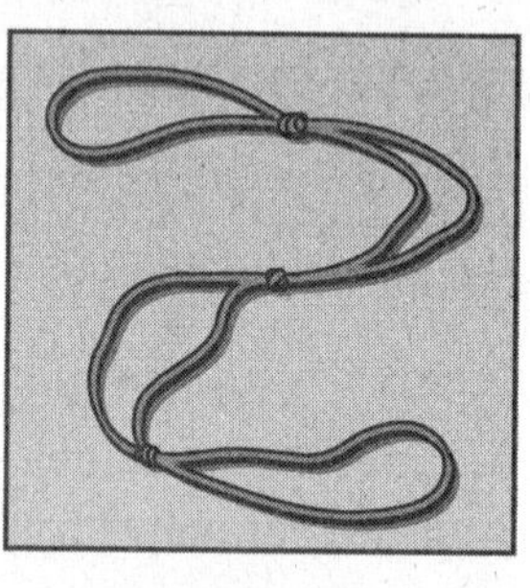
Step 4

7. Loop the rubber band chain around one of the axles inside the paper towel tube.

   a. Set the car flat on the table. Mark the top of the car with a pencil so you remember which side is the top.
   b. Push one end of the rubber band chain into the tube from the bottom of the car and wrap around the axle closest to you, pushing the rubber band toward the top of the car.
   c. Pull the rubber band out of the tube slightly and insert the other end of the chain through the loop. Pull tight.
   d. Place a small piece of tape around the axle and connected rubber band so that the chain will wrap around the axle when the wheels are turned. This will be the back axle of the car.

8. Hook a paper clip on the end of the rubber band chain that is not connected to the back axle. Drop the paper clip down into the tube and hook it onto the top of the car at the other end of the tube

9. On one of the rear tires, draw a line from the axle to the edge of the tire. When you roll the car backward to wind up the rubber band, you will count how many times the wheel turned by counting the number of times the rear wheel line revolved in a complete circle.

10. Create a racetrack for your car by clearing an area on the floor or on a flat table 1 meter wide and 2–3 meters long. Stand six dominoes on their ends at the end of the track as you did in *Task 1,* arranging the dominoes into a block so they are touching each other with no spaces between them. Make a starting line with masking tape on the other side of the racetrack.

    Tip: If you are using a long table, place the last domino in the block at the end of the table as you did for the slingshot test. If you are making a track on the floor, make a line of masking tape beside the last domino as the crash test finish line.

    CAUTION: Put on your safety goggles. Ask any students along the track to move aside.

Test your device.

11. Place the car at the starting line. Roll the car backward several times to wind up the rubber band. Count the number of times the rear wheel line revolved in a complete circle.

NOTE: If you decide to change the type of rubber band you are using to power the car, be sure to keep track of which type worked best and why.

12. Hold one of the back wheels tightly as you lift the car and place it at the starting line again. Do not let the wheels spin in the air. Then let go of the back wheel to allow the car to move.

CAUTION: Make sure that the rubber band car is pointing at the wall of dominoes and that no one is standing in the path of the car.

NOTE: It may be helpful to have someone else in your group hold the car down while you turn the wheels, especially for a large number of wheel turns.

Record your data.

13. Gather data for number of wheel turns and number of dominoes pushed off the table for three trials.

a. Record the number of times the rear wheel line revolved in a complete circle in *Data Table 1.*

b. Record the number of dominoes the car pushed off the table or past the finish line on the floor in *Data Table 1.*

c. Repeat the test two more times with a different number of wheel turns each time. Record your data for all three trials in *Data Table 1.*

Data Table 1: Different Wheel Turns

Trial	Wheel Turns	Number of dominoes
1		
2		
3		

Test your device another way.

14. Gather data for car mass and number of dominoes pushed off the table for three trials.

a. Choose a rubber band wheel turn number from *Data Table 1.* Use that number in the next three trials.

b. Measure and record the mass of your car in *Data Table 2* for the first trial.

c. Record the number of dominoes the car pushed off the table or past the finish line on the floor in *Data Table 2* for the first trial.

d. Add mass to the car by attaching 1 or 2 metal washers to the body of the car using paper clips. Measure and record the mass of the car again, and conduct a second trial.

e. Add more mass to the car by attaching 1 or 2 more washers. Measure and record the mass of the car, and conduct a third trial. Record all your data in *Data Table 2.*

Name: ______________________________ Date: ______________________

Performance-Based Assessment

Data Table 2: Different Car Masses

Trial	Car Mass	Number of dominoes
1		
2		
3		

TASK SUMMARY

1. Which type of rubber band from *Task 1* worked the best to power the rubber band car? Explain why you think this is the case.

2. Why did the number of dominoes pushed off the table or past the finish line change when the number of wheel turns and the mass of the car changed?

3. Look at the data in *Data Table 1* and *Data Table 2*. Use this data to explain the relationship between energy and speed of an object and energy and mass of an object.

4. Draw a picture of your car resting on the racetrack at the starting line before you rolled the car back and began the trial. Add and label arrows to show the direction of the forces acting on the car before you touch it when it is not moving before the collision.

5. Draw a picture of your rubber band car at the moment it collided with the block of dominoes. Add and label arrows to show the direction of the forces during the collision.

6. How did the rubber band car and the dominoes act as a force pair in each trial?

____

____

____

____

Name: ______________________________ Date: ______________________________

Performance-Based Assessment

Rubber Band Energy

Part 2: Collisions

Read the passage, then answer the questions that follow.

Jason is investigating changes in interactive force pairs during collisions. He placed one car at the top of the ramp and one at the bottom of the ramp. Then Jason let go of the car at the top of the ramp and made observations.

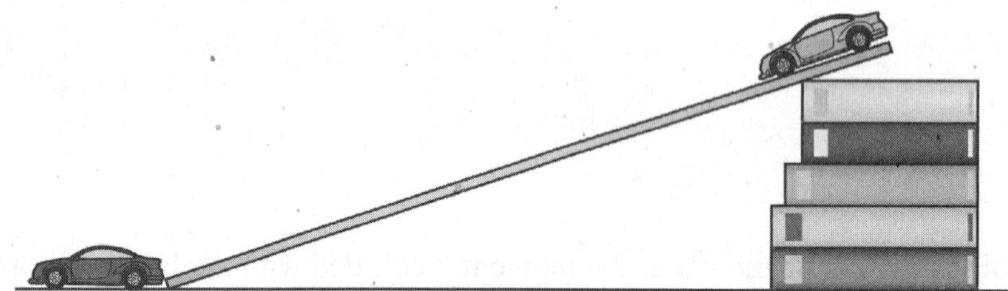

1. Jason placed a toy car at the top of the ramp and at the bottom of the ramp. What happened next? Write an X in the table to show whether each statement is true or false.

Statement	True	False
A. The bottom car transferred energy as it moved forward.		
B. The car parked at the bottom of the ramp moved forward.		
C. The top car transferred energy as it moved down the ramp.		
D. The top car transferred energy to the bottom car when they collided.		
E. The bottom car transferred energy as it sat at the bottom of the ramp.		
F. After it rolled down the ramp, the top car exerted force on the bottom car.		
G. After Jason let go of the car at the top of the ramp, it rolled down the ramp.		

2. Select the words from the drop-down lists to correctly complete the sentences about the changes in energy and movement of the cars. Write the letter of the word in the correct blank.

When Jason placed a toy car at the top of the ramp, it increased the car's __________. Jason decided to try another experiment. He placed the top car in the middle of the ramp to __________ the car's potential energy. When Jason started the top car in the middle of the ramp, the car at the bottom moved __________ when he started the car at the top of the ramp.

A. mass	**D.** lower	**G.** not as far as
B. kinetic energy	**E.** force	**H.** the same distance as
C. potential energy	**F.** raise	**I.** farther than

3. Jason wanted to know if using a more massive car on the ramp would push the bottom car farther. He chose one car to be the parked car for each test. Then he picked up five more toy cars and measured their mass.

   Predict the movement of the bottom car when Jason uses cars with more mass on the ramp.

   ____

   ____

   ____

   Describe the relationship between the mass of a toy car and kinetic energy.

   ____

   ____

   ____

4. Review the model in the passage.

   Describe the positions of the cars after the collision.

   ____

   ____

   ____

   ____

   Use force pairs to explain the movement of the cars.

   ____

   ____

   ____

   ____

Item Analysis		
Item #	**Standards**	**DOK**
1	MS-PS3-2, DCI.MS-PS3.C.1, SEP.MS.B.3	2
2	MS-PS3-2, DCI.MS-PS3.A.4	2
3	MS-PS3-1, DCI.MS-PS3.A.3, SEP.MS.F.1	2
4	MS-PS2-1, DCI.MS-PS2.A.1, SEP.MS.B.3	3

1. **A.** This is *false* because the energy transfer had already taken place in the collision.

B. This is *true* because kinetic energy is transferred from the top car to the bottom car when they collide.

C. This is *false* because energy is not transferred without a collision. Potential energy was transformed into kinetic energy.

D. This is *true* because the top car transferred kinetic energy, causing the bottom car to move.

E. This is *false* because the car at rest at the bottom of the ramp has neither potential nor kinetic energy.

F. This is *true* because the bottom car was parked at the bottom of the ramp and the top car exerted a force when they collided, causing the bottom car to move.

G. This is *true* because gravitational force will pull the car down the ramp.

2. *Potential energy* is correct because positioning the car at the top of the ramp raises it off the ground, and the higher off the ground something is, the more potential energy it has.

Lower is correct because positioning the car in the middle of the ramp moves it closer to the ground, which lowers its potential energy.

Not as far as is correct because a car starting in the middle of the ramp has less potential energy than a car starting at the top of the ramp and therefore transfers less energy to the car at the bottom of the ramp. With less kinetic energy, the car at the bottom of the ramp will not move as far.

3. Use the rubric below to evaluate total points earned for this item. *[max point: 2]*

DCI, SEP - 2 Points	
Claims	The student is able to: 1. explain the relationship between kinetic energy and mass (DCI); and 2. predict the movement of the bottom car when Jason uses cars with more mass on the ramp (SEP).
Evidence of Mastery of Disciplinary Core Ideas	1 point for correctly describing the relationship between an object's kinetic energy and mass **Part 2:** One point is earned for that an object's mass is directly proportional to its kinetic energy. The following response, or an equivalent, is acceptable: • The more massive a car, the more kinetic energy it has when it is moving.
Evidence of Mastery of Science and Engineering Practices	1 point for correctly predicting the change in the movement of the bottom car when the mass of the top car is changed **Part 1:** One point is earned for predicting that the bottom car will move farther with increasing the mass of the top car. The following response, or an equivalent, is acceptable: • After being struck by the first car, the bottom car will roll farther each time the mass of the top car is increased.

4. Use the rubric below to evaluate total points earned for this item. *[max point: 3]*

<table>
<tr><th colspan="2">DCI, SEP - 3 Points</th></tr>
<tr><td>Claims</td><td>The student is able to:
1. apply Newton's third law to explain position and movement of objects before and after a collision (DCI); and
2. use a model to describe the position of the cars after a collision (SEP).</td></tr>
<tr><td>Evidence of Mastery of Disciplinary Core Ideas</td><td>1 point for correctly using force pairs to explain movement
Part 1: One point is earned for explaining that the bottom car moves forward and the top car slows and comes to a stop because the two cars act as a force pair, exerting equal and opposite forces on each other. The following response, or an equivalent, is acceptable.
• The cars will exert equal and opposite forces on each other, causing the bottom car to move and the top car to slow down.</td></tr>
<tr><td>Evidence of Mastery of Science and Engineering Practices</td><td>2 points for correctly using the model to describe the outcome of a collision
Part 2: Two points are earned for describing that the bottom car will move forward while the top car will slow or come to a stop. The following response, or an equivalent, is acceptable.
• After being struck by the first car, the bottom car will roll forward, away from the ramp and the top car will slow down and eventually stop.</td></tr>
</table>

Electromagnetism at Work

Task 1: Investigating Magnetic Fields and Forces

The student will conduct an investigation and evaluate the investigational design to produce data about the effect of current flow on the strength and direction of the magnetic field generated in an electromagnet.

Time Rating:

1 = less time; 4 = more time
Teacher Prep: 3
Student Prep: 2
Student Cleanup: 1
Time on Task: 45 min

Materials:

For each group

- batteries (2, size D)
- compass
- electrical tape (1 roll)
- knife switch (on/off switch)
- magnet wire (10 ft, 18 gauge or higher/thinner)
- nail (1, 16d or greater)
- paperclips (20)

For each student

- pencil
- safety goggles

Performance Expectations and 3D Learning

MS-PS2-5. Conduct an investigation and evaluate the experimental design to provide evidence that fields exist between objects exerting forces on each other even though the objects are not in contact.

Safety:

- Use caution when working with electricity. Do not to touch both ends of the battery at once.
- Use insulated wire. Never use batteries that are leaking. Dispose of at approved hazardous waste location.
- Students should not touch the battery terminals while the electromagnet is turned on.
- Students should not leave the electromagnets turned on for more than a minute or two at a time, as the nail and batteries will get hot to the touch.
- If using a doorbell button, students should not touch the underside of the button while depressing.
- Check to be sure there are no frayed wires before and after task.
- Use caution if stripping the ends of wires with scissors.
- Instruct students to use materials only as directed.
- Instruct students to wash their hands thoroughly after the investigation.
- Instruct students to use caution when using the sharp end of the nail.

Preparation Quick Tips:

- Copper speaker wire can be used instead of magnet wire but does not create as strong an electromagnet. If speaker wire is used, the outer covering will need to be removed and the wrapped wires unwound so that only a single wire is used.
- Before beginning the task, cut 10-ft wire pieces into sections that are 8 ft, 1 ft, and 1 ft in length.
- Remove approximately 1 cm of insulation from the ends of each wire in advance. Be sure to cut through the plastic, but NOT the wire.
- A doorbell button can be used as a knife (on/off) switch. If a doorbell button is used, the teacher will need a screwdriver to loosen the screws on the back of the button. Also, students will have to push the button and hold it down while collecting data in the investigation.
- Alligator clips can replace tape and wire in the electromagnet.
- Battery holder can replace tape on the batteries.
- For students who require assistance, preassemble electromagnets.

Options for Project-Based Learning:

- Students can research experimental design components, such as the purpose and independent, dependent, and controlled variables, while working through their lessons on magnetic forces, electric fields, and electromagnetism.
- Students can research magnetic fields, particularly the direction of magnetic fields, while developing their own experimental design for the task.

Task 1 – Procedure Answers:

9. Answers will vary but should resemble the sample data table shown.

Sample Data Table

Direction of current flow	Location of north pole	Location of south pole	Number of paperclips at Point A	Number of paperclips at Point B
Counter-clockwise	Point A	Point B	Answers will vary but should be similar to the number of paperclips at Point B counterclockwise.	Answers will vary but should be similar to the number of paperclips at Point A counterclockwise.
Clockwise	Point B	Point A	Answers will vary but should be similar to the number of paperclips at Point B clockwise.	Answers will vary but should be similar to the number of paperclips at Point A clockwise.

Task 1 – Summary Answers:

1. Yes. There are forces acting at a distance in this investigation. The compass does not come in direct contact with the electromagnet, yet it moves in response to the magnetic field. When the compass is removed from the magnetic field of the electromagnet, it is no longer affected.
2. The purpose of the investigation was to show that electromagnetic forces act at a distance and produce a magnetic field and to determine how current flow affects this field.
3. The independent variable is current flow direction. The two dependent variables are the locations of the north and south poles of the electromagnet and the number of paperclips attracted to the electromagnet.
4. Yes, because the data collected show that the electromagnet does have a field and that the locations of the north and south poles of the electromagnet are dependent upon the direction of current (location changes when the direction of current changes). The data also show that the strength of the magnetic field is not affected by the current flow. This could be improved by testing the number of paperclips attracted to the electromagnet at only one point. I would modify the experimental design to only determine the number of paperclips attracted to the electromagnet at Point A.
5. The current flow direction determines the locations of the north and south poles of the electromagnet. For example, when the current is flowing in a counterclockwise direction, the point where the current goes into the nail (the right end) will be the south pole. The point where the current comes out of the nail (the left end) will be the north pole. When a compass is brought close to the north end of the electromagnet, the needle will orientate itself so that the south pole, or white end, of the needle is closest to the north pole of the electromagnet.

Task 1 Performance Rubric

Rating Scale

3 Outstanding	1 Needs Improvement
2 Satisfactory	0 Did Not Demonstrate Skill
NS Did not have the opportunity to observe	

Teacher Directions:
This rubric allows for performance observation of 10 students. Make copies as needed. If students are working in groups, record the group name.

Group Name ___________

Names of Students

Skills										
DCI.MS-PS2.B.3 Types of Interactions The student demonstrates electromagnetic forces that act at a distance by indicating the direction of the field generated (using a compass) and the effect on test objects (paperclips).										
SEP.MS.C.2 Planning and Carrying Out Investigations The student conducts an investigation and records data about the effect of current flow on the strength and direction of the magnetic field generated in an electromagnet.										
SEP.MS.C.2 Planning and Carrying Out Investigations The student accurately determines the purpose of the investigation.										
SEP.MS.C.2 Planning and Carrying Out Investigations The student evaluates whether the investigational design is suitable for producing the necessary data for the purpose of the investigation and describes a modification to improve the investigation.										

Group Name ___________

Names of Students

Skills (continued)										
CCC.MS.B.2 Cause and Effect The student predicts the behavior of the compass based upon the current flow.										
CCC.MS.G.1 Stability and Change The student correctly predicts the polarity of an electromagnet based on the relationship between current flow and the direction of the forces within a magnetic field.										
Overall Achievement of Performance Expectation The student conducts an investigation and evaluates the experimental design to provide evidence that electromagnetic fields can be generated and can exert a force on an object at a distance.										
Total										

Name: Date:

Electromagnetism at Work

Task1: Investigating Magnetic Fields and Forces:

In this task, you will build an electromagnet and use it to conduct an investigation about electromagnetic forces. You will the use the collected data to determine the purpose and evaluate the design of the investigation.

OBJECTIVE

Investigate magnetic fields generated by an electromagnet.

SAFETY

MATERIALS

For each group

- batteries (2, size D)
- compass
- electrical tape (1 roll)
- knife switch (on/off switch)
- magnet wire (10 ft, cut in 3 pieces)
- nail (1, 16d or greater)
- paperclips (20)

For each student

- pencil
- safety goggles

PROCEDURE

Build an electromagnet.

1. Wrap a long piece of wire around a nail 50 or more times, making certain to leave excess wire at both ends of the nail.
2. Connect one end of the wire wrapped around the nail to the knife switch (on/off switch). Tape the other end of this wire to the positive end of one size D battery. (Use multiple pieces of tape if necessary to ensure that the wire is continually touching the battery.)
3. Connect a shorter piece of wire to the other side of the on/off switch. Tape the other end of this shorter wire to the negative end of the second size D battery.
4. Use tape and the second short piece of wire to connect the negative end of the first size D battery to the positive end of the second size D battery.

Conduct the investigation.

5. Turn the electromagnet on. The current will flow through each battery from the negative end toward the positive end in a counter-clockwise direction. Use the compass to determine the north and south poles of the electromagnet at Points A and B and record the data in the *Data Table*.

   CAUTION: Do not leave the electromagnet turned on for more than a minute at a time. It will get hot to the touch! If it does begin to get warm, turn it off until it cools.

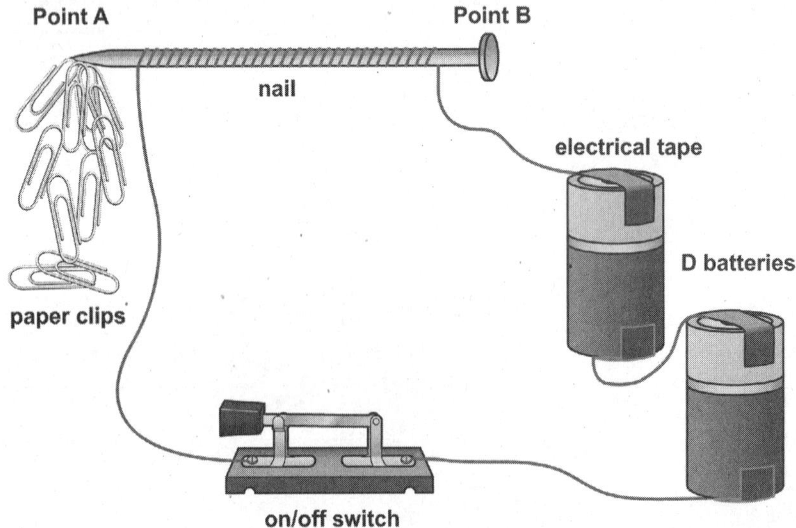

6. Hold the end of the electromagnet at Point A over the paperclips. Record in the *Data Table* the number of paperclips attracted to the electromagnet.
7. Hold the end of the electromagnet at Point B over the paperclips. Record in the *Data Table* the number of paperclips attracted to the electromagnet.
8. Remove the tape from the batteries and flip them to reverse the positive and negative poles. Tape the portion of the wire connected to the knife (on/off) switch to the positive end of one of the batteries. Tape the portion of the wire connected to the nail to the negative end of the other battery. Connect the unconnected ends of the batteries using the remaining piece of wire.
9. The current will flow from the negative end of the battery toward the positive, in a clockwise direction. Use the compass to determine the north and poles of the electromagnet at Points A and B and record the data in the *Data Table.*
10. Repeat steps 6 and 7 using this reversed set–up.
11. Record your data from Procedure steps 5 - 10 in the table.

Sample Data Table.

Direction of current flow	Location of north pole (Point A or Point B)	Location of south pole (Point A or Point B)	Number of paperclips attracted to Point A	Number of paperclips attracted to Point B
Counter-clockwise				
Clockwise				

11. Wash your hands before leaving the classroom.

Task Summary

1. Is there evidence of forces acting at a distance in this investigation? Explain your answer.

____

____

____

2. What is the purpose of this investigation?

____

____

____

____

3. The independent variable is the thing that caused a change, while the dependent variable is the thing that was affected by this change. What would be considered the independent variable and the two dependent variables in this experiment?

4. Does the data collected during the investigation provide evidence to support the purpose? Explain your reasoning and identify any changes that could be made to improve the experimental design.

5. Use the data collected to draw a conclusion about how the direction of current flow from the batteries through the electromagnet, and the locations of the north and south poles of the electromagnet, can be used to predict the behavior of a compass needle.

Electromagnetism at Work

Task 2: Push Me, Pull Me

The student will design and conduct an investigation from given materials to show that the noncontact forces created by an electromagnet can be attractive or repulsive and can influence the motion of test objects (ferromagnetic particles).

Performance Expectations and 3D Learning:

MS-PS2-2. Plan an investigation to provide evidence that the change in an object's motion depends on the sum of the forces on the object and the mass of the object.

MS-PS2-3. Ask questions about data to determine the factors that affect the strength of electric and magnetic forces.

Safety:

- Use caution when working with electricity. Do not to touch both ends of the battery at once.
- Use insulated wire. Never use batteries that are leaking. Dispose of leaking batteries at an approved hazardous waste location.
- Students should not touch the battery terminals while the electromagnet is turned on.
- Students should not leave the electromagnets turned on for more than a minute or two at a time, as the nail and batteries will get hot to the touch.
- If using a doorbell button, students should NOT touch the underside of the button while depressing.
- Ferrofluid can stain clothes and skin easily. It also should NOT be consumed, and students should be careful not to get it in their eyes.
- Instruct students to use materials only as directed.
- Instruct students to use caution when use caution when working with chemical batteries and electricity.
- Instruct students to wash their hands thoroughly after the investigation.

Tip Preparation Quick Tips:

- To make ferrofluid, mix 2 parts mineral oil, 1 part olive oil, and 2 parts black iron oxide (Fe_3O_4) powder. NOTE: It is best to order reagent grade powder rather than using synthesized iron oxide or iron filings. A particle size of 44 microns works well.
- The optional materials are extra materials that the students will not likely use in their investigational designs (if done correctly). These materials can be replaced or omitted as the teacher sees fit.
- Battery holders can replace tape on the batteries. Note that 1 mL is only an approximate amount of ferrofluid. More or less may be used.

Time Rating

1 = less time, 4 = more time

Teacher Prep 3

Student Prep 4

Student Cleanup 2

Time on Task: 1 h, 45 min

Materials:

For each group

- compass
- batteries (4, size D)
- electrical tape (1 roll)
- eyedropper (2 ml)
- ferrofluid (2 mL)
- knife (on/off) switches (2)
- magnet wire (20 ft, 18 gauge or higher/thinner)
- marker (1)
- masking tape (12 inches or greater)
- nails (2, 16d or greater)
- petri dish (1)
- plastic wrap (3-inch square piece)

Optional (for each group)

- foam cup (1)
- paper clips (20)
- plastic cup (1)
- small metal dish (1)
- water (1 mL)

For each student

- goggles
- pencil

- Students should work individually to plan the investigation and collaboratively in groups of four or five to conduct the investigation.
- Students who require extra support can work with other students whose procedure is correct or can use the sample procedure.
- If disposing of ferrofluid, a small amount may go down the drain, but too much may cause drains to clog.

Options for Project-Based Learning:

- Students may select their own materials and then plan and conduct their investigation while working through the concepts of their lessons on magnetic forces, electric fields, and electromagnetism.
- Students can rate each other's investigational design and make recommendations for improvement and understanding prior to starting Task 2.

Task 2 – Procedure Answers:

1. Answers may vary, but the student should write a testable hypothesis that demonstrates the expectation that electromagnets with opposite poles facing the ferrofluid will attract the ferrofluid, and electromagnets with the same poles facing the ferrofluid will repel the ferrofluid.
2. Sample investigational design:
   - Materials: compass, 2 electromagnet setups (4 D batteries, magnet wire, 2 nails, 2 on/off switches, electrical tape or 2 battery holders), plastic wrap, petri dish, small amount of ferrofluid, masking tape, marker, goggles, notebooks, pencils
   - Independent variable: direction of current
   - Dependent variables: type of force (attractive or repulsive) and effect on test objects (ferrofluid)
   - Controls: electromagnet, materials, and/or compass
   - Description of the type and amount of data that should be gathered to support the purpose: Qualitative data about the direction of current flow, the polarity of the electromagnets, the type of forces produced by the electromagnets (attractive or repulsive), and observations about the behavior and/or movement of the ferrofluid should be collected.
   - NOTE: For sample step-by-step directions, diagram, and table, see *Sample Procedure*.
3. For a sample diagram of setup, see *Sample Procedure*. Student diagrams should resemble that shown and should include two setups, one for clockwise and counterclockwise flow. Each diagram setup should show how the wire connects both batteries, the knife (on/off) switch, and the wire-wrapped nail together. The diagram should also show the position of the ferrofluid relative to the nail and where the plastic wrap should be located.

6. Answers/observations will vary but should include: direction of current flow, the polarity of the electromagnets, the type of forces produced by the electromagnets (attractive or repulsive), and observations about the behavior and/or movement and resemble the completed sample data table shown.

Sample Data Table:

Current flow in Setup A	Current flow in Setup B	Pole of Setup A facing ferrofluid	Pole of Setup B facing ferrofluid	Type of force	Effect on ferrofluid
clockwise	counter-clockwise	north	south	attractive	The ferrofluid bulges and the particles move upward toward Electromagnet A.
counter-clockwise	counter-clockwise	south	south	repulsive	The ferrofluid close to Electromagnet A flattens out and the particles move away from Electromagnet A.

Task 2 – Summary Answers:

1. Answers will vary but should resemble the following: The data support the purpose of the investigation because the behavior of the ferrofluid shows that both push and pull forces are created by the electromagnets.
2. Answers will vary but should resemble the following: The data show that when the direction of current flow in one of the electromagnets is changed, the location of the north and south poles changes. This causes the type of force created by the electromagnets to change.
3. Answers will vary but should resemble the following: When the directions of current flow in the two electromagnets were opposite to each other, the polarities of the ends of the electromagnets facing the ferrofluid were opposite. This caused attractive magnetic forces to pull the ferrofluid upward, toward Electromagnet A. When the directions of current flow in the two electromagnets were the same, the polarities of the ends of the electromagnets facing the ferrofluid were the same. This caused repulsive forces to push the ferrofluid away from Electromagnet A.
4. Answers will vary but should resemble the following: Daria's observation is possible because the ferrofluid moves initially in response to the forces exerted by the electromagnets. The ferrofluid is then motionless because both electromagnets are exerting equal forces on the ferrofluid, which balance each other out.
5. Answers will vary. Any two of the following specific descriptions, or equivalent, is acceptable: In order to make the ferrofluid move again, Daria will need to make a change that affects the stable system.
   - She can increase or decrease the strength of one of the electromagnets.
   - She can change her investigational setup by moving one of the electromagnets closer to the ferrofluid.
   - Daria can increase the number of times the wire is wrapped around the nail for one of the electromagnets.
   - She could use a battery of higher voltage.
   - Daria can increase the number of batteries used.
   - She can also move one of the electromagnets around or flip the current in the batteries again.

Print and distribute the *Sample Procedure* as needed.

Sample Procedure

1. Work in groups of four or five to complete the investigation. Set up two electromagnets as shown in the diagram in Task 1.
2. Flip the batteries in one electromagnet setup so that the positive end of one battery is connected to the on/off switch, and the negative end of the other battery is connected to the nail. Using the masking tape and marker, label this setup "A." (The current will now flow in the opposite direction in Setup A.) Label the other setup "B."
3. What is the direction of current flow (counterclockwise or clockwise) in Setup A?

   What is the direction of current flow in Setup B?

   Record this information in your data table.

Current flow in Setup A	Current flow in Setup B	Pole of Setup A facing ferrofluid	Pole of Setup B facing ferrofluid	Type of force	Effect on ferrofluid

4. Based on the current, which end of the electromagnet in Setup A is the north pole and which is the south pole?

   Which ends of the electromagnet are the north and south poles in Setup B?
5. Use the compass to verify the north and south poles of both electromagnets. Use the masking tape and marker to label the poles.

   NOTE: Do not cover the exposed ends of the nail. Rather, place a small piece of masking tape on top of the coiled wire on either end.
6. Cover the flat end of the nail with plastic wrap as shown in the diagram.
7. Carefully place about 1 mL of the ferrofluid into the petri dish.

   CAUTION: Ferrofluid is very messy. Do not allow it to come in contact with your skin, clothes, or electromagnets.
8. Hold the petri dish containing ferrofluid steady, above your desk or lab table.

9. Position the electromagnets as shown in the sample setup diagram, so that Electromagnet B is touching the dish and Electromagnet A is just above the surface of the ferrofluid.

   CAUTION: Do not leave the electromagnets turned on for more than a minute at a time. They will get hot to the touch! If they do begin to get warm, turn them off until they cool.

Sample setup:

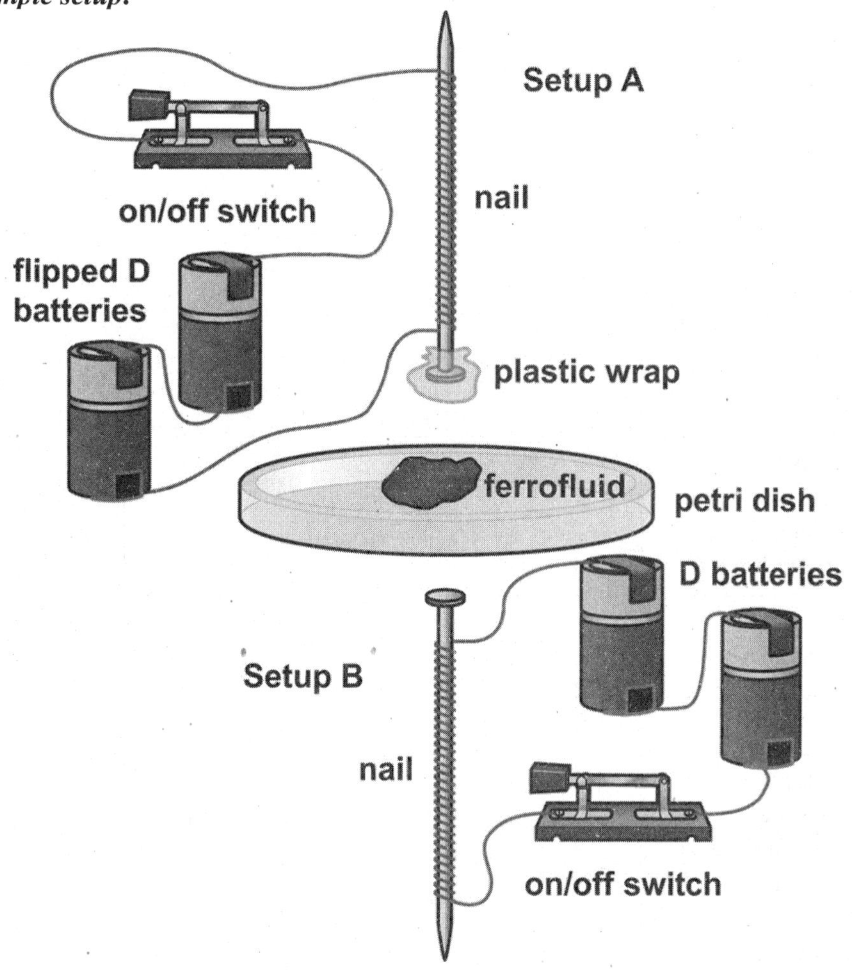

10. Observe which pole (north or south) is closest to the ferrofluid for Setup A and Setup B, and record this information in first row of the data table.
11. Determine the type of force (attractive/repulsive). Record this in the data table.
12. Observe the behavior of the ferrofluid and the movement of the tiny magnetic particles within the ferrofluid. Design a table with these column headings: Current flow in Setup A, Current flow in Setup B, Pole of Setup A facing ferrofluid, Pole of Setup B facing ferrofluid, Type of force, Effect on ferrofluid. Record your observations in the last column in the data table.
13. Flip the batteries in Setup A so that the negative end of one battery is connected to the on/off switch and the positive end of the other battery is connected to the nail. Repeat steps 8, 9, 10, and 11, recording your data in the second row of the data table.
14. Disassemble electromagnets and dispose of materials as instructed by your teacher.

Task 2 Performance Rubric

Rating Scale

3 Outstanding	1 Needs Improvement
2 Satisfactory	0 Did Not Demonstrate Skill
NS Did not have the opportunity to observe	

Teacher Directions:
This rubric allows for performance observation of 10 students. Make copies as needed. If students are working in groups, record the group name.

Group Name ___________

Names of Students

Skills										
DCI.MS-PS2.A.3 Forces and Motion The student demonstrates that noncontact forces created by an electromagnet can influence the motion of test objects (ferromagnetic particles).										
DCI.MS-PS2.B.1 Types of Interactions The student demonstrates that noncontact forces created by an electromagnet can be attractive or repulsive.										
DCI.MS-PS2.B.1 Types of Interactions The student proposes ways to change the investigational setup to demonstrate that the size of electric and magnetic (electromagnetic) forces depends on the magnitudes of the charges, currents, or magnetic strengths involved and on the distances between the interacting objects.										
SEP.MS.A.2 Asking Questions and Defining Problems The student writes a testable hypothesis that an electromagnet can generate noncontact forces that are attractive and repulsive.										
SEP.MS.C.3 Planning and Carrying Out Investigations The student plans an investigation, selects appropriate materials, identifies independent and dependent variables and controls, determines how measurements will be recorded, and identifies which data are needed to support a claim that an electromagnet can generate noncontact forces that are attractive and repulsive										

Group Name ___________

Names of Students

Skills (continued)										
CCC.MS.G.1 Stability and Change The student demonstrates the effects of stable and unstable forces on the behavior of ferrofluid.										
SEP.NOS.MS.B.1 Scientific Knowledge Is Based on Empirical Evidence The student draws a logical conclusion about the relationship between the direction of current in and the noncontact forces created by an electromagnet using evidence from the investigation										
Overall Achievement of Performance Expectation The student plans and conducts an investigation that demonstrates that an electromagnet can produce noncontact forces that are attractive and repulsive, and the size of the forced depends on current and distance.										
Total										

Name: ______________________ Date: ______________________

Performance-Based Assessment

Electromagnetism at Work

Task 2: Push Me, Pull Me:

In this task, you will plan an investigation using materials from the given list to meet a specific purpose. Once the plan is complete, you will conduct the investigation and report your results and your conclusions.

OBJECTIVE

Investigate forces generated by an electromagnet.

SAFETY

MATERIALS

For each group

- batteries (4, size D)
- electrical tape (1 roll)
- compass
- eyedropper (2 ml)
- ferrofluid (2 ml)
- foam cup
- knife (on/off) switches (2)
- magnet wire (20 feet, 18 gauge or higher/thinner)
- marker
- masking tape (12-inch piece or longer)
- nails (2, 16d or greater)
- paper clips (20)
- petri dish
- plastic cup
- plastic wrap (3-square inch piece or greater)
- water (2 ml)

For each student

- pencil
- safety goggles

PROCEDURE

Write a hypothesis.

1. The purpose of this task is to use what you learned about the direction of current in Task 1 to plan an investigation to test whether electromagnets can create forces that can both attract and repel a magnetic fluid (ferrofluid). Write a testable hypothesis that meets the purpose of the investigation.

____

____

____

Plan the investigation.

2. Plan an investigation to test your hypothesis using any of the provided materials. Your plan should include:

   - list of materials being used
   - identification of independent variable(s), dependent variable(s), and control(s)
   - step-by-step directions
   - description of the type and amount of data that should be gathered to support the purpose
   - a design for a data table

   NOTE: In your investigational plan, you may include collaboration with other students or other groups.

____

____

____

____

____

____

____

____

____

3. Sketch a diagram of your experimental setup. Add labels to your diagram.

4. Once you have written your plan, present it to the teacher for evaluation. If your plan is approved, move to the next step. If not, revise your plan as needed.

Conduct the Investigation.

5. Work in groups as assigned by your teacher to build your setup and conduct the planned investigation approved by your teacher.

6. Create a table to record your data.

7. Clean up your workspace and dispose of the ferrofluid as instructed by your teacher. Wash your hands before leaving the classroom.

Name: ______________________________ Date: ______________

Performance-Based Assessment

Task Summary

1. Explain whether your data support the purpose of the investigation.

2. How does changing the direction of current affect the forces created by the electromagnets? Use your data to support your answer.

3. Explain your observations of the ferrofluid behavior and movement using the type of force, the direction of current, and the polarity of the electromagnets.

4. Daria observes that when she positions the electromagnets above and below the ferrofluid, it moves initially and then is motionless. Explain how this is possible.

5. Describe two ways Daria could change the construction of her electromagnets to make the ferrofluid move again.

Name: ______________________ Date: ______________________

Electromagnetism at Work

Part 2: Repulsive Experiment

Read the passage, then answer the questions that follow.

Gus learns that he can make an electromagnet that can attract things made of iron, like paper clips. He wonders whether an electromagnet can be used to push (repel) an object rather than pull (attract). Gus designs an investigation to test this idea. He uses the following materials:

- refrigerator magnet
- very strong magnet
- nail
- on/off switch
- D battery
- two pieces of wire, one 3 feet long and one 12 inches long
- electrical tape
- scissors

Gus cuts the refrigerator magnet into a thin rectangular strip and tapes it to a table. He drags the very strong magnet across the length of the cut strip 20 times, always dragging the magnet in the same direction. This changes the strip into a small bar magnet, a magnetic strip.

Gus builds the electromagnet. He wraps the wire tightly around the nail 40 times. Gus connects the wire to a battery and switch, as shown in the diagram. Finally, Gus removes the tape from the magnetic strip.

Gus's Investigation Setup

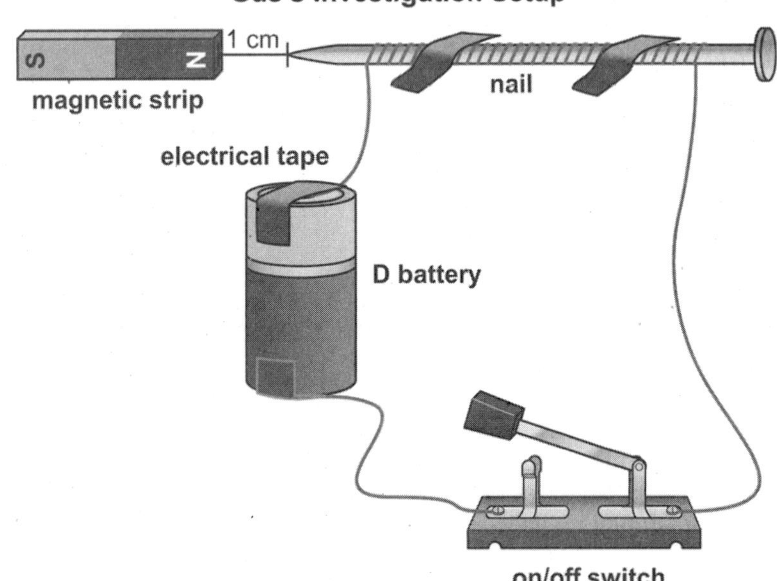

Refer to your notes from Part 1 to assist with the responses to the questions.

Name: ______________________ Date: ______________________ **Performance-Based Assessment**

1. Look at the diagram of Gus's electromagnet shown.
   - Draw an arrow to show the direction of the current in the image.
   - Draw an N and an S to label the north and south poles of the electromagnet in the image.

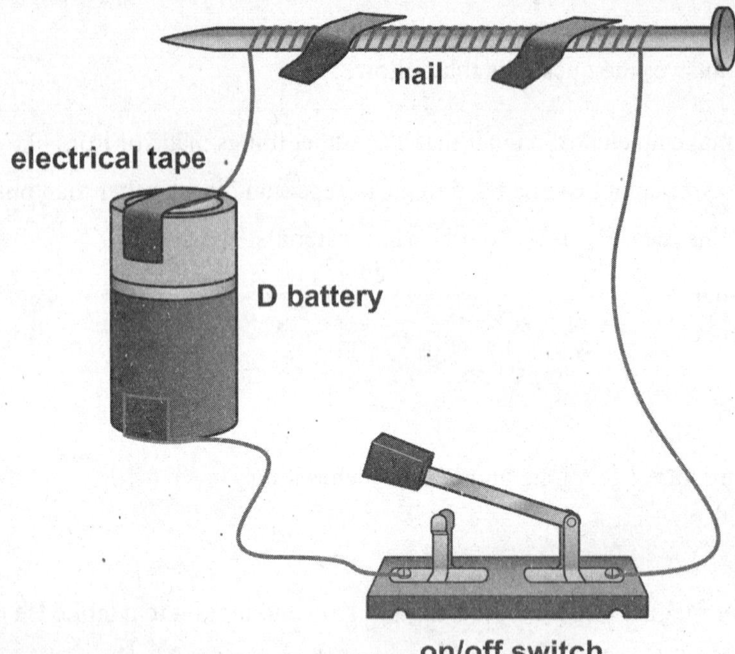

2. Gus predicts that when he turns on the current in the electromagnet, the magnetic strip will neither be attracted to nor repelled by the electromagnet because they are not touching. Write your answer on the lines.

   Explain whether Gus's prediction is correct.

   ____

   ____

   ____

   Use evidence from the diagram in the passage to support the explanation.

   ____

   ____

   ____

3. Gus arranges the setup of his investigation so that the electromagnet should repel and move the magnetic strip. When he turns on the current in the electromagnet, the magnetic strip spins and turns itself so that it is attracted to the electromagnet rather than repelled. Gus determines that he needs to revise his design. Drag each design idea into the correct position in the table to show which design ideas will repel and move the magnetic strip and which will not.

Design Idea Will Work	Design Idea Will Not Work

A. Pin magnetic strip to table.

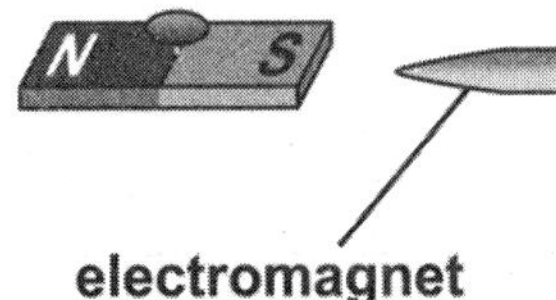

B. Tape magnetic strip to the table.

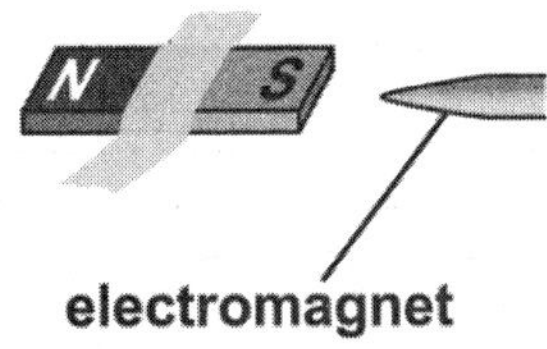

C. Suspend the magnet from two strings.

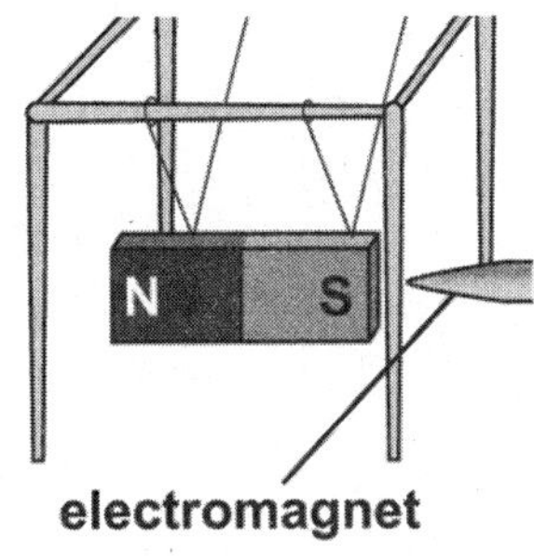

D. Place magnetic strip inside clear straw taped to table.

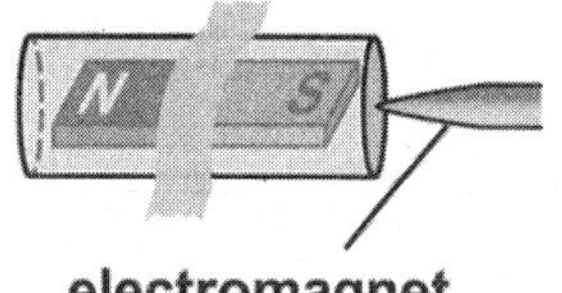

E. Tape strings to magnet; then tape string ends down to table.

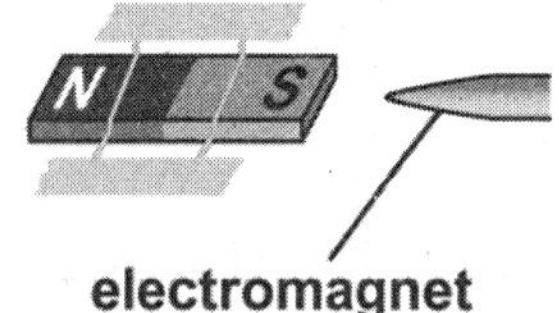

4. Gus turns on the current in the electromagnet and nothing happens to the magnetic strip. He uses a compass and determines the electromagnet is functioning. He thinks he might need to change his setup. Circle the letters of all the changes to the setup that Gus can make to produce an effect on the magnetic strip when he turns on the current.

   A. reverse the battery in the electromagnet

   B. use more batteries in the electromagnet

   C. move the magnetic strip to the opposite end of the electromagnet

   D. move the magnetic strip closer to the same end of the electromagnet

   E. move the magnetic strip so that it is next to the center of the electromagnet

   F. rebuild the electromagnet with four times the number of loops of wire around the nail

5. Consider each change to the setup that Gus can make to produce an effect on the magnetic strip when he turns on the current. Write your answers on the lines.

   Describe why the changes will likely improve Gus's investigation.

   ____

   ____

   ____

   Explain how each change will cause an improvement.

   ____

   ____

   ____

   ____

   ____

Item Analysis		
Item #	**Standards**	**DOK**
1	MS-PS2-5, DCI.MS-PS2.B.3, SEP.MS.B.1	2
2	MS-PS2-5, DCI.MS-PS2.B.3, SEP.MS.F.3	2
3	MS-PS2-2, DCI.MS-PS2.A.3, SEP.MS.C.3	3
4	MS-PS2-5, DCI.MS-PS2.B.1, SEP.MS.C.2	2
5	MS-PS2-3, DCI.MS-PS2.B.1, CCC.MS.B.2	3

1. Use the rubric below to evaluate total points earned for this item. *[max point: 2]*

DCI Only - 2 Points	
Claims	The student is able to describe the field that exists by identifying the current flow within and the north and south poles of the electromagnet (DCI).
Evidence of Mastery of Disciplinary Core Ideas	2 points for correctly identifying the current flow and the north and south poles of the electromagnet **Part 1:** One point is earned for drawing an arrow that identifies the current flow in the electromagnet as being in a clockwise direction. The following response, or an equivalent, is acceptable. **Part 2:** One point is earned for identifying the north and south poles of the electromagnet. The following response, or an equivalent, is acceptable. S N nail electrical tape D battery on/off switch

2. Use the rubric below to evaluate total points earned for this item. *[max point: 2]*

DCI Only - 2 Points	
Claims	The student is able to identify that electromagnetic forces act at a distance and predict how a field will affect a test object (the magnetic strip). (DCI)
Evidence of Mastery of Disciplinary Core Ideas	2 points for correctly identifying that the magnetic strip will be affected by the electromagnet and predicting how it will be affected One point is earned for explaining that Gus's prediction is incorrect because a field exists. The following response, or an equivalent, is acceptable. • Gus's prediction is not correct because magnets and electromagnets have fields that interact so they do not have to be touching to be attracted or repelled. One point is earned for predicting that the magnetic strip will be attracted to the electromagnet. The following response, or an equivalent, is acceptable. • Since opposite poles are facing each other, it is likely that the magnetic strip will be attracted to the electromagnet.

3. **A.** *Pin magnetic strip to table* belongs under *Design Idea Will Not Work* because the magnet will pivot around the pin when the electromagnet is on.

   B. *Tape magnetic strip to the table* belongs under *Design Idea Will Not Work* because the magnet will not be able to move when the electromagnet is on.

   C. *Suspend the magnet from two strings* belongs under *Design Idea Will Work* because the magnet will be prevented from spinning while being allowed to move towards or away from the electromagnet when it is on.

   D. *Place magnetic strip inside clear straw taped to table* belongs under *Design Idea Will Work* because the magnet is restricted from spinning but free to move towards or away from the electromagnet when it is on.

   E. *Tape strings to magnet; then tape string ends down to table* belongs under *Design Idea Will Work* because the string will prevent the magnet from spinning but allow movement toward or away from the electromagnet when it is energized.

4. **A.** This is incorrect because it only changes the polarity of the electromagnet but does not make the magnetic field any stronger.

   B. This response is correct because increasing the current (or the voltage) increases the strength of the electromagnet.

   C. This is incorrect because the strength of the field is the same at either end of the electromagnet.

   D. This is correct because shortening the distance increases the magnetic field strength experienced by the magnetic strip.

   E. This is incorrect because the field generated by an electromagnet is strongest at the poles (ends).

   F. This is correct because the force of an electromagnet is determined by the number of turns of wire around the iron core; increasing the number of turns will increase the field strength.

5. Use the rubric below to evaluate total points earned for this item. *[max point: 4]*

DCI, CCC - 4 Points	
Claims	The student is able to: 1. describe that the size of electromagnetic forces depends on the magnitude of current, magnetic strength, and distance between interacting objects (DCI); and 2. use the cause and effect relationship between the size of electromagnetic forces and the chosen factors to explain how the magnetic field strength will increase (CCC).
Evidence of Mastery of Disciplinary Core Ideas	1 point for correctly describing why the changes will improve the investigation **Part 1:** One point is earned for describing that all changes will lead to an increase in the strength of the electromagnetic forces. The following response, or an equivalent, is acceptable. • The changes will increase the forces of the electromagnet because the forces depend on the magnitude of current, magnetic strength, and distance between interacting objects.
Evidence of Mastery of Crosscutting Concepts	3 points for correctly explaining how the changes will improve the investigation **Part 2:** One point is earned for using the cause and effect relationship to explain each improvement. The following responses, or equivalents, are acceptable. • The use of more batteries in the electromagnet will cause an increase in current, which means that the number of charges moving through the wire will increase. This will increase the strength of the magnetic field around the wire. • Moving the magnetic strip closer to the electromagnet will shorten the distance between them. This will increase the force experienced by the magnetic strip since the magnetic field is strongest closest to the poles. • Increasing the number of loops of wire around the nail will concentrate the magnetic field by increasing the portions of the wire with charge moving through them that are in contact with the nail.

End-of-Module Test

Read each question. Follow the instructions to answer the questions.

1. Initially, a rubber ball sits on a level table. An upward force acts on the ball as well as the force of gravity.

   Write one letter in each blank to correctly complete the sentences.

   In order for the rubber ball to roll on the level table, a **1.** __________ is required. This quantity is measured in **2.** __________.

1.	**2.**
A. sideways unbalanced force	**E.** pounds
B. sideways balanced force	**F.** newtons
C. gravitational force	**G.** kilograms
D. magnetic force	**H.** meters per second

2. Nolan is doing an experiment in his science class in which he is making an electromagnet. Which question could he ask about the electromagnet that can lead to a practical experiment about the magnitude of the force produced?

   Circle the letter of the correct answer.

   A. How will adding more batteries affect the electromagnet?

   B. How large must the nail be in order to wrap the wire around it 100 times?

   C. How can the electromagnet be modified to pick up large objects such as cars?

   D. How can the electromagnet be built to ensure safety while handling in the classroom?

3. Write the letter of the correct word or words in the table to describe the interaction of the magnets and to identify the reason. Some options may be used more than once or not at all.

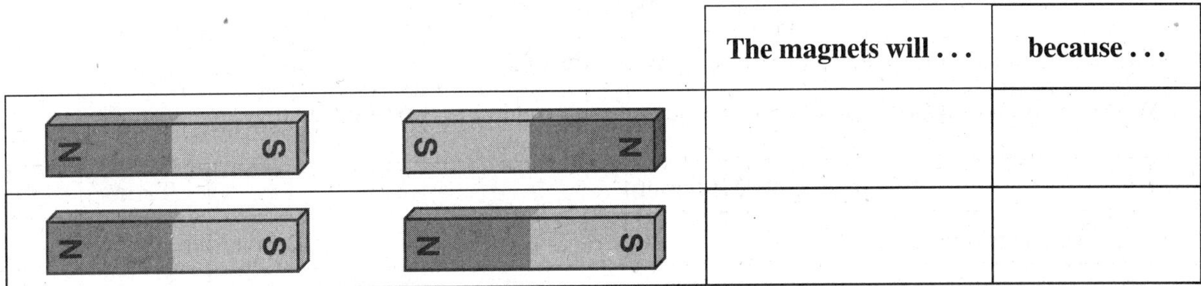

	The magnets will . . .	**because . . .**
N S — S N		
N S — N S		

The magnets will ...	**because ...**
A. repel	**D.** the magnets are not touching
B. attract	**E.** a field exists between the magnets
C. have no interaction	**F.** electricity exists between the magnets

4. A student has four objects. The objects are placed at equal distances from a fifth object. The gravitational attraction between each object and the fifth object is measured. The table shows the gravitational attractions relative to one another.

Object	Gravitational Attraction
A	37
B	31
C	60
D	5

Number the objects in the correct order from 1 to 4 with 1 as the object with the smallest mass and 4 as the object with the largest mass.

_________ A

_________ B

_________ C

_________ D

5. Two electrically charged pith balls hang from a wooden dowel as shown.

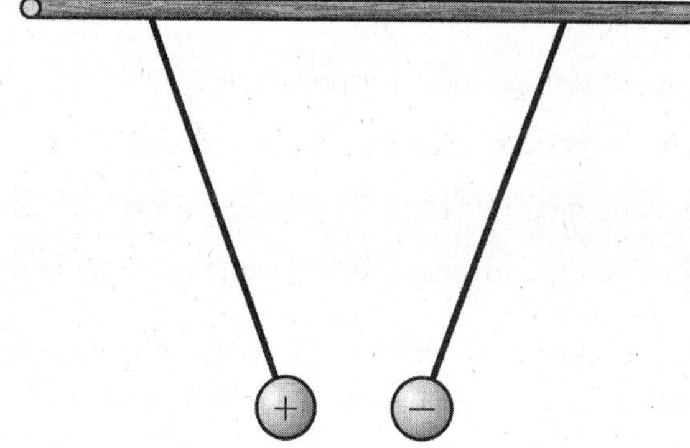

The statements describe the electric field between the balls.

Write one X in the correct box to show whether each statement is true or false.

Statement	True	False
A. The electric field has no direction.		
B. The field is strongest directly between the two balls.		
C. The field exists only between the two closest edges of the balls.		
D. The electric field causes the balls to be repelled from one another.		
E. An indicator that the field exists is that the strings holding the balls are tilted toward each other.		

6. Freddie has five objects. Each object will be paired one at a time with the other four objects so that the objects in each pair are placed exactly 1.0 meter apart. The table shows the mass of each object.

Masses of Five Objects

Object	Mass (kg)
A	80
B	20
C	70
D	40
E	90

Freddie needs to put the objects in order according to the strength of the gravitational attraction between them. She argues that A and E will have the weakest gravitational attraction because they are the most massive.

Write one letter in each blank to correctly complete the sentence.

Freddie's claim is **1.** __________ because the gravitational attraction between objects **2.** __________.

1.	**2.**
A. correct	**C.** does not depend on mass
B. incorrect	**D.** cannot be determined from the information given
	E. increases as the total mass of the objects increases
	F. increases as the total mass of the objects decreases

7. Three balls are placed on a table at the same distance from a ball in the center, as shown in the illustration. The table shows the relative strength of the gravitational attraction between each object and the center ball.

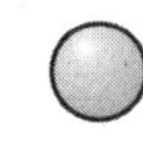

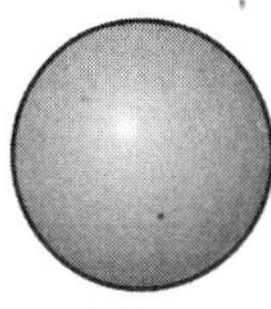

yellow ball

Ball	Gravitational Attraction
Red	14
Blue	115
Yellow	5

Number the balls in the correct order from1 to 3 with 1 as the most massive and 3 as the least massive.

__________ red ball

__________ blue ball

__________ yellow ball

8. The wire in this electromagnet is wrapped around a nail eight times.

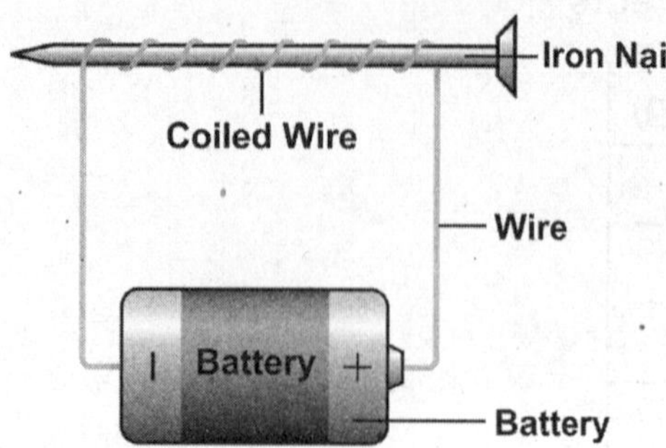

Write the letter of the statement in the box next to the correct description to indicate what would happen to the force of the electromagnet when each change is made.

Some letters may be used more than once or not at all.

Replace the nail with a plastic straw of the same size.	
Wrap the wire around the nail nine times instead of eight.	
Replace the battery with one that generates more current in the wire.	

A. The force of the electromagnet would increase.
B. The force of the electromagnet would decrease.
C. The force of the electromagnet would stay the same.

9. Anderson is investigating force and motion. To do this, he places a cart on a flat table and attaches the cart to a rope. The rope goes over a pulley and is attached to a mass. The mass generates a force on the cart. Anderson first conducts an experiment with a 20-gram mass attached to the rope. Then in a second experiment, he attaches a 40-gram mass to the rope. The diagram shows his experimental setup.

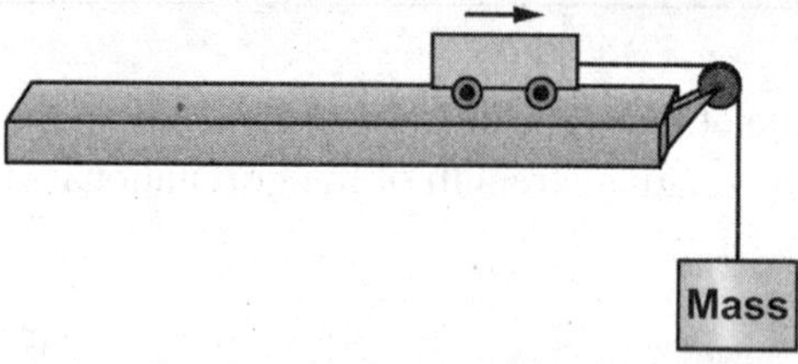

Write your answer on the lines.

Identify the independent and dependent variables in this investigation. Explain your answer.

____

____

Compare the first and second experiments. Describe the relationship that this setup can help Anderson to determine.

____

____

____

____

10. Terrell is designing an experiment using two identical toy trucks. He plans to roll one truck toward the other so they collide. The positions and speeds of the trucks before, during, and after the collision are shown.

Draw an arrow, or arrows, to show only the applied force, or forces, in the image.

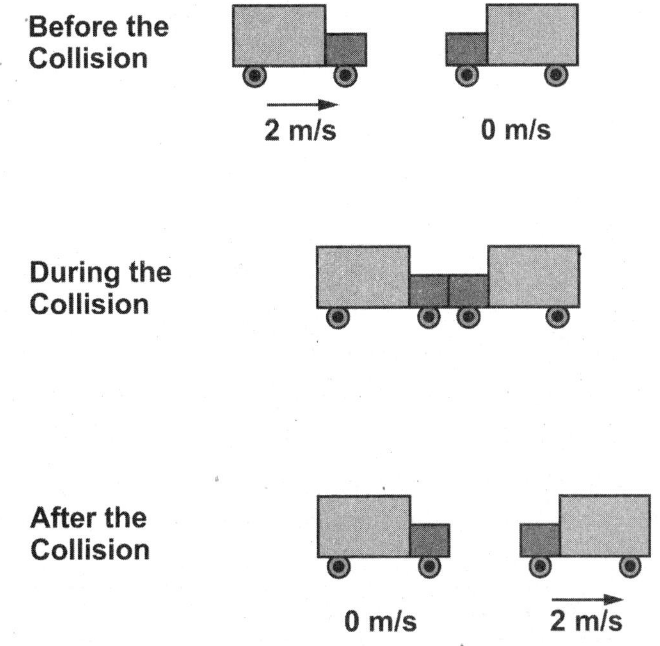

11. Scientists design an unmanned spacecraft that will collide with a meteor to break it into smaller pieces so the meteor will cause less damage if the meteor hits the moon's surface.

Circle the letter of all the statements that are correct according to Newton's third law about the meteor and the spacecraft when they collide.

A. The speeds of the meteor and spacecraft will be equal.

B. The accelerations of the meteor and spacecraft will be equal to each other.

C. The force of the spacecraft will be exerted onto the meteor at a right angle.

D. The forces of the meteor and spacecraft will be exerted on each other in opposite directions.

E. The forces of the meteor and spacecraft will be exerted on each other in the same direction.

F. The forces exerted by the meteor and the spacecraft on each other will be of equal strength.

12. The magnitude of current in the wires of an electromagnet is increased. Which describes the change that will result?

Circle the letter of the correct answer.

A. A stronger magnetic field will be generated.

B. The electromagnet will emit static electricity.

C. The polarity of the electromagnet will reverse.

D. An iron nail will be less attracted to the electromagnet.

13. Arianna is conducting several experiments about the effect of a magnetic field on different materials. In addition to the materials shown in the diagram, she has access to a very thin sheet of copper, aluminum foil, a paper napkin, a book, and a horseshoe magnet. The diagram shows Arianna's experimental setup.

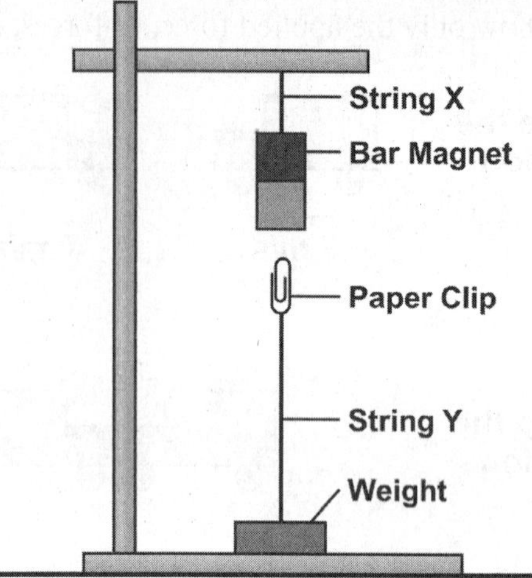

How can Arianna change her experimental setup to test the given purposes?

For each given purpose, write all of the letters representing the necessary changes to Arianna's experimental setup in the correct positions in the table. Some letters may be used more than once or not at all.

Purposes	Changes
to determine whether a magnetic field can act through different metals	
to determine whether a magnetic field can act through thin or thick materials	
to determine whether a magnetic field can act through aluminum with different types of magnets	

A. longer string Y
B. shorter string Y
C. book between magnet and paper clip
D. aluminum foil instead of bar magnet
E. horseshoe magnet instead of bar magnet
F. paper napkin between magnet and paper clip
G. aluminum foil between magnet and paper clip
H. copper sheet between magnet and paper clip

14. Ferguson has been studying the gravitational attraction between three pairs of objects. The table shows the distance between each pair and the gravitational attraction between them relative to the other pairs.

Objects	Distance Between Objects (m)	Gravitational Attraction
A and B	5	10
A and C	5	5
C and D	10	25

Explain the difference in gravitational attractions between objects A and B and objects A and C. Use the data given to support your answer.

____

____

____

____

____

Compare the masses of objects B and C using the data in the table.

____

____

____

____

____

Explain how it is possible for the gravitational force between C and D to be greater than the gravitational force between A and C.

____

____

____

____

____

15. Mellie creates a simple electromagnetic generator in her science class by spinning a magnet attached to a rod inside a small container, as shown in the diagram.

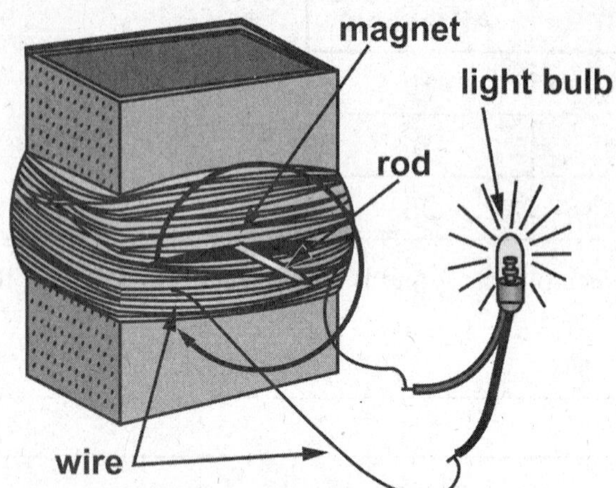

When the magnet is spun, electric current is generated in the wire coiled around the container, and the light bulb attached to the wire lights up.

Mellie is writing a hypothesis about the factors that will affect the lighting of the light bulb using the electromagnetic generator she made. She starts the hypothesis by saying, "The light bulb will light up more brightly if I change . . ."

Write one X in the correct box to show whether each factor would create a relevant or a not-relevant hypothesis.

The light bulb will light up more brightly if I change . . .	Relevant	Not Relevant
A. the length of the rod		
B. the strength of the magnet		
C. how far away the light bulb is from the magnet		
D. the speed at which the magnet is spun		
E. the number of times the wire is wrapped around the container		

16. The size of the force exerted on a rotor determines how fast the rotor spins. To test this idea, Alex made an electric motor that uses a combination of magnets and solenoids to generate movement.

The motor is shown in the diagram.

What will happen to the rotor if Alex adds an additional magnet that is orientated in the same way as the original magnet?

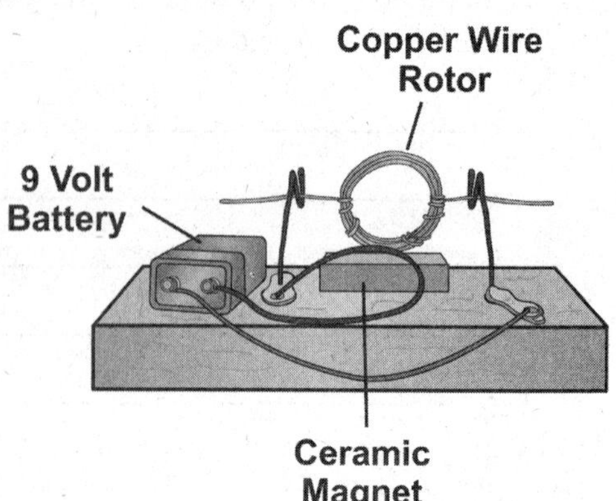

A. It will spin faster because the magnetic field will increase.

B. It will not spin because the magnetic field will be reversed.

C. It will spin more slowly because the second magnet will interrupt the current.

D. It will spin at the same speed because the number of magnets has no effect on the force.

17. The density of the field lines relates to the strength of the electric force. Two equal but opposite charged particles are shown close together and then farther apart.

Draw five arrows in each diagram to show how electric field lines are affected by distance.

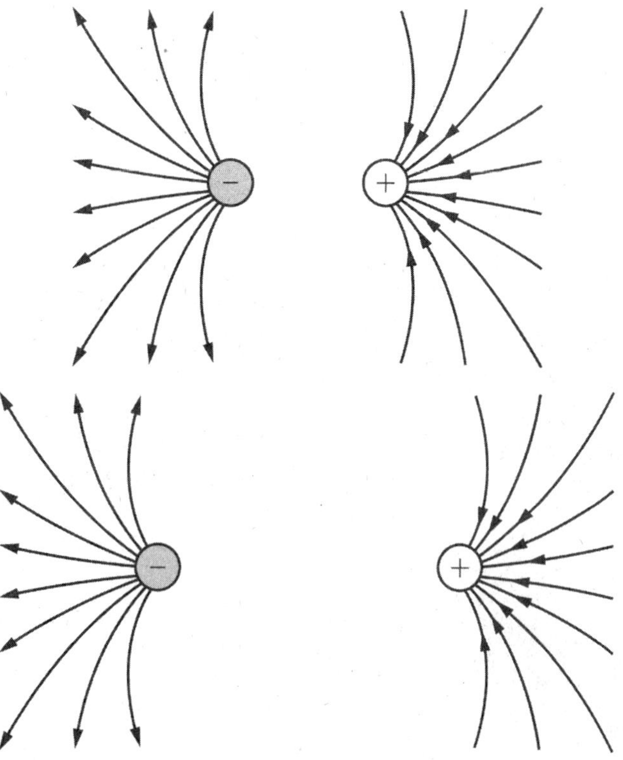

18. Two toy cars are shown traveling toward each other.

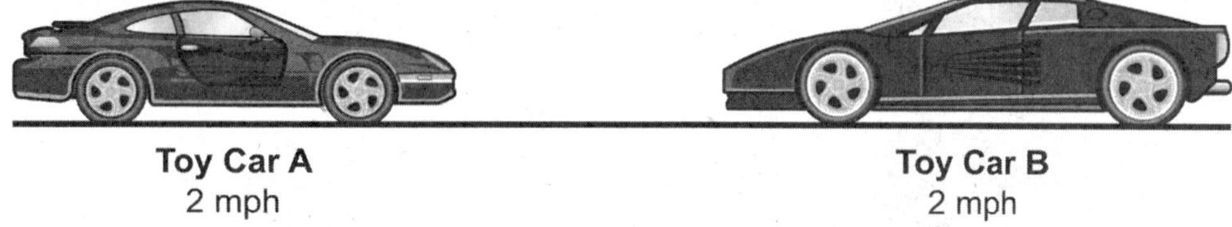

Write one letter in each blank to correctly complete the sentences.

The two toy cars are headed for each other at the same **1.** __________. The force of car A as it hits car B will be **2.** __________ the force of car B as it hits car A. The forces act in **3.** __________ directions. If car A was larger than car B, the force of car A as it hits car B will be **4.** __________ the force of car B as it hits car A.

1.	**2.** and **4.**	**3.**
A. acceleration	**D.** equal to	**G.** adjacent
B. speed	**E.** greater than	**H.** opposite
C. velocity	**F.** less than	**I.** the same

19. Lei has designed several demonstrations of the forces exerted by colliding objects using ice skates, an ice skating rink, hockey equipment, and classmates.

Write one X in the correct box to show whether or not each demonstration illustrates Newton's third law of action and reaction.

Demonstration	Illustrates Newton's Third Law	Does Not Illustrate Newton's Third Law
A. skater spinning		
B. player hitting a puck		
C. skating in line together		
D. pucks colliding		

Name: ______________________ Date: ______________________

End-of-Module
Test A

20. The diagram shows two identical carts rolling toward each other, about to collide.

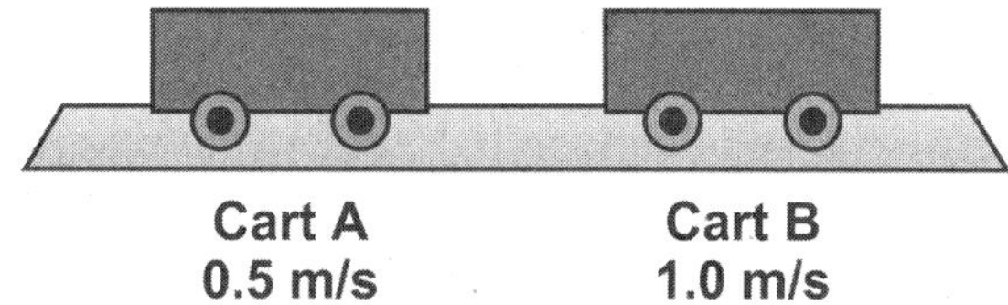

Which statement describes the direction and speed that cart A is moving before and after the collision?

Circle the letter of the correct answer.

A. Cart A moves left 0.5 m/s before the collision and to the left at a speed greater than 1.0 m/s after the collision.

B. Cart A moves left 0.5 m/s before the collision and to the right at a speed less than 0.5 m/s after the collision.

C. Cart A moves right 0.5 m/s before the collision and to the left at a speed greater than 0.5 m/s after the collision.

D. Cart A moves right 0.5 m/s before the collision and to the right at a speed less than 1.0 m/s after the collision.

21. A boy pushes against the trunk of a tree with his hands.

Write one X in the correct box to show whether each statement is true or false.

Statement	True	False
A. The tree does not exert any force on the boy.		
B. The ground exerts an upward force against the tree.		
C. The boy exerts more force on the tree than the tree exerts on the boy.		
D. The forces exerted by the boy and the tree are exerted in the same direction.		
E. Any object that touches the tree in the same way as the boy's hands will exert a force on the tree.		

22. Daniel uses a force of 5 N to push a ball with a mass of 12 kg. He puts a piece of tape on the floor to show how far the ball rolled in 1 second. Daniel wants to make a ball roll a shorter distance in 1 second than the distance the first ball rolled.

Circle the letter of all the actions Daniel could take to achieve this result.

A. push the ball down a ramp

B. mark the distance after 2 seconds

C. use a 1 N force on a ball of the same mass as in the first investigation

D. use a 1 kg ball with the same amount of force as in the first investigation

E. use a 20 N force on a ball of the same mass as in the first investigation

F. use a 20 kg ball with the same amount of force as in the first investigation

23. Two balloons are suspended from the ceiling. The picture shows the position of the balloons for a moment of time. Write your answer on the lines.

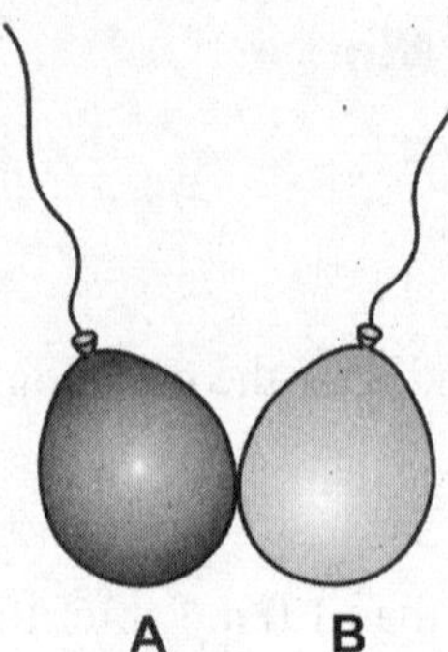

Balloon A is known to have a negative charge. Draw a conclusion about the electric charge of balloon B. Explain your reasoning.

____

____

____

____

____

Balloon A is removed from the ceiling and moved across the room. Describe what will happen to the position of balloon B. Explain your answer, including analysis of the electric force.

____

____

____

____

24. Engineers use their understanding of Newton's laws to design effective roller-coaster safety harnesses. The diagram shows a passenger at the end of the roller-coaster ride, when a device on the track slows down the roller-coaster train.

Write one letter in each blank to correctly complete the sentences.

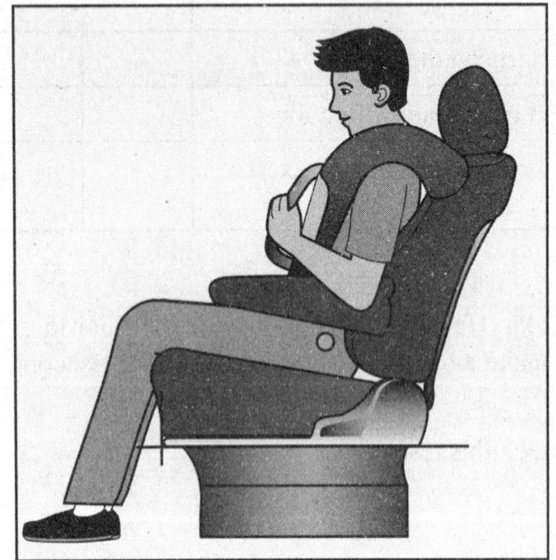

If a roller-coaster train traveling at 50 km/h collides with the stopping device with a force of 55 N, the device will exert **1.** __________ of force on the roller-coaster train. As the roller coaster slows down, the passenger's body will push forward on the safety harness. The safety harness will apply an **2.** __________ force in the **3.** __________ direction, keeping the passenger in his or her seat.

1.	2.	3.
A. 55 N	**D.** equal	**F.** same
B. 105 N	**E.** unequal	**G.** opposite
C. 110 N		

Name: ______________________________ Date: ______________________

End-of-Module
Test A

Directions: Read the passage, then answer the questions that follow.

Riley and Jessie's Experiment About Force, Mass, and Motion

Riley and Jessie are investigating the relationship between the amount of force applied to an object and the object's acceleration. In one of their experiments, Jessie uses the same force to roll a large marble and a small marble across a smooth cement floor. Riley measures the time as each marble rolls past certain marked distances. The tables show the data they record.

Masses of Marbles

	Mass (g)
Large Marble	18.5
Small Marble	14.2

Distance of Large Marble over Time

	Time (s)			
Distance (cm)	Trial 1	Trial 2	Trial 3	Average
0	0	0	0	0
25	0.270	0.250	0.250	0.260
50	0.610	0.580	0.560	0.580

Distance of Small Marble over Time

	Time (s)			
Distance (cm)	Trial 1	Trial 2	Trial 3	Average
0	0	0	0	0
25	0.200	0.190	0.210	0.200
50	0.460	0.470	0.440	0.460

25. Refer to the passage. Riley and Jessie design a new experiment to see how different surfaces affect acceleration. To do this, they put a piece of carpeting in one area of the room and also roll the marbles across the cement floor. What should Riley and Jessie use as a controlled variable for this experiment?

Circle the letter of the correct answer.

A. another type of surface

B. the original smooth floor

C. the same marbles used in the first experiment

D. the time it takes for the marbles to reach a certain distance

26. Their teacher asks Jesse and Riley for some additional information about their investigation. Use the information in the passage to determine whether each of their statements is true or false.

Write one X in the correct box to show whether each statement is true or false.

Statement	True	False
A. The frame of reference for each trial is the same.		
B. The units for force in this investigation are $\frac{g \cdot cm}{s^2}$.		
C. To know the speed of the marbles, you also have to know the direction they are moving.		
D. The reference points used in the investigation were the locations of each marble at different times.		
E. The forces that act on each marble during any time period of the experiment include gravity, the normal force, the force of the roll, and friction.		

27. Refer to the passage. What could Jessie do to make both marbles arrive at the 50 cm mark at the same time?

Circle the letter of all the correct answers.

A. Apply more force to the large marble.

B. Reduce the initial acceleration of the small marble.

C. Apply the same force to both marbles at the same time.

D. Replace the small marble with a marble of double the mass.

E. Replace the small marble with a marble of the same mass as the large marble.

28. Riley and Jessie are planning another experiment using only the small marble to test how force and acceleration are related. In this experiment, they want to double the initial acceleration of the small marble.

Write one letter in each blank to correctly complete the sentences. Some words may be used more than once or not at all.

To double the acceleration, Riley and Jessie must double the **1.** __________. In this new investigation, **2.** __________ is the dependent variable, **3.** __________ is an independent variable, and **4.** __________ is a controlled variable. To test their idea, Riley and Jessie should repeat the experiment and measure the **5.** __________ and **6.** __________.

A. acceleration	**D.** mass
B. distance	**E.** time
C. force	

29. In order to clarify their findings, Riley and Jessie carried out their experiment again using a table tennis ball and a golf ball instead of marbles, keeping all other conditions from the previous experiment the same. The table shows the data they gathered about the table tennis ball and the golf ball.

Properties of Table Tennis Ball and Golf Ball

	Diameter (mm)	Mass (g)
Table Tennis Ball	40	2.70
Golf Ball	43	45.9

If both balls are rolled across the floor with the same force, compare the accelerations of each ball. Explain your answer.

Compare and contrast the independent variables of this new investigation with the one described in the passage. Explain the reason for any differences in the two investigations.

Explain why Riley and Jessie used a table tennis ball and a golf ball in this new investigation instead of the large and small marbles.

30. A student has three masses and three spring scales. The diagram shows the springs.

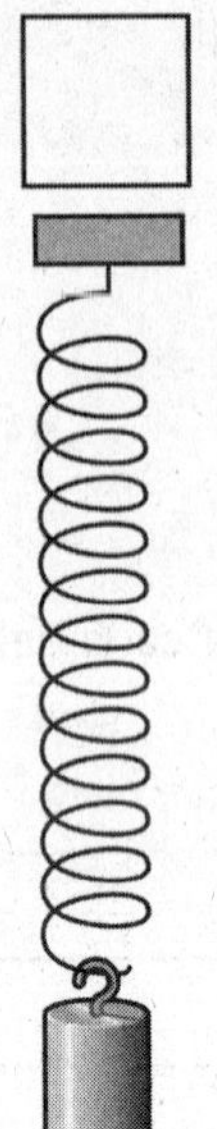
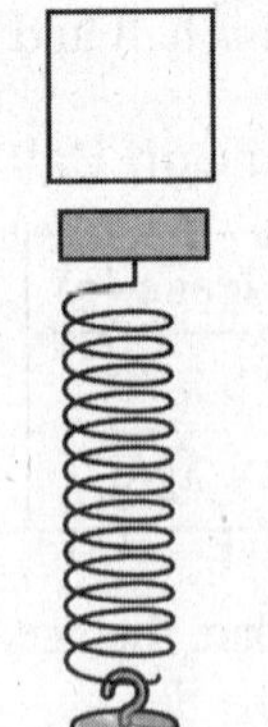
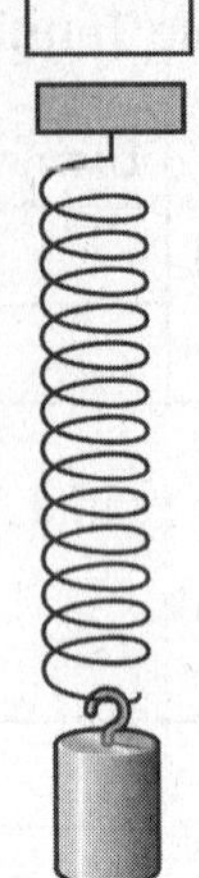

Write one letter in each box to correctly label the scales.

A. 1 N

B. 3 N

C. 9 N

31. The diagrams show magnetic field sketches made by four different students.

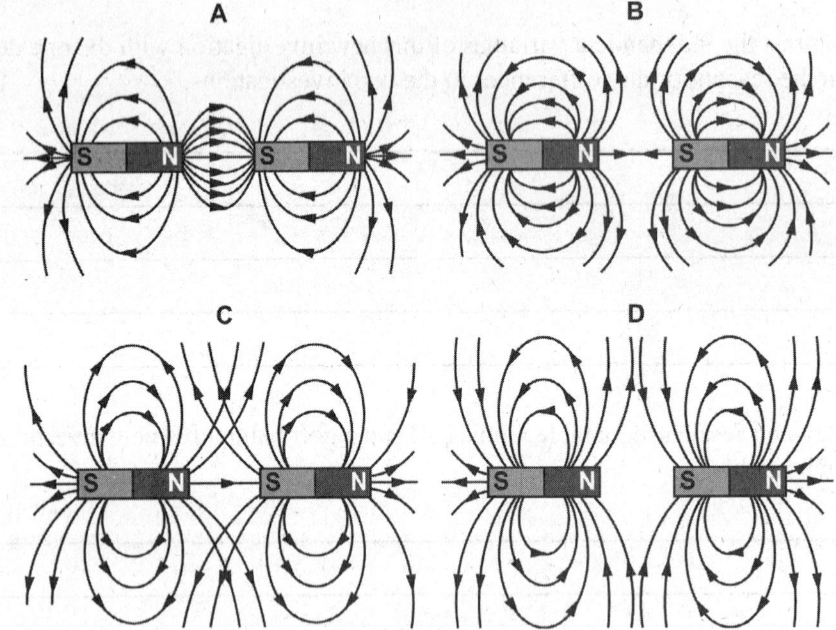

Which diagram represents the magnetic fields between the two magnets?

Circle the letter of the correct answer.

A. diagram A

B. diagram B

C. diagram C

D. diagram D

32. Pascal is standing next to his friend René. They both have mass but cannot feel any gravitational attraction between them. However, Pascal can feel the gravitational attraction of Earth on him. How do the sizes of the gravitational attractions Pascal observes compare?

Write the letter of the explanation that correctly explains the magnitude of each gravitational force in the box next to the description of the force. Some letters may be used once or not at all.

gravitational attraction between Pascal and René	
gravitational attraction between Pascal and Earth	

A. The objects' masses are relatively small.

B. The objects are very close together.

C. The objects' masses are the same.

D. One object has a mass that is very large.

E. No gravitational attraction exists between these objects.

33. Toni needs to set up a demonstration to prove that Newton's third law applies during the collision of two objects. She has a toy car, a toy truck, and two identical billiard balls. She chooses to demonstrate the action-reaction force pairs by rolling the billiard balls toward each other. Why did Toni choose billiard balls instead of the other objects to illustrate her point?

Choose the correct answer.

A. The billiard balls have the same mass, making the result of equal forces easier to see.

B. The toy truck would exert more force on the toy car, showing unequal forces instead of equal ones.

C. The billiard balls are the same diameter, showing equal forces during a collision and proving Newton's third law.

D. A collision between any of the other objects would not demonstrate Newton's third law, making the demonstration invalid.

34. Jamie has four types of objects labeled A, B, C, and D. All of the objects are 5 meters apart. The table shows the gravitational force between the objects relative to one another.

Objects	Gravitational Force
A and B	50
A and C	10
A and D	5
B and C	20
C and D	2

Write your answer on the lines.

Order the objects from the one with the smallest mass to the one with the largest mass.

Explain the relationship between mass and gravitational attraction.

Justify your ordering of the objects in terms of mass using the data in the table.

35. Sam traced the lines of force between two magnets using a compass. The diagrams show his observations.

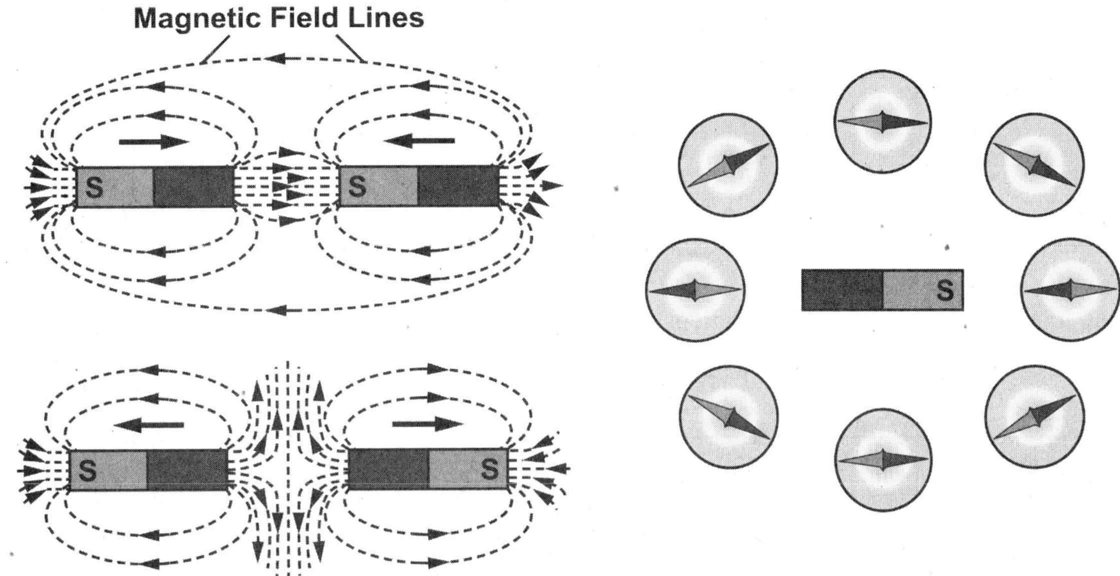

Write your answer on the lines.

Describe how the two magnets will behave when the north pole of one magnet is brought close to the south pole of the other.

Based on Sam's observations, explain how the position of the poles affects the magnetic field lines and the attractive and repulsive forces between two magnets.

Draw a conclusion about the properties of the compass needle using Sam's observations of the magnetic field lines and the effect of the magnet on the compass needle. Explain your reasoning.

36. The diagram shows two mine carts moving toward each other on a frictionless track at 2 m/s. Cart 2 has a mass that is twice that of Cart 1.

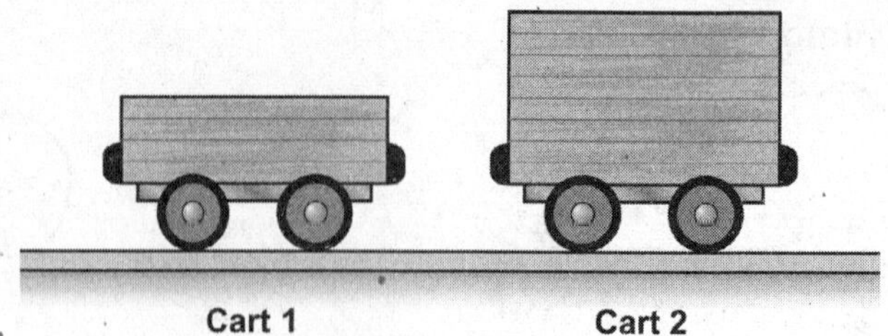

Write the letter of the arrows or words into the table to show the direction and speed of the mine carts before and after the collision. Some letters may be used more than once or not at all.

	Direction of Cart 1	Direction of Cart 2	Speed of Cart 1	Speed of Cart 2
Before Collision				
After Collision				

A. (arrow pointing left)	**C.** no motion	**E.** less than 2 m/s
B. (arrow pointing right)	**D.** equal to 2 m/s	**F.** greater than 2 m/s

37. Denise is designing an investigation to show that forces can act over a distance. Step 1 is to place a stack of textbooks on the edge of a workbench. What are the remaining steps?

Write the letter of the description in the correct box next numbered steps. Some letters will not be used.

Step 2	
Step 3	
Step 4	
Step 5	
Step 6	

A. Tie a magnet to the ruler so it hangs over the edge of the workbench.

B. Insert one end of a ruler underneath the bottom textbook.

C. Touch one pole of a second magnet to the north pole of the hanging magnet.

D. Tie a string in the middle of a bar magnet.

E. Hold one pole of a second magnet near the north pole of the hanging magnet.

F. Touch the other pole of a second magnet to the north pole of the hanging magnet.

G. Hold the other pole of a second magnet near the north pole of the hanging magnet.

H. Place a piece of paper between the magnets.

38. A class of students needs to design an experiment to demonstrate the relationship between mass and gravitational attraction. The students have access to a bungee cord and the three masses shown in the picture.

Write your answer on the lines.

Design an investigation, using the materials available, to demonstrate the relationship between mass and gravitational attraction.

____

____

____

____

____

Identify the data the students should collect during the investigation.

____

____

____

Predict how the various masses will affect the bungee cord.

____

____

____

Explain how the prediction demonstrates the relationship between mass and gravitational attraction.

____

____

____

____

39. Jackie is studying the differences in gravitational attraction that three classmates would have on the surfaces of Planet X and Planet Y. Jackie's teacher supplies the information shown in the table.

Gravitational Attraction of Classmates on Planets X and Y

Classmates	Gravitational Attraction Planet X (N)	Gravitational Attraction Planet Y (N)
Lia	980	2605
Mack	392	1042
Nadia	641	1823

Jackie argues that Planet Y must be more massive than Planet X. How do the data support or not support Jackie's claim?

A. Planet X must be more massive than Planet Y because the attraction on each student was lower on Planet X.

B. The data do not support Jackie's claim because the mass of Planet Y cannot be determined from the information given.

C. Planet Y must be more massive than Planet X because the attraction on each student was higher on Planet Y.

D. The data do not support Jackie's claim because the difference in gravitational attraction depends on the distance between Planet X and Planet Y.

Name: ______________________________ Date: ______________

End-of-Module
Test A

40. Ms. Smith hangs a spring from the classroom ceiling. Students hang four objects from the spring and measure the length of the spring for each object. The table shows the data they collected.

Object	Length of Spring (cm)
Toy Car	3
Bag of Plastic Blocks	10
Pack of Index Cards	8
Deck of Playing Cards	5

Ms. Smith asks the students to place the objects in order from largest to smallest mass. The students choose the following order: bag of plastic blocks, pack of index cards, deck of playing cards, toy car.

Explain the differences in the length of the spring for each object.

____

____

____

____

____

Explain how the experimental setup relates mass to gravitational attraction.

____

____

____

____

Justify or refute the students' ordering of the objects using the data. Explain your answer.

____

____

____

____

____

Name: ______________________________ Date: ______________________________

End-of-Module
Test B

End-of-Module Test

Read each question. Follow the instructions to answer the questions.

1. Initially, a rubber ball sits on a level table. An upward force acts on the ball as well as the force of gravity.

Write one letter in each blank to correctly complete the sentences.

In order for the rubber ball to roll on the level table, a **1.** __________ is required. This force is measured in **2.** __________.

1.	**2.**
A. sideways unbalanced force	**D.** newtons
B. sideways balanced force	**E.** kilograms
C. gravitational force	**F.** meters per second

2. Nolan is making an electromagnet. Which question could he ask about the electromagnet that can lead to a practical experiment about the magnitude of the force produced?

Circle the letter of the correct answer.

A. How will adding more batteries affect the electromagnet?

B. How large must the nail be in order to wrap the wire around it 100 times?

C. How can the electromagnet be built to ensure safety while handling in the classroom?

3. Write the letter of the correct word or words in the table to describe the interaction of the magnets and to identify the reason for the interaction. Some options may be used more than once or not at all.

	The magnets will . . .	**because . . .**
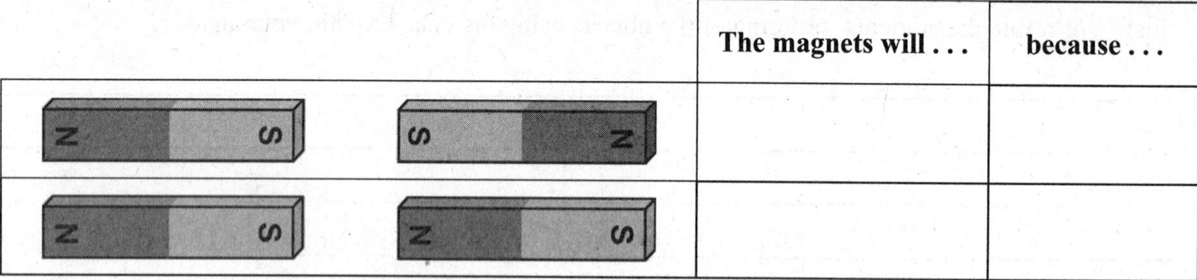		

The magnets will ...	**because ...**
A. repel	**C.** a field exists between the magnets
B. attract	**D.** electricity exists between the magnets

4. A student has four objects. The objects are placed at equal distances from a fifth object. The gravitational attraction between each object and the fifth object is measured. The table shows the gravitational attractions relative to one another.

Object	Gravitational Attraction
A	37
B	31
C	60
D	5

Number the objects in the correct order from 1 to 4 with 1 as the object with the smallest mass and 4 as the object with the largest mass.

__________ A

__________ B

__________ C

__________ D

5. Two electrically charged pith balls hang from a wooden dowel as shown.

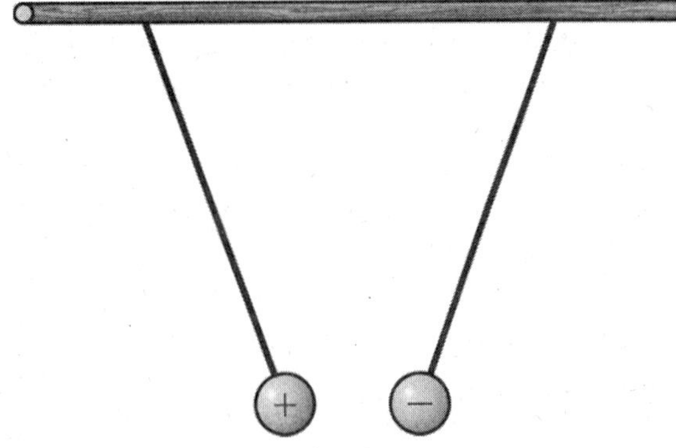

The statements describe the electric field between the balls.

Write one X in the correct box to show whether each statement is true or false.

Statement	True	False
A. The electric field has no direction.		
B. The field is strongest directly between the two balls.		
C. The electric field causes the balls to be repelled from one another.		

6. Freddie has five objects. Each object will be paired one at a time with the other four objects so that the objects in each pair are placed exactly 1.0 meter apart. The table shows the mass of each object.

Masses of Five Objects

Object	Mass (kg)
A	80
B	20
C	70
D	40
E	90

Freddie needs to put the objects in order according to the strength of the gravitational attraction between them. She argues that A and E will have the weakest gravitational attraction because they are the most massive.

Write one letter in each blank to correctly complete the sentence.

Freddie's claim is **1.** __________ because the gravitational attraction between objects **2.** __________.

1.	**2.**
A. correct	**C.** does not depend on mass
B. incorrect	**D.** increases as the total mass of the objects increases

7. Three balls are placed on a table at the same distance from a ball in the center, as shown in the illustration. The table shows the relative strength of the gravitational attraction between each object and the center ball.

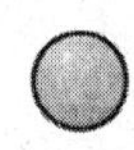

blue ball

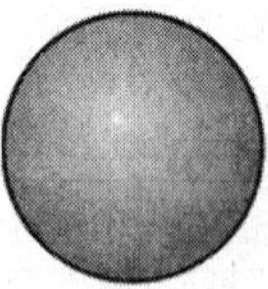

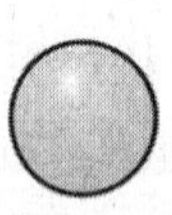

yellow ball

red ball

Ball	Gravitational Attraction
Red	14
Blue	115
Yellow	5

Number the balls in the correct order from1 to 3 with 1 as the most massive and 3 as the least massive.

__________ red ball

__________ blue ball

__________ yellow ball

8. The wire in this electromagnet is wrapped around a nail eight times.

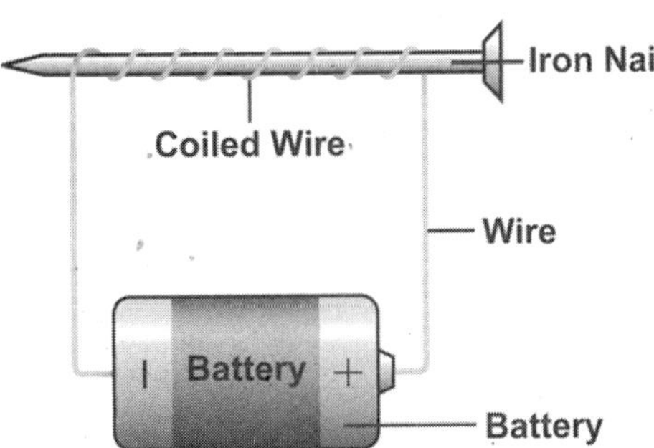

Write the letter of the statement in the box next to the correct description to show what would happen to the force of the electromagnet when each change is made.

Some letters may be used more than once or not at all.

Replace the nail with a plastic straw of the same size.	
Wrap the wire around the nail nine times instead of eight.	

A. The force of the electromagnet would increase.

B. The force of the electromagnet would decrease.

C. The force of the electromagnet would stay the same.

9. Anderson is investigating force and motion. He places a cart on a flat table and attaches the cart to a rope. The rope goes over a pulley and is attached to a mass. The mass creates a force on the cart. Anderson first conducts an experiment with a 20-gram mass attached to the rope. Then in a second experiment, he attaches a 40-gram mass to the rope. The diagram shows his experimental setup.

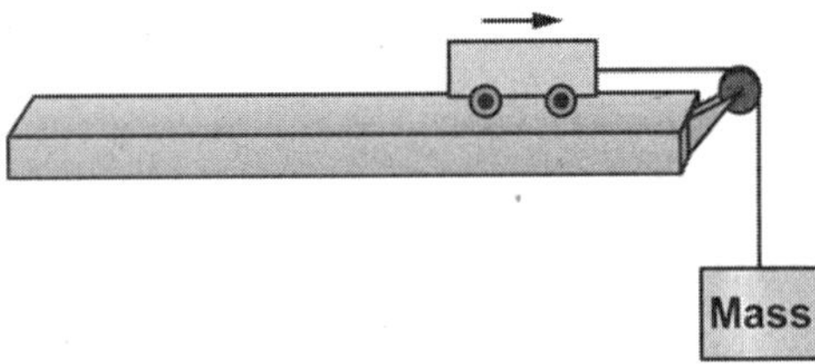

Write your answer on the lines.

Identify the independent and dependent variables in this investigation. Explain your answer.

____

____

Describe what this setup can show Anderson about the relationship between force and motion.

____

____

____

____

Name: Date:

End-of-Module
Test B

10. Terrell rolls a truck toward another, identical truck so they collide. The positions and speeds of the trucks before, during, and after the collision are shown.

Draw an arrow, or arrows, to show only the applied force, or forces, in the image. Some parts of the image may not be used.

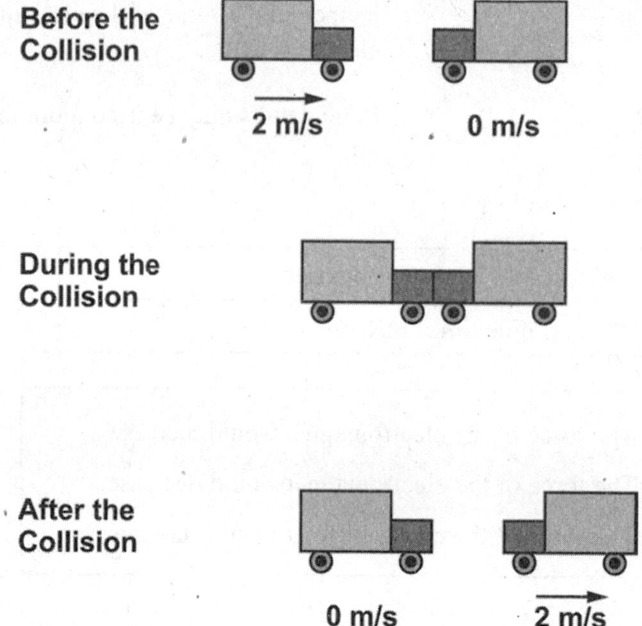

11. Scientists design an unmanned spacecraft that will collide with a meteor. The collision will break the meteor into smaller pieces, so it will cause less damage if the meteor hits the moon's surface.

Circle the letter of all the statements that are correct according to Newton's third law about the meteor and the spacecraft when they collide.

A. The accelerations of the meteor and spacecraft will be equal to each other.

B. The forces of the meteor and spacecraft will be exerted on each other in opposite directions.

C. The forces of the meteor and spacecraft will be exerted on each other in the same direction.

D. The forces exerted by the meteor and the spacecraft on each other will be of equal strength.

12. The magnitude of current in the wires of an electromagnet is increased. Which describes the change that will result?

Circle the letter of the correct answer.

A. A stronger magnetic field will be generated.

B. The electromagnet will emit static electricity.

C. The polarity of the electromagnet will reverse.

13. Arianna is conducting several experiments about the effect of a magnetic field on different materials. She has access to the materials shown in the diagram. She also has access to a very thin sheet of copper, aluminum foil, a paper napkin, a book, and a horseshoe magnet. The diagram shows Arianna's experimental setup.

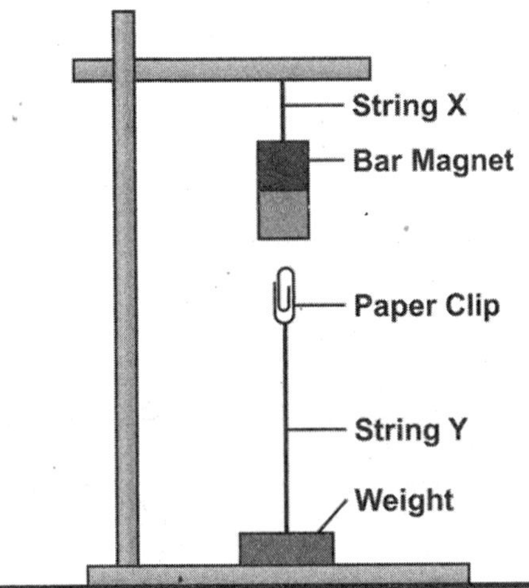

How can Arianna change her experimental setup to test the given purposes?

For each given purpose, write all of the letters representing the necessary changes to Arianna's experimental setup in the correct positions in the table. Some letters may be used more than once or not at all.

Purposes	Changes
to determine whether a magnetic field can act through different metals	
to determine whether a magnetic field can act through thin or thick materials	
to determine whether a magnetic field can act through aluminum	

A. book between magnet and paper clip
B. aluminum foil between magnet and paper clip
C. copper sheet between magnet and paper clip

14. Ferguson has been studying the gravitational attraction between three pairs of objects. The table shows the distance between each pair and the gravitational attraction between them relative to the other pairs.

Objects	Distance Between Objects (m)	Gravitational Attraction
A and B	5	10
A and C	5	5
C and D	10	25

Explain the difference in gravitational attractions between objects A and B and objects A and C. Use the data given to support your answer.

____

____

____

____

____

Compare the masses of objects B and C using the data in the table.

____

____

____

____

____

15. Mellie creates a simple electromagnetic generator in her science class by spinning a magnet attached to a rod inside a small container, as shown in the diagram.

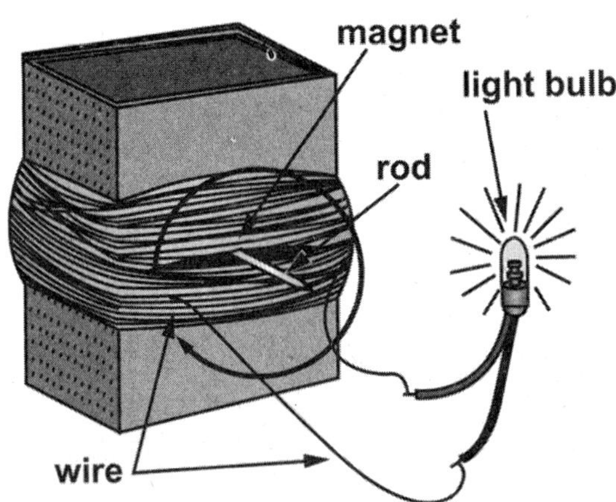

When the magnet is spun, electric current is generated in the wire coiled around the container, and the light bulb attached to the wire lights up.

Mellie is writing a hypothesis about which factors will affect the lighting of the light bulb. She starts the hypothesis by saying, "The light bulb will light up more brightly if I change . . ."

Write one X in the correct box to show whether each factor would create a relevant or a not-relevant hypothesis.

The light bulb will light up more brightly if I change . . .	Relevant	Not Relevant
A. the length of the rod		
B. the strength of the magnet		
C. how far away the light bulb is from the magnet		

16. The size of the force exerted on a rotor determines how fast the rotor spins. To test this idea, Alex made an electric motor. The motor is shown in the diagram.

The motor is shown in the diagram.

What will happen to the rotor if Alex adds an additional magnet that is orientated in the same way as the original magnet?

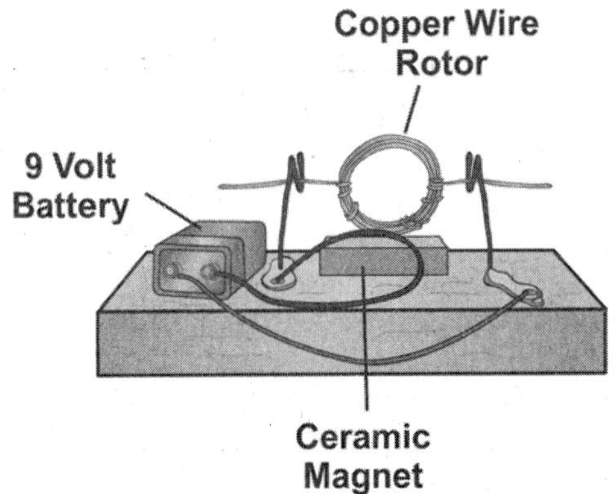

A. It will spin faster because the magnetic field will increase.

B. It will not spin because the magnetic field will be reversed.

C. It will spin at the same speed because the number of magnets has no effect on the force.

17. The density of the field lines relates to the strength of the electric force. Two equal but opposite charged particles are shown close together and then farther apart.

Draw five arrows in each diagram to show how electric field lines are affected by distance.

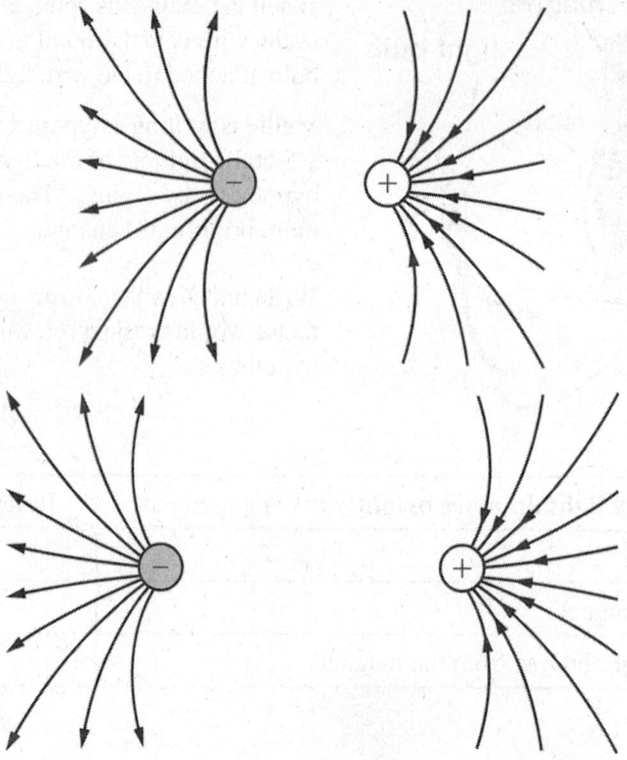

18. Two toy cars are shown traveling toward each other.

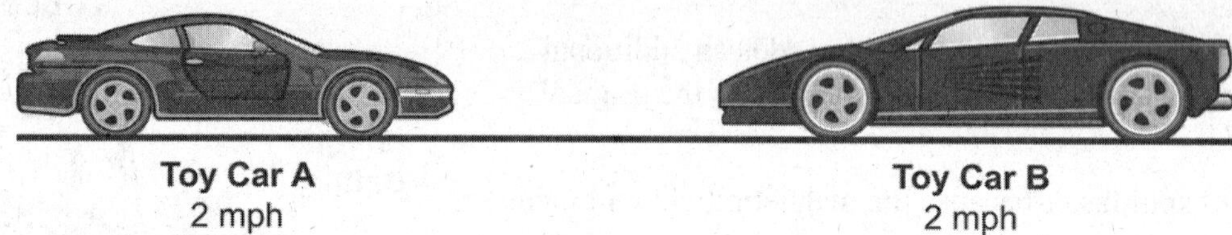

Write one letter in each blank to correctly complete the sentences.

The two toy cars are headed for each other at the same **1.** __________. The force of car A as it hits car B will be **2.** __________ the force of car B as it hits car A. The forces act in **3.** __________ directions. If car A was larger than car B, the force of car A as it hits car B will be **4.** __________ the force of car B as it hits car A.

1.	**2.** and **4.**	**3.**
A. acceleration	**C.** equal to	**E.** opposite
B. speed	**D.** greater than	**F** the same

19. Lei has designed several demonstrations of the forces exerted by colliding objects using ice skates, an ice skating rink, hockey pucks, and classmates.

Write one X in the correct box to show which demonstration illustrates Newton's third law of action and reaction.

	Demonstration	Illustrates Newton's Third Law
A. 	skater spinning	
B. 	pucks colliding	

20. The diagram shows two identical carts rolling toward each other, about to collide.

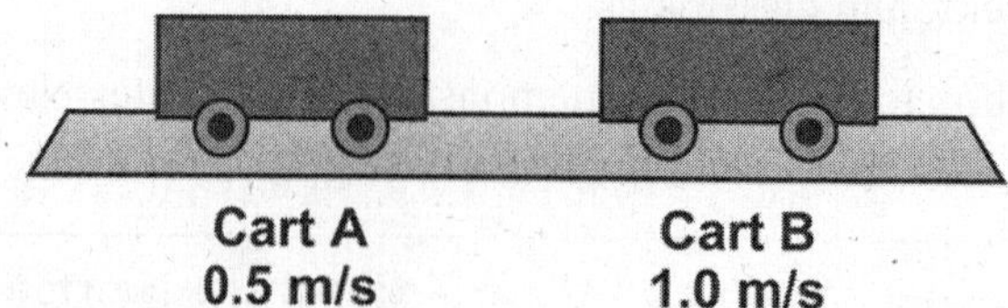

Which statement describes the direction and speed that cart A is moving before and after the collision?

Circle the letter of the correct answer.

A. Cart A moves left 0.5 m/s before the collision and to the right at a speed less than 0.5 m/s after the collision.

B. Cart A moves right 0.5 m/s before the collision and to the left at a speed greater than 0.5 m/s after the collision.

C. Cart A moves right 0.5 m/s before the collision and to the right at a speed less than 1.0 m/s after the collision.

21. A boy pushes against the trunk of a tree with his hands.

Write one X in the correct box to show whether each statement is true or false.

Statement	True	False
A. The ground exerts an upward force against the tree.		
B. The boy exerts more force on the tree than the tree exerts on the boy.		
C. The forces exerted by the boy and the tree are exerted in the same direction.		

22. Daniel uses a force of 5 N to push a ball with a mass of 12 kg. He puts a piece of tape on the floor to show how far the ball rolled in 1 second. Daniel wants to make a ball roll a shorter distance in 1 second than the distance the first ball rolled.

Circle the letter of all the actions Daniel could take to achieve this result.

A. use a 1 N force on a ball of the same mass as in the first investigation

B. use a 1 kg ball with the same amount of force as in the first investigation

C. use a 20 N force on a ball of the same mass as in the first investigation

D. use a 20 kg ball with the same amount of force as in the first investigation

23. Two balloons are suspended from the ceiling. The picture shows the position of the balloons for a moment of time. Write your answer on the lines.

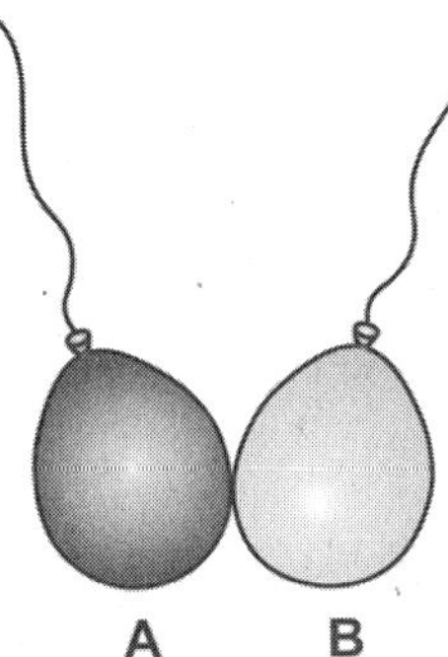

Balloon A is known to have a negative charge. Draw a conclusion about the electric charge of balloon B. Explain your reasoning.

____
____
____
____
____

Balloon A is removed from the ceiling and moved across the room. Describe what will happen to the position of balloon B. Explain your answer, including analysis of the electric force.

____
____
____
____

24. Engineers use their understanding of Newton's laws to design effective roller-coaster safety harnesses. The diagram shows a passenger at the end of the roller-coaster ride, when a device on the track slows down the roller-coaster train.

Write one letter in each blank to correctly complete the sentences.

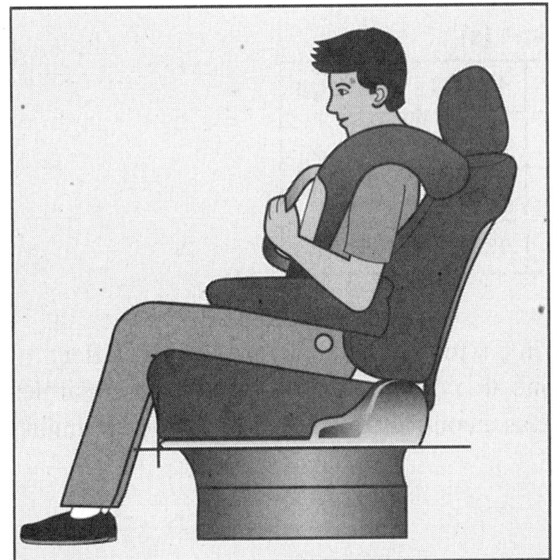

If a roller-coaster train traveling at 50 km/h collides with the stopping device with a force of 55 N, the device will exert **1.** __________ of force on the roller-coaster train. As the roller coaster slows down, the passenger's body will push forward on the safety harness. The safety harness will apply an **2.** __________ force in the **3.** __________ direction, keeping the passenger in his or her seat.

1.	**2.**	**3.**
A. 55 N	**C.** equal	**E.** same
B. 105 N	**D.** unequal	**F.** opposite

Name: ______________________ Date: ______________________

End-of-Module

Test B

Directions: Read the passage, then answer the questions that follow.

Riley and Jessie's Experiment About Force, Mass, and Motion

Riley and Jessie are investigating the relationship between the amount of force applied to an object and the object's acceleration. In one of their experiments, Jessie uses the same force to roll a large marble and a small marble across a smooth cement floor. Riley measures the time as each marble rolls past certain marked distances. The tables show the data they record.

Masses of Marbles

	Mass (g)
Large Marble	18.5
Small Marble	14.2

Distance of Large Marble over Time

	Time (s)			
Distance (cm)	Trial 1	Trial 2	Trial 3	Average
0	0	0	0	0
25	0.270	0.250	0.250	0.260
50	0.610	0.580	0.560	0.580

Distance of Small Marble over Time

	Time (s)			
Distance (cm)	Trial 1	Trial 2	Trial 3	Average
0	0	0	0	0
25	0.200	0.190	0.210	0.200
50	0.460	0.470	0.440	0.460

25. Refer to the passage. Riley and Jessie design a new experiment to see how different surfaces affect acceleration. To do this, they put a piece of carpeting in one area of the room and also roll the marbles across the cement floor. What should Riley and Jessie use as a controlled variable for this experiment?

Circle the letter of the correct answer.

A. another type of surface

B. the original smooth floor

C. the same marbles used in the first experiment

26. Their teacher asks Jessie and Riley for some additional information about their investigation. Use the information in the passage to determine whether each of their statements is true or false.

Write one X in the correct box to show whether each statement is true or false.

Statement	True	False
A. The frame of reference for each trial is the same.		
B. The units for force in this investigation are $\frac{g \cdot cm}{s^2}$.		
C. The reference points used in the investigation were the locations of each marble at different times.		
D. The forces that act on each marble during any time period of the experiment include gravity, the normal force, the force of the roll, and friction.		

27 Refer to the passage. What could Jessie do to make both marbles arrive at the 50 cm mark at the same time?

Circle the letter of all the correct answers.

A. Apply more force to the large marble.

B. Reduce the initial acceleration of the small marble.

C. Apply the same force to both marbles at the same time.

D. Replace the small marble with a marble of the same mass as the large marble.

28. Riley and Jessie are planning another experiment using only the small marble to test how force and acceleration are related. In this experiment, they want to double the initial acceleration of the small marble.

Write one letter in each blank to correctly complete the sentences. Some words may be used more than once or not at all.

To double the acceleration, Riley and Jessie must double the **1.** __________. In this new investigation, **2.** __________ is the dependent variable, **3.** __________ is an independent variable, and **4.** __________ is a controlled variable. To test their idea, Riley and Jessie should repeat the experiment and measure the **5.** __________ and time.

A. acceleration	**C.** force
B. distance	**D.** mass

29. In order to clarify their findings, Riley and Jessie carried out their experiment again using a table tennis ball and a golf ball instead of marbles, keeping all other conditions from the previous experiment the same. The table shows the data they gathered about the table tennis ball and the golf ball.

Properties of Table Tennis Ball and Golf Ball

	Diameter (mm)	Mass (g)
Table Tennis Ball	40	2.70
Golf Ball	43	45.9

If both balls are rolled across the floor with the same force, compare the accelerations of each ball. Explain your answer.

Compare and contrast the independent variables of this new investigation with the one described in the passage. Explain the reason for any differences in the two investigations.

30. A student has three masses and three spring scales. The diagram shows the springs.

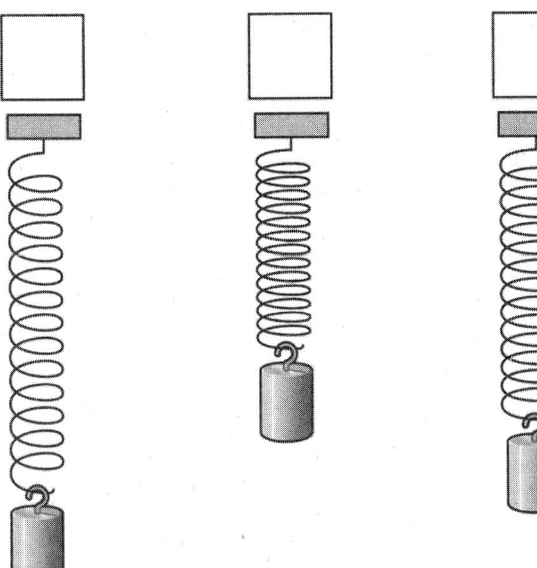

Write one letter in each box to correctly label the scales.

A. 1 N

B. 3 N

C. 9 N

31. The diagrams show magnetic field sketches made by four different students.

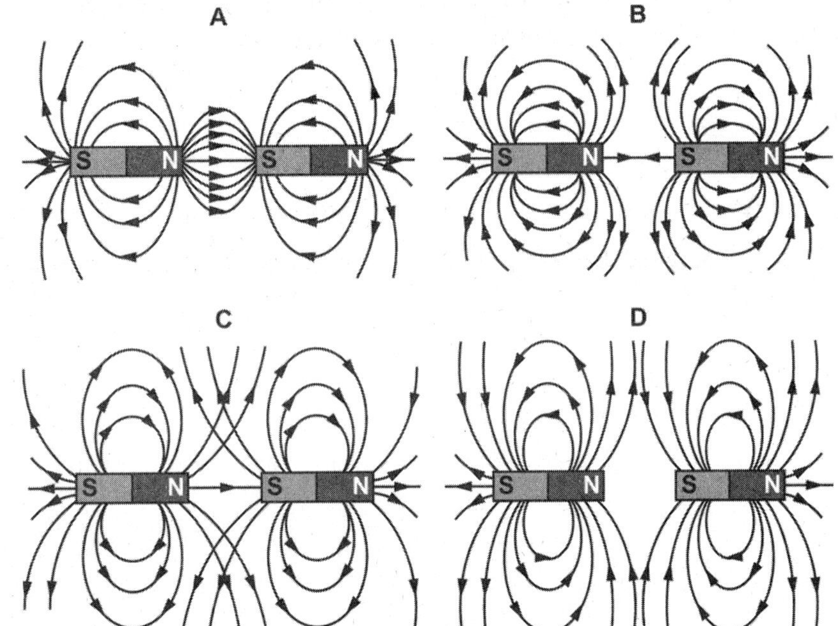

Which diagram represents the magnetic fields between the two magnets?

Circle the letter of the correct answer.

A. diagram A

B. diagram B

C. diagram C

32. Pascal is standing next to his friend René. They both have mass but cannot feel any gravitational attraction between them. However, Pascal can feel the gravitational attraction of Earth on him. What explains the difference in gravitational attractions that Pascal observes?

Write the letter of the explanation that correctly explains the magnitude of each gravitational force in the box next to the description of the force. Some letters may be used once or not at all.

gravitational attraction between Pascal and René	
gravitational attraction between Pascal and Earth	

A. The objects' masses are relatively small.

B. The objects are very close together.

C. One object has a mass that is very large.

D. No gravitational attraction exists between these objects.

33. Toni needs to set up a demonstration to prove that Newton's third law applies during the collision of two objects. She has a small toy car, a big toy truck, and two identical billiard balls. She chooses to demonstrate the action-reaction force pairs by rolling the billiard balls toward each other. Why did Toni choose billiard balls instead of the other objects to illustrate her point?

Choose the correct answer.

A. The billiard balls have the same mass, making the result of equal forces easier to see.

B. The toy truck would exert more force on the toy car, showing unequal forces instead of equal ones.

C. The billiard balls are the same diameter, showing equal forces during a collision and proving Newton's third law.

34. Jamie has four types of objects labeled A, B, C, and D. All of the objects are 5 meters apart. The table shows the gravitational force between the objects relative to one another.

Objects	Gravitational Force
A and B	50
A and C	10
A and D	5
B and C	20
C and D	2

Write your answer on the lines.

Order the objects from the one with the smallest mass to the one with the largest mass.

Justify your ordering of the objects using the relationship between mass and gravitational attraction.

35. Sam traced the lines of force between two magnets using a compass. The diagrams show his observations.

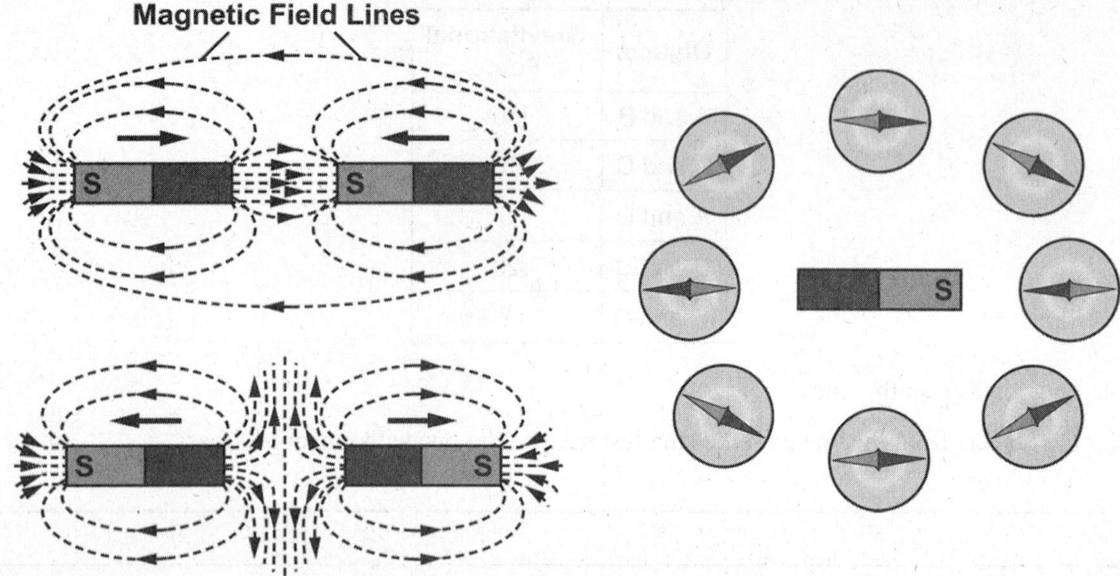

Write your answer on the lines.

Describe how the two magnets will behave when the north pole of one magnet is brought close to the south pole of the other.

____

____

____

____

Draw a conclusion about the properties of the compass needle using Sam's observations of the magnetic field lines and the effect of the magnet on the compass needle. Explain your reasoning.

____

____

____

____

36. The diagram shows two mine carts moving toward each other on a frictionless track at 2 m/s. Cart 2 has a mass that is twice that of Cart 1.

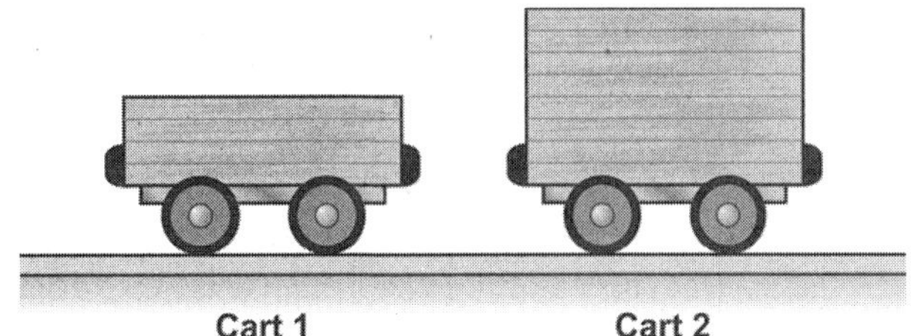

Write the letter of the arrows or words into the table to show the direction and speed of the mine carts before and after the collision. Some letters may be used more than once or not at all.

	Direction of Cart 1	Direction of Cart 2	Speed of Cart 1	Speed of Cart 2
Before Collision				
After Collision				

A. 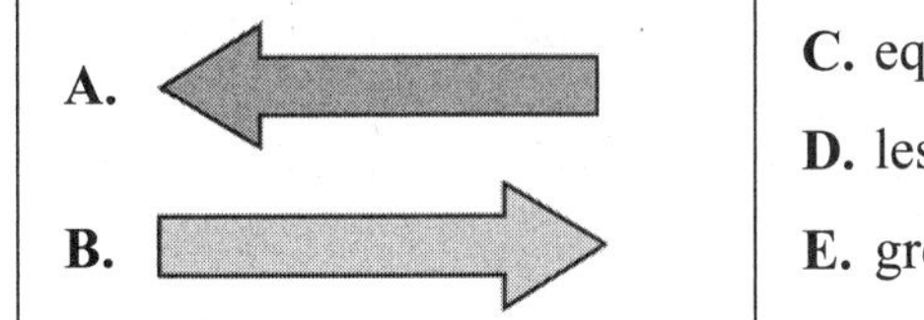 B.	C. equal to 2 m/s D. less than 2 m/s E. greater than 2 m/s

37. Denise is designing an investigation to show that forces can act over a distance. Step 1 is to place a stack of textbooks on the edge of a workbench. What are the remaining steps?

Write the letter of the description in the correct box next numbered steps. Some letters will not be used.

Step 2	
Step 3	
Step 4	
Step 5	

A. Tie a magnet to the ruler so it hangs over the edge of the workbench.

B. Insert one end of a ruler underneath the bottom textbook.

C. Touch one pole of a second magnet to the north pole of the hanging magnet.

D. Hold one pole of a second magnet near the north pole of the hanging magnet.

E. Touch the other pole of a second magnet to the north pole of the hanging magnet.

F. Hold the other pole of a second magnet near the north pole of the hanging magnet.

38. A class of students needs to design an experiment to demonstrate the relationship between mass and gravitational attraction. The students have access to a bungee cord and the three masses shown in the picture.

Identify the data the students should collect during the investigation.

Explain the relationship between mass and gravitational attraction that the students will see in this investigation.

39. Jackie is studying the differences in gravitational attraction that three classmates would have on the surfaces of Planet X and Planet Y. Jackie's teacher supplies the information shown in the table.

Gravitational Attraction of Classmates on Planets X and Y

Classmates	Gravitational Attraction Planet X (N)	Gravitational Attraction Planet Y (N)
Lia	980	2605
Mack	392	1042
Nadia	641	1823

Jackie argues that Planet Y must be more massive than Planet X. How do the data support or not support Jackie's claim?

A. Planet X must be more massive than Planet Y because the attraction on each student was lower on Planet X.

B. Planet Y must be more massive than Planet X because the attraction on each student was higher on Planet Y.

C. The data do not support Jackie's claim because the difference in gravitational attraction depends on the distance between Planet X and Planet Y.

40. Ms. Smith hangs a spring from the classroom ceiling. Students hang four objects from the spring and measure the length of the spring for each object. The table shows the data they collected.

Object	Length of Spring (cm)
Toy Car	3
Bag of Plastic Blocks	10
Pack of Index Cards	8
Deck of Playing Cards	5

Ms. Smith asks the students to place the objects in order from largest to smallest mass. The students choose the following order: bag of plastic blocks, pack of index cards, deck of playing cards, toy car.

Explain the differences in the length of the spring for each object.

Describe the relationship between mass and gravitational attraction in this setup.

Justify or refute the students' ordering of the objects using the data.

Unit 1 Forces and Motion

Unit 1 Pretest

Item Analysis			
Item #	**Key**	**Standards**	**DOK**
1	B	MS-PS2-2	1
2	C	MS-PS2-2, DCI.MS-PS2.A.3	1
3	C	MS-PS2-1, DCI.MS-PS2.A.1	2
4	A	MS-PS2-2, DCI.MS-PS2.A.3	2
5	C	MS-PS2-2	1
6	D	MS-PS2-2, DCI.MS-PS2.A.2	1
7	B	MS-PS2-4, DCI.MS-PS2.B.2, SEP.NOS.MS.B.1	2
8	A	MS-PS2-1, DCI.MS-PS2.A.1	3
9	C	MS-PS2-4	2
10	C	MS-PS2-4, DCI.MS-PS2.B.2, SEP.NOS.MS.B.1	3
11	D	MS-PS2-2, DCI.MS-PS2.A.2	1
12	D	MS-PS2-2, DCI.MS-PS2.A.3	1
13	A	MS-PS2-4, DCI.MS-PS2.B.2	2
14	B	MS-PS2-4	1
15	D	MS-PS2-1, DCI.MS-PS2.A.1	2

Unit 1 Lesson 1 Quiz – Introduction to Forces

Item Analysis				
Item #	**Key**	**Standards**	**Page #**	**DOK**
1	D	MS-PS2-5	1–15	1
2	C	MS-PS2-2	15	2
3	A	MS-PS2-2	17	2
4	D	MS-PS2-4	4–23	2
5	B	MS-PS2-5	15	2
6	C	MS-PS2-2	13–15	2
7	B	MS-PS2-5	13–15	2
8	Rubric	MS-PS2-2	9	2
9	Rubric	MS-PS2-2, CCC.MS.G.1, DCI.MS-PS2.A.2	10–18	3
10	Rubric	MS-PS2-2, DCI.MS-PS2.A.2	10–12, 17, 18	2

8. Use the rubric below to evaluate total points earned for this item. *[max point: 1]*

NGSS Constructed Response Answer – 1 Point	
Evidence of Mastery	Sample answers: • The bird has a speed of 17 meters per second when flying with the wind. • The bird has a speed of 8 meters per second when flying against the wind.

9. Use the rubric below to evaluate total points earned for this item. *[max point: 1]*

NGSS Constructed Response Answer – 1 Point	
Evidence of Mastery	Sample answers: • Marek exerts a force in the direction of the arrow. • Friction is a force working in the direction opposite to the arrow. • Gravity is a force pushing down on the box. • The floor is pushing up with a force on the box. • To make the box move, Marek needs to push with a larger force than the force of friction.

10. Use the rubric below to evaluate total points earned for this item. *[max point: 1]*

NGSS Constructed Response Answer – 1 Point	
Evidence of Mastery	Sample answers: • The net force is found by combining the forces acting on the box. If the forces are in the same direction, the forces add together. If the forces are in opposite directions, the smaller force is subtracted from the larger force, and the net force is in the direction of the larger force. • The upward force and the downward force are the same size and in opposite directions, so the net force is 25 N – 25 N = 0 N. • The force toward the right is larger than the force to the left, so the net force is 100 N – 50 N = 50 N to the right. • The box will accelerate to the right due to the net force.

Unit 1 Lesson 2 Quiz – Gravity and Friction

Item Analysis				
Item #	**Key**	**Standards**	**Page #**	**DOK**
1	A	MS-PS2-4, DCI.MS-PS2.B.2	26-28	2
2	C	MS-PS2-4, DCI.MS-PS2.B.2	30	2
3	D	MS-PS2-2	32-33	2
4	D	MS-PS2-4, DCI.MS-PS2.B.2	28-30	2
5	D	MS-PS2-4, DCI.MS-PS2.B.2	28-30	3
6	D	MS-PS2-2	32-38	2
7	C	MS-PS2-4	26-28	2
8	Rubric	MS-PS2-4, DCI.MS-PS2.B.2, SEP.MS.G.1	26-31	2
9	Rubric	MS-PS2-2	32-35	3
10	Rubric	MS-PS2-4, CCC.MS.D.2, DCI.MS-PS2.B.2, SEP.NOS.MS.B.1	26-31	3

8. Use the rubric below to evaluate total points earned for this item. *[max point: 1]*

NGSS Constructed Response Answer – 1 Point	
Evidence of Mastery	Sample answer: • The pilot is correct because the planet will exert a gravitational force on the spaceship, pulling it toward the planet on its own.

9. Use the rubric below to evaluate total points earned for this item. *[max point: 1]*

NGSS Constructed Response Answer – 1 Point	
Evidence of Mastery	Sample answers: • The friction decreased. • The sandpaper is rough, and it caused small bumps on the surface of the wood to be removed, which made the surface smoother. Smoother surfaces have less friction.

10. Use the rubric below to evaluate total points earned for this item. *[max point: 1]*

NGSS Constructed Response Answer – 1 Point	
Evidence of Mastery	Sample answer: • The combined masses of C and D must be greater than the combined masses of A and B in order for the gravitational attraction between C and D to be larger even though these objects are farther apart.

Unit 1 Lesson 3 Quiz – Newton's Laws of Motion

Item Analysis				
Item #	**Key**	**Standards**	**Page #**	**DOK**
1	C	MS-PS2-2, DCI.MS-PS2.A.2	55-59	3
2	C	MS-PS2-1, DCI.MS-PS2.A.1	60-63	2
3	C	MS-PS2-2	50-51	2
4	A	MS-PS2-1, DCI.MS-PS2.A.1	60	2
5	B	MS-PS2-1, DCI.MS-PS2.A.3	47	2
6	B	MS-PS2-2, DCI.MS-PS2.A.2	50-51, 55	2
7	D	MS-PS2-2, DCI.MS-PS2.A.2	50-57	2
8	Rubric	MS-PS2-2, DCI.MS-PS2.A.2	55-59	2
9	Rubric	MS-PS2-1, CCC.MS.G.1, DCI.MS-PS2.A.1	52	2
10	Rubric	MS-PS2-1, DCI.MS-PS2.A.1	55-59	3

8. Use the rubric below to evaluate total points earned for this item. *[max point: 1]*

NGSS Constructed Response Answer – 1 Point	
Evidence of Mastery	Sample answer: • Newton's second law says $F = ma$. Therefore the net force is $F = (1 \text{ kg})(5 \text{ m/s2}) = 5$ N. • The object is accelerating, which means its speed is increasing.

9. Use the rubric below to evaluate total points earned for this item. *[max point: 1]*

NGSS Constructed Response Answer – 1 Point	
Evidence of Mastery	Sample answer: • The gravitational force of Earth pulls down on the person. The sidewalk pushes back up with a force equal and opposite to the gravitational force. The forces are balanced. If the person started walking, he or she would have to exert a sideways force on the sidewalk, and the sidewalk would exert a force in the opposite direction that is equal and opposite. This causes the forces to be unbalanced so the person can move.

10. Use the rubric below to evaluate total points earned for this item. *[max point: 1]*

NGSS Constructed Response Answer – 1 Point	
Evidence of Mastery	Sample answer: • The opposing forces are the same. The skater with the greater mass will have the lesser acceleration since a= F/m.

Unit 1 Lesson 4 Quiz – Engineer It • Collisions Between Objects

Item Analysis				
Item #	**Key**	**Standards**	**Page #**	**DOK**
1	C	MS-PS2-1, DCI.MS-PS2.A.1	72-73	3
2	A	MS-PS2-1	73	2
3	D	MS-PS2-1	70-73	3
4	C	MS-PS2-2, DCI.MS-PS2.A.2	72, 80	2
5	C	MS-PS2-1, CCC.MS.D.2, DCI.MS-PS2.A.1	72-76	2
6	Rubric	MS-ETS1-1, DCI.MS-ETS1.A.1	77-80	3
7	Rubric	MS-PS2-1, CCC.MS.D.2, DCI.MS-PS2.A.1	77-80	2
8	Rubric	MS-PS2-1, DCI.MS-PS2.A.1	73-74	2
9	B	MS-PS2-1	70-74	2
10	B	MS-PS2-1	70-74	2

6. Use the rubric below to evaluate total points earned for this item. *[max point: 1]*

NGSS Constructed Response Answer – 1 Point	
Evidence of Mastery	Sample answer: • The material will need to be soft in order to absorb the energy of any potential collisions.

7. Use the rubric below to evaluate total points earned for this item. *[max point: 1]*

NGSS Constructed Response Answer – 1 Point	
Evidence of Mastery	Sample answer: • If the ball collides with a player's head, the ball will rebound in the opposite direction after the collision. The player's head will feel the same force, but the helmet deforms, which absorbs energy so the person's head does not change its motion as much as it would if she was not wearing a helmet. The force is the same, but the acceleration is less.

8. Use the rubric below to evaluate total points earned for this item. *[max point: 1]*

NGSS Constructed Response Answer – 1 Point	
Evidence of Mastery	Sample answer: • According to Newton's third law, objects exert equal, opposing forces on each other when they collide. If the two bumper cars have the same mass, they would have the same acceleration because, according to Newton's second law, "$F = ma$ and $a = F/m$."

Unit 1 Unit Test A – Forces and Motion

Item Analysis		
Item #	**Standards**	**DOK**
1	MS-PS2-2	1
2	MS-PS2-2, DCI.MS-PS2.A.2, CCC.MS.G.1	1
3	MS-PS2-1, DCI.MS-PS2.A.1	2
4	MS-PS2-4, DCI.MS-PS2.B.2, SEP.NOS.MS.B.1	2
5	MS-PS2-1, DCI.MS-PS2.A.1	2
6	MS-PS2-4, DCI.MS-PS2.B.2, CCC.MS.D.2	2
7	MS-PS2-2	2
8	MS-PS2-2	1
9	MS-PS2-2	1
10	MS-PS2-2, SEP.MS.B.3	2
11	MS-PS2-4, DCI.MS-PS2.B.2, SEP.MS.G.1	2
12	MS-PS2-2, DCI.MS-PS2.A.2, SEP.MS.C.3	2
13	MS-ETS1-1, DCI.MS-ETS1.A.1, SEP.MS.A.3	3
14	MS-PS2-2, DCI.MS-PS2.A.2, CCC.MS.G.1	2
15	MS-PS2-2, DCI.MS-PS2.A.2, SEP.MS.E.1	3
16	MS-PS2-2, DCI.MS-PS2.A.2, CCC.MS.F.2	3
17	MS-ETS1-1, DCI.MS-ETS1.A.1	2
18	MS-ETS1-2, DCI.MS-ETS1.B.2, SEP.MS.G.2	2
19	MS-PS2-1, DCI.MS-PS2.A.1, CCC.MS.D.2	2
20	MS-PS2-1, DCI.MS-PS2.A.1, SEP.MS.F.4	3

1. A. This is incorrect because a pull is only one type of force; some forces also push on objects.

B. This is incorrect because the weight, a measurement of how heavy an object is, is an example of the force of gravity acting on an object.

C. This is correct because every force is either a push or a pull that is exerted on an object.

D. This is incorrect because a change in the direction of an object's motion is a sign that there is a force acting on an object, but an object can also have forces acting on it without changing its motion.

2. A. This is correct because the type of force that opposes motion is the friction force, and since the motion of the block does not change, the forces must be balanced.

B. This is incorrect because the gravitational force points downward, while Sasha's force points in the direction of the motion of the block; therefore, these two forces do not balance one another.

C. This is incorrect because in order for an object's motion to change, there must be unbalanced forces acting on it.

D. This is incorrect because if there were no forces acting on it, then the motion of the block would not change; therefore, it would move at a constant velocity.

3. **A.** This is incorrect because the sun and the comet exert equal and opposite forces on each other.
   B. This is incorrect because gravitational forces are exerted on objects that are not touching.
   C. This is incorrect because the sun and the comet apply equal and opposite forces on each other. In addition, the speed of the comet does not affect the magnitude of the force.
   D. This is correct because Newton's law says that there are equal and opposite forces applied, but because the sun is very massive, the effect of the force on the sun does not affect its motion enough to notice.

4. **A.** This is correct because the table shows that object A has a larger weight than objects C and D on planet 2 and that object A has a larger weight than object B on planet 3. Therefore, object A has the largest mass and will, thus, have the highest mass and weight on Earth.
   B. This is incorrect because the table shows that object B has a lower weight than object D on planet 1, that object B has a lower weight than objects A and D on planet 3, and that object B has a lower weight than object A on planet 4. Therefore, object B has a lower mass than objects A and D and will, thus, have a lower mass and weight on Earth.
   C. This is incorrect because the table shows that object C has a lower weight than objects B and D on planet 1, that object C has a lower weight than objects A and D on planet 2, and that object C has a lower weight than objects A and B on planet 4. Therefore, object C has a lower mass than all of the other objects and will, thus, have a lower mass and weight on Earth.
   D. This is incorrect because the table shows that object D has a lower weight than object A on planet 2 and that object D has a lower weight than object A on planet 3. Therefore, object D has a lower mass than object A and will, thus, have a lower mass and weight on Earth.

5. **A.** This is incorrect because the force on the ball from the target and the force on the target from the ball are an action-reaction pair, and, therefore, are the same magnitude. How bouncy the ball is might affect the result of the force (whether the ball changes direction or shape) but does not affect the size of the force.
   B. This is incorrect because the force on the ball from the target and the force on the target from the ball are an action-reaction pair, and, therefore, are the same magnitude. Since the target has a larger mass than the ball, its motion will change less than that of the ball rather than more.
   C. This is correct because the force on the target from the ball and the force on the ball from the target are the same size but in different directions.
   D. This is incorrect because the force on the ball from the target and the force on the target from the ball are an action-reaction pair, and, therefore, are the same magnitude. The mass of the ball is less than that of the target, so the change in motion of the ball will be larger than the change in motion of the target, but the forces are equal.

6. **A.** This is incorrect because the force that causes the spring to stretch is the weight of the object, and the number of striped segments that are pulled out of the tube shows how much the spring stretches. Since the fewest number of striped segments are outside of the tube for object A, this object has the smallest weight.
   B. This is incorrect because the force that causes the spring to stretch is the weight of the object, and the number of striped segments that are pulled out of the tube shows how much the spring stretches. The picture shows that object B causes fewer striped segments to be pulled out of the tube than object D; therefore, it has a smaller weight than object D.
   C. This is incorrect because the force that causes the spring to stretch is the weight of the object, and the number of striped segments that are pulled out of the tube shows how much the spring stretches. The picture shows that object C causes fewer striped segments to be pulled out of the tube than objects B and D; therefore, it has a smaller weight than these objects.
   D. This is correct because the force that causes the spring to stretch is the weight of the object, and the number of striped segments that are pulled out of the tube shows how much the spring stretches. The picture shows that object D causes the largest number of striped segments to be pulled out of the tube; therefore, it causes the spring to stretch by the largest amount and, thus, must have the largest weight.

7. **A.** This is incorrect because although Car 1 reaches a larger maximum speed, its acceleration is over a longer time and, therefore, is smaller than the acceleration of Car 2. Also, average speed is given by distance divided by time, and Car 2 takes a shorter amount of time to travel the same distance.

B. This is correct because the acceleration of Car 2 is (20 m/s)/(20 s) = 1 m/s^2, which is larger than the acceleration of Car 1, (20 m/s)/(30 s) = 0.67 m/s^2. Also, Car 2 takes a shorter total amount of time (30 s) than Car 1 (35 s) to travel the same distance and, therefore, has a larger average speed since average speed is the distance traveled divided by the amount of time it takes.

C. This is incorrect because although Car 2 does have a larger average speed than Car 1, Car 1 does not have a larger acceleration than Car 2. The acceleration of Car 1 is over a longer time, and acceleration is equal to change in speed divided by time.

D. This is incorrect because Car 2 has a larger acceleration than Car 1 and its average speed is also larger than the average speed of Car 1 because it takes a shorter total amount of time to travel the same distance.

8. The number list should be 4, 2, 1, 3, 5. The correct order from fastest to slowest is glass, chromium, steel, aluminum, and titanium vanadium alloy because the higher the friction, the stronger the force that opposes the motion of the block down the ramp. Therefore, the objects with the smallest coefficient of friction will reach the bottom of the ramp the fastest. The table shows that glass will have the lowest friction force on the steel ramp, while titanium vanadium alloy will have the highest friction force on the ramp.

9. **A.** *Noncontact* is correct because the gravitational force acts at a distance between objects that are not touching.

B. *Contact* is correct because objects need to be touching in order for there to be a frictional force.

C. *Contact* is correct because air resistance is a type of force in which air particles moving past an object create friction.

D. *Noncontact* is correct because magnetic objects can attract or repel other objects by magnetic fields without touching.

E. *Contact* is correct because when a person applies force to an object by pushing with his or her hands, he or she is in contact with the object.

10. **A.** The picture of the box with a short arrow to the left and two short arrows to the right belongs in the *Starts moving to the right* column because the sum of the two rightward arrows is larger than the leftward arrow.

B. The picture of the box with a short arrow to the right and a long arrow to the left belongs in the *Starts moving to the left* column because the left arrow is longer than the right arrow.

C. The picture of the box with two short arrows to the left and one long arrow to the right belongs in the *Stays at rest* column because the sum of the two leftward arrows is the same as the length of the rightward arrow, so the forces are balanced.

D. The picture of the box with equally sized arrows to the right and left belongs in the *Stays at rest* column because the two forces are the same size but in opposite directions, so the forces are balanced.

11. **A.** *Object 1* belongs in the second blank because as the 10 kg object moves from point A to point E, it moves farther away from Object 1; therefore, the gravitational force decreases. The data in the table support this fact.

B. *Object 2* belongs in the first blank because as the 10 kg object moves from point A to point E, it moves closer to Object 2; therefore, the gravitational force increases. The data in the table support this fact.

C. *Both objects* does not belong in any blank because as the 10 kg object moves from point A to point E, it moves closer to Object 2 but farther from Object 1, and gravitational force gets stronger as objects move closer together and weaker as objects move farther apart.

D. *Neither object* does not belong in any blank because as the 10 kg object moves from point A to point E, it moves closer to Object 2 but farther from Object 1, and gravitational force gets stronger as objects move closer together and weaker as objects move farther apart.

E. *Correct* does not belong in any blank because the evidence shows that the force of gravity due to Object 1 is always larger than the force of gravity due to Object 2 between point A and point E; therefore, the evidence does not support the claim that there is a point in which the forces are equal.

F. *Incorrect* belongs in the third blank because the evidence shows that the force of gravity due to Object 1 is always larger than the force of gravity due to Object 2 between point A and point E; therefore, the evidence does not support the claim that there is a point in which the forces are equal.

12. A. The picture showing two fans facing each other with a ball in between does not match with any of the options because this setup will test the motion of an object with balanced forces.

B. The picture showing one fan pointing across the path of a ball matches *investigation setup* because the force from the fan will change the direction of the ball in different amounts depending on the inertia of the ball.

C. *Mass of the ball* matches *independent variable* because the mass is being varied and the inertia of a ball is related to its mass; the higher the mass, the more inertia.

D. *Color of the ball* does not match with any of the options because this variable is not being changed and does not affect the forces or motion of the ball.

E. *Mass of the fan or fans* does not match with any of the options because this variable should remain constant throughout the investigation.

F. *Speed of the fan or fans* does not match with any of the options because this variable should remain constant throughout the investigation.

G. *Direction of motion of the ball* matches *dependent variable* because this is what is measured and what changes as a result of the mass of the ball.

H. *Direction of the fan or fans* does not match with any of the options because this variable should remain constant throughout the investigation.

13. 1C. *More secure* is correct because if the stakes are large then they will be less likely to be pulled out of the ground.

2E. *More force* is correct because if the stakes are larger, then it takes more force to get them to drive them into the ground.

3G. *More* is correct because a heavy mallet will provide more force because the mallet is more massive.

4I. *Mass* is correct because force is equal to mass times acceleration.

14. Use the rubric below to evaluate total points earned for this item. *[max point: 3]*

	DCI, CCC - 3 Points
Claims	The student is able to: 1. identify the forces acting on the hockey puck in opposite directions (DCI); and 2. explain how balanced forces acting on a puck result in a stable position (CCC); and 3. describe that a change in the force applied to the puck affect the stability of the puck's position (CCC).
Evidence of Mastery of Disciplinary Core Ideas	1 point for correctly identifying the forces acting on the puck **Part 1:** One point is earned for identifying that the forces acting on the puck are the pushes from the hockey sticks, acting in opposite directions. Any one of the following responses, or an equivalent, is acceptable. • Each player is pushing on the puck in a different direction. • There are two forces on the puck, one force from the first hockey stick, and the other force in the opposite direction from the other hockey stick.

Evidence of Mastery of Crosscutting Concepts	1 point for correctly explaining why the puck does not move **Part 2:** One point is earned for explaining that the forces acting on the puck are balanced, and as a result, the puck does not move. The following response, or an equivalent, is acceptable. • The two forces acting on the puck are balanced at first, because both players are pushing in opposite directions with equal force. 1 point for correctly describing how to get the puck to move **Part 3:** One point is earned for describing that a change in the size or direction of one of the forces would cause the puck to move. Any of the following responses, or an equivalent, is acceptable. • One of the players will have to push harder than the opposing player. • One player will have to push in a different direction. If one of the players pushes the puck to the side instead, the puck will move sideways.

15. Use the rubric below to evaluate total points earned for this item. *[max point: 3]*

DCI, SEP - 3 Points	
Claims	The student is able to: 1. explain that the greater the mass of an object, the greater the force needed to achieve the same change in motion (DCI); and 2. use the mathematical representation of Newton's second law of motion to calculate force (SEP); and 3. use the mathematical representation of Newton's second law of motion to calculate acceleration (SEP).
Evidence of Mastery of Disciplinary Core Ideas	1 point for correctly identifying and explaining how Christian could reach the same speed while carrying the cargo **Part 3:** One point is earned for explaining that the heavier the total mass, the greater the force needed to achieve the same acceleration. Any one of the following responses, or an equivalent, is acceptable. • After he adds the cargo, the total mass is larger, and therefore Christian cannot reach the same acceleration with the same force. He will need to exert a larger force to reach the same speed. • After he adds the cargo, the total mass is larger, and therefore Christian cannot reach the same acceleration with the same force. Since the acceleration is smaller, he needs to exert the force for a longer amount of time to reach the same speed.
Evidence of Mastery of Science and Engineering Practices	1 point for correctly calculating the force before picking up the cargo **Part 1:** One point is earned for using Newton's second law to calculate the force that is applied on the system without the cargo. Force is equal to mass times acceleration, so $F = (54\text{ kg})(0.44\text{ m/s}^2) = 23.8\text{ N}$. The following response, or an equivalent, is acceptable. • 23.8 N 1 point for correctly calculating the acceleration when the cargo is added **Part 2:** One point is earned for using Newton's second law to calculate the acceleration on the system with the cargo. Acceleration is equal to force divided by mass, so $a = (23.8\text{ N})/(54\text{ kg} + 12\text{ kg}) = 0.36\text{ m/s}^2$. The following response, or an equivalent, is acceptable. • 0.36 m/s^2

16. Use the rubric below to evaluate total points earned for this item. *[max point: 3]*

<table>
<tr><th colspan="2">DCI, CCC - 3 Points</th></tr>
<tr><td>Claims</td><td>The student is able to:
1. identify and describe the forces acting on the skier using knowledge that the motion of an object is determined by the sum of the forces acting on it (DCI); and
2. describe how materials can be designed to suit a particular purpose (CCC); and
3. describe how structure can be modified to fit a particular function (CCC).</td></tr>
<tr><td>Evidence of Mastery of Disciplinary Core Ideas</td><td>1 point for correctly identifying and describing the forces acting on the skier
Part 1: One point is earned for identifying and describing that gravity and opposing forces are acting on the skier and that she will move when gravity is larger. The following response, or an equivalent, is acceptable.
• Gravity pulls the skier down the slope. Friction and air resistance are forces that oppose the motion. When the force of gravity is larger than the forces of friction and air resistance, the skier will move.</td></tr>
<tr><td>Evidence of Mastery of Crosscutting Concepts</td><td>1 point for correctly describing how the skier can increase her maximum speed
Part 2: One point is earned for describing one way the skier can reduce the air resistance or friction to increase her acceleration. Any one of the following responses, or an equivalent, is acceptable.
• She could reduce the friction between her skis and the snow by rubbing them with wax so there is less force opposing gravity and so she has a greater acceleration.
• She could choose skis made of a material that has the smallest amount of friction between the skis and the snow so there is less force opposing gravity and so she has a greater acceleration.
• She could choose clothing that reduces the air resistance so there is less force opposing gravity and so she has a greater acceleration.
1 point for correctly describing how the skier can increase or decrease her velocity
Part 3: One point is earned for describing how the skier can speed up or slow down by changing her body position to affect the force due to the air resistance. The following response, or an equivalent, is acceptable.
• The skier can reduce the amount of air resistance by crouching down, which will make the net force down the hill larger, so she can have a greater acceleration.</td></tr>
</table>

17. A. This is correct because the lighter the material, the easier and less expensive it is to launch the spacecraft.

B. This is incorrect because although hard materials might protect the spaceship from some objects, they are more likely to cause damage for faster or larger objects, as demonstrated by steel plates in the passage.

C. This is incorrect because if the material is heavy, it will be difficult to launch into space.

D. This is incorrect because the main expense comes from launching the spaceship out of the atmosphere, not from the cost of the materials.

E. This is correct because when the spaceship is launched, there is a lot of air resistance from the atmosphere. This causes a lot of heat, which can degrade the material if it is not heat resistant.

F. This is correct because the material must be able to absorb the impact of a meteoroid when it collides with the spaceship in order for the contents of the spaceship to be protected; this is demonstrated by the foam layers in the passage.

G. This is incorrect because meteoroids are more easily able to go through a thin material; the thicker the material, the less likely that it will be affected by the collision.

18. A. This is incorrect because the criteria state that the material could be transparent or mostly transparent, and Material 2 is mostly transparent.

B. This is incorrect because the astronauts have extra shielding to protect from a large number of meteors, so the material does not need to provide this protection.

C. This is incorrect because the weight of the material was not one of the criteria listed.

D. This is correct because the ability to protect from different-sized meteoroids and being transparent or mostly transparent are the criteria that the material must meet.

19. Use the rubric below to evaluate total points earned for this item. *[max point: 2]*

DCI, CCC - 2 Points	
Claims	The student is able to: 1. complete a model to show that the force exerted by the first object on the second object is equal in strength to the force that the second object exerts on the first, but in the opposite direction (DCI); and 2. complete a model in order to track changes in motion before and after a collision by drawing arrows to represent motion (CCC).
Evidence of Mastery of Disciplinary Core Ideas	1 point for correctly drawing arrows to represent the forces acting during the collision **Part 1:** One point is earned for drawing arrows of the same size but opposite directions for the spaceship and meteoroid to represent the forces acting during the collision. See sample answer.
Evidence of Mastery of Crosscutting Concepts	1 point for correctly drawing arrows to represent motion after the collision **Part 2:** One point is earned for drawing arrows pointing to the right for the spaceship and meteoroid to represent the direction of velocity after the collision. The following response, or an equivalent, is acceptable. Before / During / After

20. Use the rubric below to evaluate total points earned for this item. *[max point: 4]*

DCI, SEP - 4 Points	
Claims	The student is able to: 1. explain an application of Newton's laws of motion (DCI); and 2. apply scientific knowledge about collisions to design a demonstration (SEP).
Evidence of Mastery of Disciplinary Core Ideas	2 points for correctly explaining how Newton's second and third laws of motion apply to the demonstration **Part 2:** One point is earned for explaining that the two objects exert equal and opposite forces on each other. The following response, or an equivalent, is acceptable. • The model spaceship exerts a force on the marble. The marble bounces off the spaceship, exerting an equal and opposite force on the spaceship as well. **Part 2:** One point is earned for explaining how the masses of the objects affect their motion in response to the forces. The following response, or an equivalent, is acceptable. • Since the spaceship is much larger and heavier than the marble, but the forces are the same, it does not change its motion very much. However, the marble has a very small mass compared with the spaceship so it will show a large change in motion when acted on by a force of the same size.

Evidence of Mastery of Science and Engineering Practices	2 points for correctly identifying and explaining which materials to use in the demonstration **Part 1:** One point is earned for identifying materials that can be used to demonstrate how Newton's second and third laws apply to a collision between a spaceship and a meteoroid. The following response, or an equivalent, is acceptable. • The student should tie the string to the spaceship, hang it from the lab stand, and use marbles to represent the meteoroids. **Part 1:** One point is earned for explaining why the student should use each of the materials in the demonstration. The following response, or an equivalent, is acceptable. • The model spaceship represents the real spaceship, and it is hung by a string to represent space. The marble represents the meteoroid because it is much smaller than the model spaceship but also not too light to be thrown at a high speed toward the spaceship to show the collision.

Unit 1 Unit Test B – Forces and Motion

Item Analysis		
Item #	**Standards**	**DOK**
1	MS-PS2-2	1
2	MS-PS2-2, DCI.MS-PS2.A.2, CCC.MS.G.1	1
3	MS-PS2-1, DCI.MS-PS2.A.1	2
4	MS-PS2-4, DCI.MS-PS2.B.2, SEP.NOS.MS.B.1	2
5	MS-PS2-1, DCI.MS-PS2.A.1	2
6	MS-PS2-4, DCI.MS-PS2.B.2, CCC.MS.D.2	2
7	MS-PS2-2	2
8	MS-PS2-2	1
9	MS-PS2-2	1
10	MS-PS2-2, SEP.MS.B.3	2
11	MS-PS2-4, DCI.MS-PS2.B.2, SEP.MS.G.1	2
12	MS-PS2-2, DCI.MS-PS2.A.2, SEP.MS.C.3	2
13	MS-ETS1-1, DCI.MS-ETS1.A.1, SEP.MS.A.3	3
14	MS-PS2-2, DCI.MS-PS2.A.2, CCC.MS.G.1	2
15	MS-PS2-2, DCI.MS-PS2.A.2, SEP.MS.E.1	3
16	MS-PS2-2, DCI.MS-PS2.A.2, CCC.MS.F.2	3
17	MS-ETS1-1, DCI.MS-ETS1.A.1	2
18	MS-ETS1-2, DCI.MS-ETS1.B.2, SEP.MS.G.2	2
19	MS-PS2-1, DCI.MS-PS2.A.1, CCC.MS.D.2	2
20	MS-PS2-1, DCI.MS-PS2.A.1, SEP.MS.F.4	3

1. **A.** This is incorrect because a pull is only one type of force; some forces also push on objects.
   B. This is correct because every force is either a push or a pull that is exerted on an object.
   C. This is incorrect because a change in the direction of an object's motion is a sign that there is a force acting on an object, but an object can also have forces acting on it without changing its motion.

2. **A.** This is correct because the type of force that opposes motion is the friction force, and since the motion of the block does not change, the forces must be balanced.

   B. This is incorrect because the gravitational force points downward, while Sasha's force points in the direction of the motion of the block; therefore, these two forces do not balance one another.

   C. This is incorrect because if there were no forces acting on it, then the motion of the block would not change; therefore, it would move at a constant velocity.

3. **A.** This is incorrect because gravitational forces are exerted on objects that are not touching.

   B. This is incorrect because the sun and the comet apply equal and opposite forces on each other. In addition, the speed of the comet does not affect the magnitude of the force.

   C. This is correct because Newton's law says that there are equal and opposite forces applied, but because the sun is very massive, the effect of the force on the sun does not affect its motion enough to notice.

4. **A.** This is correct because the table shows that object A has a larger weight than objects C and D on planet 2 and that object A has a larger weight than object B on planet 3. Therefore, object A has the largest mass and will, thus, have the highest mass and weight on Earth.

   B. This is incorrect because the table shows that object B has a lower weight than object D on planet 1, that object B has a lower weight than objects A and D on planet 3, and that object B has a lower weight than object A on planet 4. Therefore, object B has a lower mass than objects A and D and will, thus, have a lower mass and weight on Earth.

   C. This is incorrect because the table shows that object C has a lower weight than objects B and D on planet 1, that object C has a lower weight than objects A and D on planet 2, and that object C has a lower weight than objects A and B on planet 4. Therefore, object C has a lower mass than all of the other objects and will, thus, have a lower mass and weight on Earth.

   D. This is incorrect because the table shows that object D has a lower weight than object A on planet 2 and that object D has a lower weight than object A on planet 3. Therefore, object D has a lower mass than object A and will, thus, have a lower mass and weight on Earth.

5. **A.** This is incorrect because the force on the ball from the target and the force on the target from the ball are an action-reaction pair, and, therefore, are the same magnitude. Since the target has a larger mass than the ball, its motion will change less than that of the ball rather than more.

   B. This is correct because the force on the target from the ball and the force on the ball from the target are the same size but in different directions.

   C. This is incorrect because the force on the ball from the target and the force on the target from the ball are an action-reaction pair, and, therefore, are the same magnitude. The mass of the ball is less than that of the target, so the change in motion of the ball will be larger than the change in motion of the target, but the forces are equal.

6. **A.** This is incorrect because the force that causes the spring to stretch is the weight of the object, and the number of striped segments that are pulled out of the tube shows how much the spring stretches. Since the fewest number of striped segments are outside of the tube for object A, this object has the smallest weight.

   B. This is incorrect because the force that causes the spring to stretch is the weight of the object, and the number of striped segments that are pulled out of the tube shows how much the spring stretches. The picture shows that object B causes fewer striped segments to be pulled out of the tube than object D; therefore, it has a smaller weight than object D.

   C. This is incorrect because the force that causes the spring to stretch is the weight of the object, and the number of striped segments that are pulled out of the tube shows how much the spring stretches. The picture shows that object C causes fewer striped segments to be pulled out of the tube than objects B and D; therefore, it has a smaller weight than these objects.

   D. This is correct because the force that causes the spring to stretch is the weight of the object, and the number of striped segments that are pulled out of the tube shows how much the spring stretches. The picture shows that object D causes the largest number of striped segments to be pulled out of the tube; therefore, it causes the spring to stretch by the largest amount and, thus, must have the largest weight.

7. **A.** This is incorrect because although Car 1 reaches a larger maximum speed, its acceleration is over a longer time and, therefore, is smaller than the acceleration of Car 2. Also, average speed is given by distance divided by time, and Car 2 takes a shorter amount of time to travel the same distance.

   B. This is correct because the acceleration of Car 2 is (20 m/s)/(20 s) = 1 m/s^2, which is larger than the acceleration of Car 1, (20 m/s)/(30 s) = 0.67 m/s^2. Also, Car 2 takes a shorter total amount of time (30 s) than Car 1 (35 s) to travel the same distance and, therefore, has a larger average speed since average speed is the distance traveled divided by the amount of time it takes.

   C. This is incorrect because although Car 2 does have a larger average speed than Car 1, Car 1 does not have a larger acceleration than Car 2. The acceleration of Car 1 is over a longer time, and acceleration is equal to change in speed divided by time.

8. The number list should be 4, 2, 1, 3, 5. The correct order from fastest to slowest is *glass, chromium, steel, aluminum,* and *titanium vanadium alloy* because the higher the friction, the stronger the force that opposes the motion of the block down the ramp. Therefore, the objects with the smallest coefficient of friction will reach the bottom of the ramp the fastest. The table shows that glass will have the lowest friction force on the steel ramp, while titanium vanadium alloy will have the highest friction force on the ramp.

9. **A.** *Noncontact* is correct because the gravitational force acts at a distance between objects that are not touching.

   B. *Contact* is correct because air resistance is a type of force in which air particles moving past an object create friction.

   C. *Noncontact* is correct because magnetic objects can attract or repel other objects by magnetic fields without touching.

   D. *Contact* is correct because when a person applies force to an object by pushing with his or her hands, he or she is in contact with the object.

10. **A.** The picture of the box with a short arrow to the left and two short arrows to the right belongs in the *Starts moving to the right* column because the sum of the two rightward arrows is larger than the leftward arrow.

    B. The picture of the box with a short arrow to the right and a long arrow to the left belongs in the *Starts moving to the left* column because the left arrow is longer than the right arrow.

    C. The picture of the box with two short arrows to the left and one long arrow to the right belongs in the *Stays at rest* column because the sum of the two leftward arrows is the same as the length of the rightward arrow, so the forces are balanced.

11. **A.** *Object 1* belongs in the second box because as the 10 kg object moves from point A to point E, it moves farther away from Object 1; therefore, the gravitational force decreases. The data in the table support this fact.

    B. *Object 2* belongs in the first box because as the 10 kg object moves from point A to point E, it moves closer to Object 2; therefore, the gravitational force increases. The data in the table support this fact.

    C. *Correct* does not belong in any box because the evidence shows that the force of gravity due to Object 1 is always larger than the force of gravity due to Object 2 between point A and point E; therefore, the evidence does not support the claim that there is a point in which the forces are equal.

    D. *Incorrect* belongs in the third box because the evidence shows that the force of gravity due to Object 1 is always larger than the force of gravity due to Object 2 between point A and point E; therefore, the evidence does not support the claim that there is a point in which the forces are equal.

12. **A.** The picture showing two fans facing each other with a ball in between does not match with any of the options because this setup will test the motion of an object with balanced forces.

    B. The picture showing one fan pointing across the path of a ball matches *investigation setup* because the force from the fan will change the direction of the ball in different amounts depending on the inertia of the ball.

C. *Mass of the ball* matches *independent variable* because the mass is being varied and the inertia of a ball is related to its mass; the higher the mass, the more inertia.

D. *Direction of motion of the ball* matches *dependent variable* because this is what is measured and what changes as a result of the mass of the ball.

13. 1B. *More secure* is correct because if the stakes are large then they will be less likely to be pulled out of the ground.

2D. *More force* is correct because if the stakes are larger, then it takes more force to drive them into the ground.

3F. *Mass* is correct because force is equal to mass times acceleration.

14. Use the rubric below to evaluate total points earned for this item. *[max point: 3]*

DCI, CCC - 3 Points	
Claims	The student is able to: 1. identify the forces acting on the hockey puck in opposite directions (DCI); and 2. explain how balanced forces acting on a puck result in a stable position (CCC); and
Evidence of Mastery of Disciplinary Core Ideas	1 point for correctly identifying the forces acting on the puck **Part 1:** One point is earned for identifying that the forces acting on the puck are the pushes from the hockey sticks, acting in opposite directions. Any one of the following responses, or an equivalent, is acceptable. • Each player is pushing on the puck in a different direction. • There are two forces on the puck, one force from the first hockey stick, and the other force in the opposite direction from the other hockey stick.
Evidence of Mastery of Crosscutting Concepts	2 points for correctly explaining why the puck does not move **Part 2:** Two points are earned for explaining that the forces acting on the puck are balanced, and as a result, the puck does not move. The following response, or an equivalent, is acceptable. • The two forces acting on the puck are balanced at first, because both players are pushing in opposite directions with equal force.

15. Use the rubric below to evaluate total points earned for this item. *[max point: 3]*

DCI, SEP - 3 Points	
Claims	The student is able to: 1. explain that the greater the mass of an object, the greater the force needed to achieve the same change in motion (DCI); and 2. use the mathematical representation of Newton's second law of motion to calculate force (SEP)
Evidence of Mastery of Disciplinary Core Ideas	2 points for correctly identifying and explaining how Christian could reach the same speed while carrying the cargo **Part 2:** Two points are earned for explaining that the heavier the total mass, the greater the force needed to achieve the same acceleration. Any one of the following responses, or an equivalent, is acceptable. • After he adds the cargo, the total mass is larger, and therefore Christian cannot reach the same acceleration with the same force. He will need to exert a larger force to reach the same speed. • After he adds the cargo, the total mass is larger, and therefore Christian cannot reach the same acceleration with the same force. Since the acceleration is smaller, he needs to exert the force for a longer amount of time to reach the same speed.

Evidence of Mastery of Science and Engineering Practices	1 point for correctly calculating the force before picking up the cargo **Part 1:** One point is earned for using Newton's second law to calculate the force that is applied on the system without the cargo. Force is equal to mass times acceleration, so F = (54 kg)(0.44 m/s^2) = 23.8 N. The following response, or an equivalent, is acceptable. • 23.8 N

16. Use the rubric below to evaluate total points earned for this item. *[max point: 3]*

DCI, CCC - 3 Points	
Claims	The student is able to: 1. identify and describe the forces acting on the skier using knowledge that the motion of an object is determined by the sum of the forces acting on it (DCI); and 2. describe how materials can be designed to suit a particular purpose (CCC); and
Evidence of Mastery of Disciplinary Core Ideas	1 point for correctly identifying and describing the forces acting on the skier **Part 1:** One point is earned for identifying and describing that gravity and opposing forces are acting on the skier and that she will move when gravity is larger. The following response, or an equivalent, is acceptable. • Gravity pulls the skier down the slope. Friction and air resistance are forces that oppose the motion. When the force of gravity is larger than the forces of friction and air resistance, the skier will move.
Evidence of Mastery of Crosscutting Concepts	2 points for correctly describing how the skier can increase her speed **Part 2:** One point is earned for describing one way the skier can reduce the air resistance or friction to increase her acceleration. Any one of the following responses, or an equivalent, is acceptable. • She could reduce the friction between her skis and the snow by rubbing them with wax so there is less force opposing gravity and so she has a greater acceleration. • She could choose skis made of a material that has the smallest amount of friction between the skis and the snow so there is less force opposing gravity and so she has a greater acceleration. • She could choose clothing that reduces the air resistance so there is less force opposing gravity and so she has a greater acceleration.

17. A. This is correct because the lighter the material, the easier and less expensive it is to launch the spacecraft.

B. This is incorrect because although hard materials might protect the spaceship from some objects, they are more likely to cause damage for faster or larger objects, as demonstrated by steel plates in the passage.

C. This is incorrect because the main expense comes from launching the spaceship out of the atmosphere, not from the cost of the materials.

D. This is correct because when the spaceship is launched, there is a lot of air resistance from the atmosphere. This causes a lot of heat, which can degrade the material if it is not heat resistant.

E. This is correct because the material must be able to absorb the impact of a meteoroid when it collides with the spaceship in order for the contents of the spaceship to be protected; this is demonstrated by the foam layers in the passage.

F. This is incorrect because meteoroids are more easily able to go through a thin material; the thicker the material, the less likely that it will be affected by the collision.

18. A. This is incorrect because the criteria state that the material could be transparent or mostly transparent, and Material 2 is mostly transparent.

B. This is incorrect because the weight of the material was not one of the criteria listed.

C. This is correct because the ability to protect from different-sized meteoroids and being transparent or mostly transparent are the criteria that the material must meet.

19. Use the rubric below to evaluate total points earned for this item. *[max point: 2]*

DCI, CCC - 2 Points	
Claims	The student is able to: 1. complete a model to show that the force exerted by the first object on the second object is equal in strength to the force that the second object exerts on the first, but in the opposite direction (DCI); and 2. complete a model in order to track changes in motion before and after a collision by drawing arrows to represent motion (CCC).
Evidence of Mastery of Disciplinary Core Ideas	1 point for correctly drawing arrows to represent the forces acting during the collision **Part 1:** One point is earned for drawing arrows of the same size but opposite directions for the spaceship and meteoroid to represent the forces acting during the collision. See sample answer.
Evidence of Mastery of Crosscutting Concepts	1 point for correctly drawing arrows to represent motion after the collision **Part 2:** One point is earned for drawing arrows pointing to the right for the spaceship and meteoroid to represent the direction of velocity after the collision. The following response, or an equivalent, is acceptable. Before During After

20. Use the rubric below to evaluate total points earned for this item. *[max point: 4]*

DCI, SEP - 4 Points	
Claims	The student is able to: 1. explain an application of Newton's laws of motion (DCI); and 2. apply scientific knowledge about collisions to design a demonstration (SEP).
Evidence of Mastery of Disciplinary Core Ideas	2 points for correctly explaining how Newton's second and third laws of motion apply to the demonstration **Part 2:** One point is earned for explaining that the two objects exert equal and opposite forces on each other. The following response, or an equivalent, is acceptable. • The model spaceship exerts a force on the marble. The marble bounces off the spaceship, exerting an equal and opposite force on the spaceship as well. **Part 2:** One point is earned for explaining how the masses of the objects affect their motion in response to the forces. The following response, or an equivalent, is acceptable. • Since the spaceship is much larger and heavier than the marble, but the forces are the same, it does not change its motion very much. However, the marble has a very small mass compared with the spaceship so it will show a large change in motion when acted on by a force of the same size.

Evidence of Mastery of Science and Engineering Practices	2 points for correctly identifying and explaining which materials to use in the demonstration **Part 1:** One point is earned for identifying materials that can be used to demonstrate how Newton's second and third laws apply to a collision between a spaceship and a meteoroid. The following response, or an equivalent, is acceptable. • The student should tie the string to the spaceship, hang it from the lab stand, and use marbles to represent the meteoroids. **Part 1:** One point is earned for explaining why the student should use each of the materials in the demonstration. The following response, or an equivalent, is acceptable. • The model spaceship represents the real spaceship, and it is hung by a string to represent space. The marble represents the meteoroid because it is much smaller than the model spaceship but also not too light to be thrown at a high speed toward the spaceship to show the collision.

Unit 2 Electric and Magnetic Forces

Unit 2 Pretest

Item Analysis			
Item #	**Key**	**Standards**	**DOK**
1	A	MS-PS2-3, DCI.MS-PS2.B.1	1
2	C	MS-PS2-3	2
3	A	MS-PS2-5, DCI.MS-PS2.B.3	1
4	D	MS-PS2-3	1
5	A	MS-PS2-3	1
6	A	MS-PS2-5, DCI.MS-PS2.B.3	1
7	B	MS-PS2-5, DCI.MS-PS2.B.3	1
8	A	MS-PS2-3	1
9	C	MS-PS2-3	1
10	B	MS-PS2-3, DCI.MS-PS2.B.1	2
11	C	MS-PS2-3	2
12	C	MS-PS2-3	1
13	D	MS-PS2-5, DCI.MS-PS2.B.3	1
14	C	MS-PS2-3, DCI.MS-PS2.B.1	2
15	A	MS-PS2-3	2

Unit 2 Lesson 1 Quiz – Magnetic Forces

Item Analysis				
Item #	**Key**	**Standards**	**Page #**	**DOK**
1	D	MS-PS2-3, CCC.MS.B.2, DCI.MS-PS2.B.1	97-100	2
2	C	MS-PS2-3, DCI.MS-PS2.B.1	97-100	2
3	C	MS-PS2-3	104-105	1
4	B	MS-PS2-5	104	2
5	D	MS-PS2-3	104-105	1

6	A	MS-PS2-3, CCC.MS.B.2, DCI.MS-PS2.B.1	97-99, 103, 109-110	2
7	A	MS-PS2-3	104-106	1
8	Rubric	MS-PS2-5, DCI.MS-PS2.B.3, SEP.MS.C.2	100-103	3
9	Rubric	MS-PS2-3, DCI.MS-PS2.B.1, SEP.MS.C.2	98-106	2
10	Rubric	MS-PS2-3, DCI.MS-PS2.B.1, SEP.MS.B.1	104-105	2

8. Use the rubric below to evaluate total points earned for this item. *[max point: 1]*

NGSS Constructed Response Answer – 1 Point	
Evidence of Mastery	Sample answer: • Place a paper clip close to each magnet, and observe the maximum distance at which the magnet will attract the paper clip.

9. Use the rubric below to evaluate total points earned for this item. *[max point: 1]*

NGSS Constructed Response Answer – 1 Point	
Evidence of Mastery	Sample answers: • which materials become magnetic when they are brought near a magnet • He can move the magnet near each end of the rod instead of the center.

10. Use the rubric below to evaluate total points earned for this item. *[max point: 1]*

NGSS Constructed Response Answer – 1 Point	
Evidence of Mastery	Sample answers: • If the material became magnetized, the arrows in the domains would all be aligned in the same direction. • In the original model, the arrows are randomly aligned, so the magnetic fields cancel out. In a model of a magnet, all of the domains are aligned so that the arrows point in the same direction, forming a magnetic field around the entire material.

Unit 2 Lesson 2 Quiz – Electric Forces

Item Analysis				
Item #	**Key**	**Standards**	**Page #**	**DOK**
1	A	MS-PS2-3	120	1
2	C	MS-PS2-3	114-117	2
3	B	MS-PS2-5	114-117	2
4	C	MS-PS2-3	118-120	2
5	C	MS-PS2-3, DCI.MS-PS2.B.1	118-121	2
6	B	MS-PS2-3	114-117	2
7	A	MS-PS2-3, DCI.MS-PS2.B.1	118-121	2
8	Rubric	MS-PS2-3	114-117	2
9	Rubric	MS-PS2-3	114-117	2
10	Rubric	MS-PS2-3, CCC.MS.B.2, DCI.MS-PS2.B.1	114-117	2

8. Use the rubric below to evaluate total points earned for this item. *[max point: 1]*

NGSS Constructed Response Answer – 1 Point	
Evidence of Mastery	To earn full credit, students must state that electric charge is a physical property that results in static electricity. The following response, or an equivalent, is acceptable. In this situation, electric charge represents a physical property of the balloon and the hair that results in static electricity because each object has charges that are not moving.

9. Use the rubric below to evaluate total points earned for this item. *[max point: 1]*

NGSS Constructed Response Answer – 1 Point	
Evidence of Mastery	Sample answer: • The charges in the neutral object move around because of the nearby charged object. The negative charges in the neutral object that are closest to the negatively charged object are repelled, and the neutral object becomes positively charged on the side closest to the charged object. As a result, the neutral object becomes attracted to the charged object.

10. Use the rubric below to evaluate total points earned for this item. *[max point: 1]*

NGSS Constructed Response Answer – 1 Point	
Evidence of Mastery	To earn full credit, students must the state that the rod will be able to pick up more paper because the magnitude of charge increases, causing an increase in the electric force. The following response, or an equivalent, is acceptable. The rod will be able to pick up more paper when it is rubbed for an additional period of time because it acquires more charge, which will make the electric force between the rod and paper stronger.

Unit 2 Lesson 3 Quiz – Fields

Item Analysis				
Item #	**Key**	**Standards**	**Page #**	**DOK**
1	C	MS-PS2-5, DCI.MS-PS2.B.3	136	1
2	D	MS-PS2-5, DCI.MS-PS2.B.3	135-138	2
3	C	MS-PS2-5, DCI.MS-PS2.B.3	136	3
4	B	MS-PS2-5, DCI.MS-PS2.B.3	135	4
5	D	MS-PS2-5	136-138	5
6	C	MS-PS2-5, DCI.MS-PS2.B.3	134, 141, 143	6
7	A	MS-PS2-5, DCI.MS-PS2.B.3	135-136	7
8	Rubric	MS-PS2-5, DCI.MS-PS2.B.3, SEP.MS.C.2	141-143	8
9	Rubric	MS-PS2-5, CCC.MS.B.2, DCI.MS-PS2.B.3	135-136	9
10	Rubric	MS-PS2-5, CCC.MS.B.2, DCI.MS-PS2.B.3	132, 134, 136	10

8. Use the rubric below to evaluate total points earned for this item. *[max point: 1]*

NGSS Constructed Response Answer – 1 Point	
Evidence of Mastery	Sample answer: • What is the shape of the magnetic field lines from a bar magnet?

9. Use the rubric below to evaluate total points earned for this item. *[max point: 1]*

NGSS Constructed Response Answer – 1 Point	
Evidence of Mastery	Sample answers: • The electric field lines go out from the positive particle, and in toward the negative particle. The force between the two particles is attractive. • If both were positively charged, the electric field lines would go outward from both particles. In between the two particles, the field lines will bend away from each other. The force between the particles is repulsive.

10. Use the rubric below to evaluate total points earned for this item. *[max point: 1]*

NGSS Constructed Response Answer – 1 Point	
Evidence of Mastery	To get full credit, students must use the model to identify and explain that object B is a magnet and that object B will move away from object A when released. The following response, or an equivalent, is acceptable. When two magnetic objects are near each other, attractive or repulsive magnetic forces between the objects will cause a change to the shape of the magnetic field. Since object B caused a change to the shape of object A's magnetic field, this means object B must be a magnetized material. Object B caused the magnetic field lines of object A to move closer together, which means that the magnetic force between object B and object A is repulsive. Therefore, object B must be a magnet, and when it is released, it will move away from object A.

Unit 2 Lesson 4 Quiz – Electromagnetism

Item Analysis				
Item #	**Key**	**Standards**	**Page #**	**DOK**
1	C	MS-PS2-3	153	1
2	B	MS-PS2-3, CCC.MS.B.2, DCI.MS-PS2.B.1	154-157	2
3	B	MS-PS2-3	150	3
4	D	MS-PS2-3	159-162	4
5	B	MS-PS2-3, DCI.MS-PS2.B.1	152-153	5
6	D	MS-PS2-3	154-156	6
7	D	MS-PS2-3	152-153, 166, 168-170	7
8	Rubric	MS-PS2-3, CCC.MS.B.2, DCI.MS-PS2.B.1	154-158	8
9	Rubric	MS-PS2-3 SEP.MS.F.4	159-162	9
10	Rubric	MS-PS2-3, CCC.MS.B.2	160-162	10

8. Use the rubric below to evaluate total points earned for this item. *[max point: 1]*

NGSS Constructed Response Answer – 1 Point	
Evidence of Mastery	Sample answers: • An aluminum nail is not a ferromagnetic material like iron. Because of this, the aluminum nail does not become magnetized when an electric current is in the wires, and so it does not pick up any paper clips. • Pamela could use the iron nail in the electromagnet. Then, she could wrap the copper wire more times around the iron nail so that it has a stronger magnetic field.

9. Use the rubric below to evaluate total points earned for this item. *[max point: 1]*

NGSS Constructed Response Answer – 1 Point	
Evidence of Mastery	Sample answers: • When the magnet starts to spin, it causes electric charges to flow through the coil of wire. • This process is known as electromagnetic induction. • The person could modify the machine by attaching the coil of copper wire to the turbine blades. This way, the coil of wire will spin around the magnet when the wind blows. This will produce the same effect as the original design because electric current is produced when a magnet moves in a coil of wire or when a wire moves between the poles of a magnet.

10. Use the rubric below to evaluate total points earned for this item. *[max point: 1]*

NGSS Constructed Response Answer – 1 Point	
Evidence of Mastery	To earn full credit, students must predict that the current will reverse direction and identify that Idra could increase the strength of the current by moving the magnets faster or increasing the number of wire coils around the plastic tube. The following response, or an equivalent, is acceptable. Reversing the poles of the magnets as they move through the tube will reverse the direction of the current. To increase the strength of the current, Idra could coil the wire more times around the plastic tube.

Unit 2 Unit Test A – Electric and Magnetic Forces

Item Analysis		
Item #	**Standards**	**DOK**
1	MS-PS2-3, DCI.MS-PS2.B.1, SEP.MS.D.1	2
2	MS-PS2-3	1
3	MS-PS2-3	1
4	MS-PS2-3	1
5	MS-PS2-3	2
6	MS-PS2-5, DCI.MS-PS2.B.3, CCC.MS.B.2	3
7	MS-PS2-3, DCI.MS-PS2.B.1	1
8	MS-PS2-5, DCI.MS-PS2.B.3, CCC.MS.B.2	2
9	MS-PS2-5, DCI.MS-PS2.B.3	2
10	MS-PS2-3, DCI.MS-PS2.B.1	2
11	MS-PS2-3, DCI.MS-PS2.B.1, SEP.MS.B.3	2
12	MS-PS2-5, DCI.MS-PS2.B.3, CCC.MS.B.2	2

13	MS-PS2-3, DCI.MS-PS2.B.1, SEP.MS.B.3	3
14	MS-PS2-3, DCI.MS-PS2.B.1, SEP.MS.A.3	3
15	MS-PS2-5, DCI.MS-PS2.B.3	2
16	MS-PS2-5, DCI.MS-PS2.B.3, SEP.MS.B.1	3
17	MS-PS2-5, DCI.MS-PS2.B.3, SEP.MS.B.1	3
18	MS-PS2-3, DCI.MS-PS2.B.1, SEP.MS.A.2	1
19	MS-PS2-3, DCI.MS-PS2.B.1, CCC.MS.B.2	2
20	MS-PS2-5, DCI.MS-PS2.B.3, SEP.MS.C.2	2

1. **A.** This is correct because the two magnets Jesse warmed, magnets A and C, have reduced magnetic forces, but magnet B, which Jesse did not warm, has the same strength as in the first trial. This is because warming a magnet scrambles the magnetic domains and weakens the magnetic field produced by the magnet.

   B. This is incorrect because if magnets naturally lost strength over time, all three magnets would have had a reduced magnetic force. Magnets A and C produced weaker forces because warming the magnets scrambled the magnetic domains, not because they were tested at a later time. A permanent magnet becomes weaker when its magnetic domains become unaligned, which happens due to an increase in temperature, a sharp force, or the presence of a stronger magnetic field.

   C. This is incorrect because magnetic fields extend to infinity, meaning that magnetic forces can act at any distance. Although it is true that the magnets that were warmed held fewer paper clips afterward, this happened because the magnetic fields became weaker, not because the magnetic field extended to a shorter distance.

   D. This is incorrect because magnetic forces between a magnet and a paper clip are always attractive, regardless of the orientation of the magnet's poles.

2. **A.** This is incorrect because electric forces involve charges rather than magnets. The picture shows magnetic attraction. Also, in order for electric forces to be attractive, the charges must be opposite.

   B. This is incorrect because when like poles come together, they repel one another. The picture shows magnetic attraction between opposite poles.

   C. This is incorrect because electric forces involve charges rather than magnets. The picture shows magnetic attraction.

   D. This is correct because the picture shows magnetic attraction between opposite poles. Opposite magnetic poles like north and south attract one another.

3. **A.** This is incorrect because the magnetic field is not changing, so no current will be induced in the wire.

   B. This is incorrect because the magnetic field is not changing, so no current will be induced in the loop.

   C. This is correct because moving the magnet through the loop changes the magnetic field around the loop, which induces a current in the loop. The quicker speed of the magnet means that the magnetic field is changing more quickly, which induces a larger current.

   D. This is incorrect. Although moving the wire loop above the magnet does cause the loop to move through a changing magnetic field, because the loop moves slowly, the magnetic field changes slowly, and the current induced is not as large as if the loop was moved quickly.

4. **A.** This is correct because the negatively charged particle is transferred from the cloth to the balloon. Charge is conserved, so in order for a neutral object to become charged, charge must be transferred between objects. It cannot be created or destroyed.

   B. This is incorrect because balloons, like most objects, tend to be neutrally charged. Balloons can be easily charged, but they do not often start out that way.

C. This is incorrect because charge is not created or destroyed. Charge can be transferred, but it cannot appear.

D. This is incorrect because charge is not created or destroyed. Charge can be transferred, but it cannot be destroyed.

5. A. This is incorrect because plastic is not magnetic. Therefore, the paper clips Rohit tests will not produce magnetic forces that will cause the compass to change direction.

B. This is incorrect because wood is not magnetic. Therefore, the doorknob does not produce magnetic forces that can cause the compass to change direction.

C. This is correct because there are charges moving through the wire while the cell phone is being charged. Moving electric charges produce a magnetic field. Therefore, the wire produces magnetic forces that will cause the compass to change direction.

D. This is incorrect because the lamp is unlit, so there are no moving charges in the wire and no magnetic field is produced. Therefore, the wire does not produce magnetic forces that will cause the compass to change direction.

6. A. This is incorrect because if A attracts to both D and C, then one of the bars must be a temporary magnet, like iron, not a permanent magnet. Temporary magnets will temporarily produce a magnetic field when they are near a permanent magnet, but they will not produce a magnetic field otherwise. If bar AB always produced a magnetic field, it would be a permanent magnet, and would repel like poles and attract opposite poles, and would therefore be attracted to only one end of CD.

B. This is incorrect because B would attract to C whether AB was a permanent magnet or a temporary magnet, so the result will not allow her to draw any conclusion. Permanent magnets will always produce a magnetic field, while temporary magnetic fields produce a magnetic field when they are near a permanent magnet, but they will not produce a magnetic field otherwise. If AB were a permanent magnet, then A and D would be opposite poles, which means that B and C would also be opposite poles, and therefore B would attract to C. But if AB were a temporary magnet, B would still attract to C because the temporary magnetic field would be set up so that the bar always would always attract to either pole.

C. This is incorrect because B would attract to C whether AB is a permanent magnet or a temporary magnet, so the result will not allow her to draw any conclusion. Permanent magnets will always produce a magnetic field, while temporary magnetic fields produce a magnetic field when they are near a permanent magnet, but they will not produce a magnetic field otherwise. If AB were a permanent magnet, then A and D would be opposite poles, which means that B and C would also be opposite poles, and therefore B would attract to C. But if AB were a temporary magnet, B would still attract to C because the temporary magnetic field would be set up so that the bar always will attract to either pole.

D. This is correct because magnetic fields produced by a bar magnet are strong at the poles and weak in the center. If end A is weakly attracted to the center of CD, then this shows that AB does not produce its own magnetic field, because if it did, A would be a pole and therefore it would have a strong field, and would have attracted to CD. Since Sachdev knows that A does attract to end D, then this means bar CD must produce a magnetic field that can attract bar AB. She can conclude that bar CD is a permanent magnet and therefore always produces a magnetic field, but bar AB is a magnetic material, like iron, which only temporarily produces a magnetic field when it is close to a magnetic material.

7. The ends of the magnet, labeled *N* and *S*, should be circled because the strength of magnetic forces increases as the distance from the magnetic poles decreases, and these locations are closest to the poles. In other words, the magnetic forces will be strongest at magnetic poles and become weaker as the object is moved farther from the poles.

8. The number list should be 2, 4, 1, 3 because all of the charges have the same magnitude, and the strength of the electric force increases when the distance between the charges decreases. Only the direction, but not the strength, of the force will vary (attractive or repulsive) when the sign of the charge is changed.

9. The sentence *The magnetic field around Magnet A exerts a force on Magnet B, so Magnet B moves downward and to the right* should be circled because this sentence provides an explanation of Magnet B's motion. Magnetic fields extend in all directions around magnetic objects, and describe areas where objects experience magnetic forces. Magnetic forces between like poles are repulsive, while magnetic forces between unlike poles are attractive. The repulsive force will push Magnet B downward and to the right. The phrase cancel each other out is not selected because the fields do not cancel each other out, and if they did cancel each other out, there would be zero magnetic force and therefore Magnet B would not move.

10. A. *Reverse the wires to switch the charges on the plates* belongs in the *no change in strength* category. The strength of the electric force is directly proportional to the magnitude of the charges and inversely proportional to the distance between the plates. The direction of the electric field does not affect the strength of the electric force. Therefore, switching the charges on the plates will not change the strength of the force.

    B. *Increase the thickness of the insulating material* belongs in the *decrease strength* category. Increasing the thickness of the insulating material will increase the distance between the plates. The strength of the electric force is inversely proportional to the distance between charges. Therefore, if the distance between the plates increases, the strength of the electric force will decrease.

    C. *Increase the thickness of the plastic coating* belongs in the *no change in strength* category. The strength of the electric force is directly proportional to the magnitude of the charges and inversely proportional to the distance between the plates. Changing the thickness of the plastic coating may affect how much electric force is felt by someone touching the capacitor, but it does not affect the strength of the electric force between the plates.

    D. *Decrease the current in the wires* belongs in the *decrease strength* category. Decreasing the current will decrease the amount of charge on the plates. The strength of the electric force is directly proportional to the magnitude of the charges. Therefore, if the electric charge on the plates decreases, the strength of the electric force will decrease.

    E. *Decrease the length of the wires* belongs in the *no change in strength* category. Changing the length of the wires does not change the amount of charge on the plates, so this does not affect the strength of the electric force between the plates.

11. A. The picture showing arrows pointing in all different directions is correct for *diagram 1* because when a ferromagnetic material is brought near a nonmagnetic material, its domains do not line up; they go in random directions, canceling one another out.

    B. The picture showing arrows all pointing in the same direction, from left to right, is correct for both the left half and the right half of the magnet in *diagram 3* because magnets have aligned magnetic domains that do not change; cutting a magnet in half will produce two magnets, each with north and south poles and domains pointing in the same direction.

    C. The picture showing the arrows nearest the magnetic material (on the right side of the picture) oriented in the same direction is correct for d*iagram 2* because when a ferromagnetic material is brought near a magnetic material, its domains nearest the magnet become aligned.

12. A. *Does not move* is not used because the magnetic force between the magnets will push or pull the car toward or away from the wall, causing the car to move.

    B. *Moves more slowly toward the wall* matches *He positions the car farther from the wall and reverses the orientation of the magnet on the wall* because moving the car farther from the wall decreases the strength of the force between the magnets. Reversing the orientation of the magnet on the wall makes the magnets attract instead of repel. When the car is released, the weaker attractive force will cause a smaller acceleration toward the wall.

    C. *Moves more quickly toward wall* matches *He positions the car closer to the wall and reverses the orientation of the magnet on the car* because moving the car closer to the wall increases the strength of the force between the magnets. Reversing the orientation of the magnet on the car makes the magnets attract instead of repel. When the car is released, the stronger attractive force will cause a greater acceleration toward the wall.

D. *Moves more slowly away from wall* is not used because the car only moves away from the wall if the orientation of the magnets is kept the same. Also, the car would move more slowly if the magnetic force between the magnets was decreased. Gundeep did not make a change to the experiment that would decrease the magnetic force while keeping the orientation of the magnets the same.

E. *Moves more quickly away from wall* matches *He positions the car closer to the wall* and *He replaces the bar magnet on the wall with a stronger magnet* because moving the car closer to the wall increases the strength of the repelling force between the magnets. Also, increasing the strength of the magnet increases the strength of the magnetic force between the magnets. When the car is released, the stronger repelling force will cause a greater acceleration away from the wall.

13. Use the rubric below to evaluate total points earned for this item. *[max point: 4]*

DCI, SEP - 4 Points	
Claims	The student is able to: 1. identify attractive and repulsive electric forces (DCI); and 2. complete a model to predict movement of charged objects based on attractive/repulsive electric forces (SEP).
Evidence of Mastery of Disciplinary Core Ideas	1 point for correctly identifying positively charged objects in the image in order to show attractive/repulsive electric forces **Part 1:** One point is earned for drawing a plus sign in the middle of each positively charged object in the image. See sample answer.
Evidence of Mastery of Science and Engineering Practices	3 points for determining the direction each pair of objects moves **Part 2:** One point is earned for not drawing any arrows below the objects in the top left corner of the image. The objects both have equal numbers of positive and negative particles and are therefore both neutral and will not move. See sample answer. **Part 2:** One point is earned for drawing arrows pointing toward each other below the objects in the bottom left corner and in the bottom right corner of the image. One of the objects in the bottom left corner is negatively charged and the other is positively charged. Positively and negatively charged objects cause an attractive electric force so the objects will move toward each other. One of the objects in the bottom right corner is positively charged and the other is neutral. The negatively charged particles in the neutral object will temporarily move closer to the side next to the positively charged object, causing an attractive electric force so the objects will move toward each other. See sample answer **Part 2:** One point is earned for drawing arrows pointing away from each other below the object in the top right corner of the image. Both objects are positively charged, causing a repulsive electric force. The objects will therefore move away from each other. The following response, or an equivalent, is acceptable.

14. A. This criterion can be satisfied by both an *electromagnet* and a *permanent magnet* because iron is a magnetic material, while sand is not; all magnets will attract iron but not affect sand.

B. This is *not a criterion for Karin's device* because the device does not need to scoop up the mixture in order to separate the two substances.

C. This criterion can be satisfied only by an *electromagnet* because, unlike permanent magnets, electromagnets can be turned on and off. When the electromagnet has been turned off, the iron shavings will fall off into a separate container.

D. This criterion can be satisfied by both an *electromagnet* and a *permanent magnet* because an electromagnet is a coil of wire that has a soft iron core. The list of things Karin found in her home contains a battery, an iron substance, wire, and wire cutters, which can be used to construct an electromagnet. Karin also found permanent magnets in her home.

15. Use the rubric below to evaluate total points earned for this item. *[max point: 2]*

DCI Only - 2 Points	
Claims	The student is able to: 1. Explain that magnetic forces act at a distance (DCI); and 2. Explain that magnetic forces are caused by magnetic fields that extend through space (DCI).
Evidence of Mastery of Disciplinary Core Ideas	1 point for correctly explaining why the needle rotated **Part 1:** One point is earned for explaining that magnetic forces between the magnet and needle caused the needle to move. The following response, or an equivalent, is acceptable. • There was a magnetic force from the magnet on the needle. This magnetic force pulled on the end of the needle, making it to rotate toward the magnet. 1 point for correctly explaining why the motion of the needle provides evidence to support Mia's claim **Part 2:** One point is earned for explaining that the motion of the needle provides evidence that a magnetic field exists between the objects. The following response, or an equivalent, is acceptable. • The needle can move only if there's a force on it, but the magnet and needle were not in contact. Therefore, there must be a magnetic field between the magnet and needle to provide the magnetic force.

16. Use the rubric below to evaluate total points earned for this item. *[max point: 3]*

DCI, SEP - 3 Points	
Claims	The student is able to: 1. explain that forces that act at a distance can be explained by fields that extend into space (DCI); and 2. use a model to describe the unobservable mechanism of a gravitational field (SEP); and 3. develop a model to describe the unobservable mechanism of a gravitational field and make a prediction (SEP).
Evidence of Mastery of Disciplinary Core Ideas	1 point for correctly explaining that the arrows represent gravitational fields **Part 1:** One point is earned for explaining that planets produce gravitational fields, which are regions where gravitational forces act on other objects. The following response, or an equivalent, is acceptable. • The arrows in the model represent the gravitational fields of the planets.

Evidence of Mastery of Science and Engineering Practices	1 point for correctly describing how the gravitational fields of the planets differ **Part 2:** One point is earned for describing that the density of the arrows indicates the strength of the gravitational fields. The following response, or an equivalent, is acceptable. • Planet A has more arrows around it, which shows that the gravitational field of Planet A is stronger than the gravitational field of Planet B. 1 point for describing how the path of the spacecraft would be affected **Part 3:** One point is earned for using the model to predict that the stronger gravitational field of Planet A would make the path of a spacecraft curve more than that of Planet B because fields are the mechanism that produces gravitational forces. The following response, or an equivalent, is acceptable. • The gravitational field of Planet A is stronger than the gravitational field of Planet B, so Planet A would exert a stronger gravitational force on the spacecraft than Planet B would. When a spacecraft is flying by, the gravitational force will cause its path to curve toward the planet. The amount that it curves will be greater for Planet A than for Planet B because the gravitational force is stronger.

17. Use the rubric below to evaluate total points earned for this item. *[max point: 3]*

DCI, SEP - 3 Points	
Claims	The student is able to: 1. explain that forces that act at a distance can be explained by fields that extend into space (DCI); and 2. use a model to describe the unobservable mechanism of an electric field (SEP); and 3. develop a model to describe the mechanism of an electric field and make a prediction (SEP).
Evidence of Mastery of Disciplinary Core Ideas	1 point for correctly explaining what the arrows represent **Part 1:** One point is earned for explaining that charged objects produce electric fields, which are regions where electric forces can act on other objects. The arrows represent these regions. The following response, or an equivalent, is acceptable. • The arrows in the model represent the electric fields of the charged objects. Electric fields are areas around objects where electric forces can act.
Evidence of Mastery of Science and Engineering Practices	1 point for correctly determining the charges of the objects **Part 2:** One point is earned for using the model to determine the charges of objects A and B. The field lines between the positive charge and object A repel each other between the charges, which means that the force is repulsive. Electric field lines that connect two charged objects show that the force is attractive. The following response, or an equivalent, is acceptable. • Like charges repel, so object A must also have a positive charge. Because the arrows connect objects A and B, the objects are attracting. Since object A is positive, and opposites attract, object B must be negative. 1 point for correctly describing how the model would change **Part 3:** One point is earned for describing that the strength of the field is represented by the density of the field lines, and that doubling the charge will increase the number of field lines in the model. The following response, or an equivalent, is acceptable. • If the charge of object A is doubled, then it has a stronger electric field, so there should be twice as many lines to represent the increased strength of the electric field around it.

18. **A.** This is incorrect because Leisha does not test metals other than iron.
B. This is correct because Leisha tests the bar magnet and iron at different distances from the electromagnet's poles.
C. This is incorrect because Leisha's experiment tests only attractive forces.
D. This is incorrect because Leisha does not test both poles of the electromagnet.

19. **A.** This is incorrect because increasing the number of wire coils will increase the strength of the magnetic field, not decrease it; therefore the distance at which the iron feels a strong enough force to start moving must increase, not decrease.
B. This is correct because increasing the number of coils will increase the strength of the magnetic field, which means the field will be strong enough to cause the iron to move when it is at a greater distance. Therefore, the iron will begin to move when the electromagnet is more than 6 cm away.
C. This is incorrect because increasing the number of wire coils will increase the strength of the magnetic field, which means the field can be felt strongly enough to start to move at a greater distance away. Therefore the distance at which the iron begins to move must increase, not stay the same.
D. This is incorrect because the strength of the magnetic forces produced by an electromagnet is proportional to the number of wire coils, so increasing the number of coils will increase the strength of the electromagnet.

20. Use the rubric below to evaluate total points earned for this item. *[max point: 3]*

DCI, SEP - 3 Points	
Claims	The student is able to: 1. explain that magnetic forces act at a distance to attract or repel other objects (DCI); and 2. evaluate experimental designs to see if they will meet the goals of the investigation (SEP).
Evidence of Mastery of Disciplinary Core Ideas	2 points for correctly explaining what the modifications can tell Leisha about the magnetic force **Part 2:** Two points are earned for explaining that Leisha can map the magnetic forces by observing their effect on test objects. The following response, or an equivalent, is acceptable. • Connecting the wires to different ends of the battery will reverse the current. She can use the paper clips to see if the strength of the magnetic force changed after she changed the direction of the current because if the magnet is stronger, it will hold more paper clips. She can use the bar magnet to test the direction of the magnetic field because the electromagnet will repel the like pole or attract the opposite pole.
Evidence of Mastery of Science and Engineering Practices	1 point for identifying the modifications that Leisha should use **Part 1:** One point is earned for evaluating the modifications and determining that all of 1, 2, and 3 together will provide the required data to show how the magnetic field changes when the direction of the electric current is reversed. The following response, or an equivalent, is acceptable. • Leisha should use 1, 2, and 3.

Unit 2 Unit Test B – Electric and Magnetic Forces

Item Analysis		
Item #	**Standards**	**DOK**
1	MS-PS2-3, DCI.MS-PS2.B.1, SEP.MS.D.1	2
2	MS-PS2-3	1
3	MS-PS2-3	1
4	MS-PS2-3	1
5	MS-PS2-3	2

6	MS-PS2-5, DCI.MS-PS2.B.3, CCC.MS.B.2	3
7	MS-PS2-3, DCI.MS-PS2.B.1	1
8	MS-PS2-5, DCI.MS-PS2.B.3, CCC.MS.B.2	2
9	MS-PS2-5, DCI.MS-PS2.B.3	2
10	MS-PS2-3, DCI.MS-PS2.B.1	2
11	MS-PS2-3, DCI.MS-PS2.B.1, SEP.MS.B.3	2
12	MS-PS2-5, DCI.MS-PS2.B.3, CCC.MS.B.2	2
13	MS-PS2-3, DCI.MS-PS2.B.1, SEP.MS.B.3	3
14	MS-PS2-3, DCI.MS-PS2.B.1, SEP.MS.A.3	3
15	MS-PS2-5, DCI.MS-PS2.B.3	2
16	MS-PS2-5, DCI.MS-PS2.B.3, SEP.MS.B.1	3
17	MS-PS2-5, DCI.MS-PS2.B.3, SEP.MS.B.1	3
18	MS-PS2-3, DCI.MS-PS2.B.1, SEP.MS.A.2	1
19	MS-PS2-3, DCI.MS-PS2.B.1, CCC.MS.B.2	2
20	MS-PS2-5, DCI.MS-PS2.B.3, SEP.MS.C.2	2

1. **A.** This is correct because the two magnets that were warmed, magnets A and C, have reduced magnetic forces, but magnet B, which did not warm, has the same strength as in the first trial. This is because warming a magnet scrambles the magnetic domains and weakens the magnetic field produced by the magnet.

B. This is incorrect because magnetic fields extend to infinity, meaning that magnetic forces can act at any distance. Although it is true that the magnets that were warmed held fewer paper clips afterward, this happened because the magnetic fields became weaker, not because the magnetic field extended to a shorter distance.

C. This is incorrect because magnetic forces between a magnet and a paper clip are always attractive, regardless of the orientation of the magnet's poles.

2. **A.** This is incorrect because electric forces involve charges rather than magnets. The picture shows magnetic attraction. Also, in order for electric forces to be attractive, the charges must be opposite.

B. This is incorrect because electric forces involve charges rather than magnets. The picture shows magnetic attraction.

C. This is correct because the picture shows magnetic attraction between opposite poles. Opposite magnetic poles like north and south attract one another.

3. **A.** This is incorrect because the magnetic field is not changing, so no current will be induced in the wire.

B. This is incorrect because the magnetic field is not changing, so no current will be induced in the loop.

C. This is correct because moving the magnet through the loop changes the magnetic field around the loop, which induces a current in the loop. The quicker speed of the magnet means that the magnetic field is changing more quickly, which induces a larger current.

4. **A.** This is correct because the negatively charged particle is transferred from the cloth to the balloon. Charge is conserved, so in order for a neutral object to become charged, charge must be transferred between objects. It cannot be created or destroyed.

B. This is incorrect because balloons, like most objects, tend to be neutrally charged. Balloons can be easily charged, but they do not often start out that way.

C. This is incorrect because charge is not created or destroyed. Charge can be transferred, but it cannot be destroyed.

5. **A.** This is incorrect because plastic is not magnetic. Therefore, the paper clips Rohit tests will not produce magnetic forces that will cause the compass to change direction.

   B. This is correct because there are charges moving through the wire while the cell phone is being charged. Moving electric charges produce a magnetic field. Therefore, the wire produces magnetic forces that will cause the compass to change direction.

   C. This is incorrect because the lamp is unlit, so there are no moving charges in the wire and no magnetic field is produced. Therefore, the wire does not produce magnetic forces that will cause the compass to change direction.

6. **A.** This is incorrect because B would attract to C whether AB was a permanent magnet or a temporary magnet, so the result will not allow her to draw any conclusion. Permanent magnets will always produce a magnetic field, while temporary magnetic fields produce a magnetic field when they are near a permanent magnet, but they will not produce a magnetic field otherwise. If AB were a permanent magnet, then A and D would be opposite poles, which means that B and C would also be opposite poles, and therefore B would attract to C. But if AB were a temporary magnet, B would still attract to C because the temporary magnetic field would be set up so that the bar always would attract to either pole.

   B. This is incorrect because B would attract to C whether AB is a permanent magnet or a temporary magnet, so the result will not allow her to draw any conclusion. Permanent magnets will always produce a magnetic field, while temporary magnetic fields produce a magnetic field when they are near a permanent magnet, but they will not produce a magnetic field otherwise. If AB were a permanent magnet, then A and D would be opposite poles, which means that B and C would also be opposite poles, and therefore B would attract to C. But if AB were a temporary magnet, B would still attract to C because the temporary magnetic field would be set up so that the bar always will attract to either pole.

   C. This is correct because magnetic fields produced by a bar magnet are strong at the poles and weak in the center. If end A is weakly attracted to the center of CD, then this shows that AB does not produce its own magnetic field, because if it did, A would be a pole and therefore it would have a strong field, and would have attracted to CD. Since Sachdev knows that A does attract to end D, then this means bar CD must produce a magnetic field that can attract bar AB. She can conclude that bar CD is a permanent magnet and therefore always produces a magnetic field, but bar AB is a magnetic material, like iron, which only temporarily produces a magnetic field when it is close to a magnetic material.

7. The ends of the magnet, labeled N and S, should be circled because the strength of magnetic forces increases as the distance from the magnetic poles decreases, and these locations are closest to the poles. The south pole of another magnet would be most strongly repelled or attracted at the poles, and less strongly affected farther from the poles.

8. The number list should be 2, 3, 1. The objects should be ordered from largest to smallest distance: *+q and +q at a distance of 3.0 cm*, *+q and +q at a distance of 2.0 cm*, and *+q and +q at a distance of 1.0 cm*, because all of the charges have the same magnitude, and the strength of the electric force increases when the distance between the charges decreases.

9. The sentence *The magnetic field around Magnet A exerts a force on Magnet B, so Magnet B moves* should be circled because this sentence provides an explanation of Magnet B's motion. Magnetic fields extend in all directions around magnetic objects, and describe areas where objects experience magnetic forces. Magnetic forces between like poles are repulsive, while magnetic forces between unlike poles are attractive. The repulsive force will push Magnet B downward and to the right. The phrase *cancel each other out* is not selected because the fields do not cancel each other out, and if they did cancel each other out, there would be zero magnetic force and therefore Magnet B would not move.

10. **A.** *Reverse the wires to switch the charges on the plates* belongs in the *no change in strength* category. The strength of the electric force is directly proportional to the magnitude of the charges and inversely proportional to the distance between the plates. The direction of the electric field does not affect the strength of the electric force. Therefore, switching the charges on the plates will not change the strength of the force.

B. *Increase the thickness of the insulating material* belongs in the *decrease strength* category. Increasing the thickness of the insulating material will increase the distance between the plates. The strength of the electric force is inversely proportional to the distance between charges. Therefore, if the distance between the plates increases, the strength of the electric force will decrease.

C. *Increase the thickness of the plastic coating* belongs in the *no change in strength* category. The strength of the electric force is directly proportional to the magnitude of the charges and inversely proportional to the distance between the plates. Changing the thickness of the plastic coating may affect how much electric force is felt by someone touching the capacitor, but it does not affect the strength of the electric force between the plates.

11. A. The picture showing arrows pointing in all different directions does not belong in any box because a magnet has aligned domains, meaning the arrows would all be pointing the same direction.

B. This picture belongs in both boxes because magnets have aligned magnetic domains that do not change; cutting a magnet in half will produce two magnets, each with north and south poles and domains pointing in the same direction.

C. The picture showing arrows pointing in all different directions does not belong in any box because a magnet has aligned domains, meaning the arrows would all be pointing the same direction.

12. A. *Does not move* is not used because the magnetic force between the magnets will push or pull the car toward or away from the wall, causing the car to move.

B. *Moves more slowly toward the wall* matches *He positions the car farther from the wall and reverses the orientation of the magnet on the wall* because moving the car farther from the wall decreases the strength of the force between the magnets. Reversing the orientation of the magnet on the wall makes the magnets attract instead of repel. When the car is released, the weaker attractive force will cause a smaller acceleration toward the wall.

C. *Moves more quickly toward wall* matches *He positions the car closer to the wall and reverses the orientation of the magnet on the car* because moving the car closer to the wall increases the strength of the force between the magnets. Reversing the orientation of the magnet on the car makes the magnets attract instead of repel. When the car is released, the stronger attractive force will cause a greater acceleration toward the wall.

D. *Moves more slowly away from wall* is not used because the car only moves away from the wall if the orientation of the magnets is kept the same. Also, the car would move more slowly if the magnetic force between the magnets was decreased. Gundeep did not make a change to the experiment that would decrease the magnetic force while keeping the orientation of the magnets the same.

E. *Moves more quickly away from wall* matches *He positions the car closer to the wall* and *He replaces the bar magnet on the wall with a stronger magnet* because moving the car closer to the wall increases the strength of the repelling force between the magnets. Also, increasing the strength of the magnet increases the strength of the magnetic force between the magnets. When the car is released, the stronger repelling force will cause a greater acceleration away from the wall.

13. Use the rubric below to evaluate total points earned for this item. *[max point: 4]*

DCI, SEP - 4 Points	
Claims	The student is able to: 1. identify attractive and repulsive electric forces (DCI); and 2. complete a model to predict movement of charged objects based on attractive/repulsive electric forces (SEP).
Evidence of Mastery of Disciplinary Core Ideas	1 point for correctly identifying positively charged objects in the image in order to show attractive/repulsive electric forces **Part 1:** One point is earned for drawing a plus sign in the middle of each positively charged object in the image. See sample answer.
Evidence of Mastery of Science and Engineering Practices	3 points for determining the direction each pair of objects moves **Part 2:** One point is earned for not drawing any arrows below the objects in the top left corner of the image. The objects both have equal numbers of positive and negative particles and are therefore both neutral and will not move. See sample answer. **Part 2:** One point is earned for drawing arrows pointing toward each other below the objects in the bottom left corner and in the bottom right corner of the image. One of the objects in the bottom left corner is negatively charged and the other is positively charged. Positively and negatively charged objects cause an attractive electric force so the objects will move toward each other. One of the objects in the bottom right corner is positively charged and the other is neutral. The negatively charged particles in the neutral object will temporarily move closer to the side next to the positively charged object, causing an attractive electric force so the objects will move toward each other. See sample answer **Part 2:** One point is earned for drawing arrows pointing away from each other below the object in the top right corner of the image. Both objects are positively charged, causing a repulsive electric force. The objects will therefore move away from each other. The following response, or an equivalent, is acceptable. 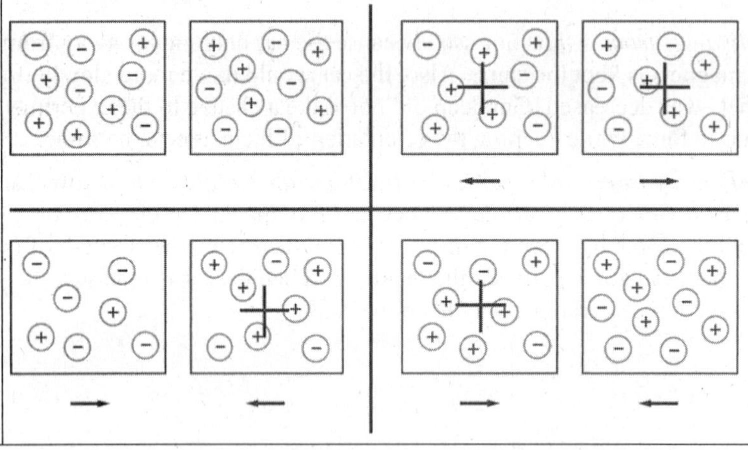

14. A. This is true for both an *electromagnet* and a *permanent magnet* because all magnets will attract iron but not affect sand.

B. This is true for only an *electromagnet* because, unlike permanent magnets, electromagnets can be turned on and off. When the electromagnet has been turned off, the iron shavings will fall off into a separate container.

C. This is true for both an *electromagnet* and a *permanent magnet* because an electromagnet is a coil of wire that has a soft iron core. The list of things Karin found in her home includes batteries, iron bolts, and wire, which can be used to construct an electromagnet. Karin also found permanent magnets in her home.

15. Use the rubric below to evaluate total points earned for this item. *[max point: 2]*

DCI Only - 2 Points	
Claims	The student is able to explain that magnetic fields extend through space to exert forces on objects at a distance (DCI).
Evidence of Mastery of Disciplinary Core Ideas	2 points for correctly explaining why the needle rotated **Part 1:** Two points are earned for explaining that magnetic forces between the magnet and needle caused the needle to move. The following response, or an equivalent, is acceptable. • There was a magnetic force from the magnet on the needle. This magnetic force pulled on the end of the needle, making it rotate toward the magnet.

16. Use the rubric below to evaluate total points earned for this item. *[max point: 3]*

DCI, SEP - 3 Points	
Claims	The student is able to: 1. explain that forces that act at a distance can be explained by fields that extend into space (DCI); and 2. use a model to describe the unobservable mechanism of a gravitational field (SEP).
Evidence of Mastery of Disciplinary Core Ideas	1 point for correctly explaining that the arrows represent gravitational fields **Part 1:** One point is earned for explaining that planets produce gravitational fields, which are regions where gravitational forces act on other objects. The following response, or an equivalent, is acceptable. • The arrows in the model represent the gravitational fields of the planets.
Evidence of Mastery of Science and Engineering Practices	2 points for correctly describing how the two planets differ **Part 2:** Two points are earned for describing that the density of the arrows indicates the strength of the gravitational fields. The following response, or an equivalent, is acceptable. • Planet A has more arrows around it, which shows that the gravitational field of Planet A is stronger than the gravitational field of Planet B.

17. Use the rubric below to evaluate total points earned for this item. *[max point: 3]*

DCI, SEP - 3 Points	
Claims	The student is able to: 1. explain that forces that act at a distance can be explained by fields that extend into space (DCI); and 2. use a model to describe the unobservable mechanism of an electric field (SEP)
Evidence of Mastery of Disciplinary Core Ideas	1 point for correctly explaining what the arrows represent **Part 1:** One point is earned for explaining that charged objects produce electric fields, which are regions where electric forces can act on other objects. The arrows represent these regions. The following response, or an equivalent, is acceptable. • The arrows in the model represent the electric fields of the charged objects. Electric fields are areas around objects where electric forces can act.

Evidence of Mastery of Science and Engineering Practices	2 points for correctly determining the charges of the objects **Part 2:** Two points are earned for using the model to determine the charges of objects A and B. The field lines between the positive charge and object A repel each other between the charges, which means that the force is repulsive. Electric field lines that connect two charged objects show that the force is attractive. The following response, or an equivalent, is acceptable. • Like charges repel, so object A must also have a positive charge. Because the arrows connect objects A and B, the objects are attracting. Since object A is positive, and opposites attract, object B must be negative.

18. **A.** This is incorrect because Leisha does not test metals other than iron.

B. This is correct because Leisha tests the bar magnet and iron at different distances from the electromagnet's poles.

C. This is incorrect because Leisha does not test both poles of the electromagnet.

19. **A.** This is incorrect because increasing the number of wire coils will increase the strength of the magnetic field, not decrease it; therefore, the distance at which the iron feels a strong enough force to start moving must increase, not decrease.

B. This is correct because increasing the number of coils will increase the strength of the magnetic field, which means the field will be strong enough to cause the iron to move when it is at a greater distance. Therefore, the iron will begin to move when the electromagnet is more than 6 cm away.

C. This is incorrect because increasing the number of wire coils will increase the strength of the magnetic field, which means the field can be felt strongly enough to start to move at a greater distance away. Therefore, the distance at which the iron begins to move must increase, not stay the same.

20. Use the rubric below to evaluate total points earned for this item. *[max point: 3]*

DCI, SEP - 3 Points	
Claims	The student is able to: 1. explain that magnetic forces act at a distance to attract or repel other objects (DCI); and 2. evaluate experimental designs to see if they will meet the goals of the investigation (SEP).
Evidence of Mastery of Disciplinary Core Ideas	2 points for correctly explaining what the modifications can tell Leisha about the magnetic force **Part 2:** Two points are earned for explaining that Leisha can map the magnetic forces by observing their effect on test objects. The following response, or an equivalent, is acceptable. • Connecting the wires to different ends of the battery will reverse the current. She can use the paper clips to see if the strength of the magnetic force changed after she changed the direction of the current because if the magnet is stronger, it will hold more paper clips. She can use the bar magnet to test the direction of the magnetic field because the electromagnet will repel the like pole or attract the opposite pole.
Evidence of Mastery of Science and Engineering Practices	1 point for identifying the modifications that Leisha should use **Part 1:** One point is earned for evaluating the modifications and identifying that all of 1, 2, and 3 together will provide the required data to show how the magnetic field changes when the direction of the electric current is reversed. The following response, or an equivalent, is acceptable. • Leisha should use 1, 2, and 3.

End-of-Module Test A – Forces, Motion, & Fields

Item Analysis		
Item #	**Standards**	**DOK**
1	MS-PS2-2, DCI.MS-PS2.A.3	1
2	MS-PS2-3, DCI.MS-PS2.B.1, SEP.MS.A.2	1
3	MS-PS2-5, DCI.MS-PS2.B.3	1
4	MS-PS2-4, DCI.MS-PS2.B.2	2
5	MS-PS2-5, DCI.MS-PS2.B.3	2
6	MS-PS2-4, DCI.MS-PS2.B.2, SEP.MS.G.1	2
7	MS-PS2-4, DCI.MS-PS2.B.2	2
8	MS-PS2-3, DCI.MS-PS2.B.1	2
9	MS-PS2-2, DCI.MS-PS2.A.2, SEP.MS.C.3	2
10	MS-PS2-1, DCI.MS-PS2.A.1, SEP.MS.F.4	2
11	MS-PS2-1, DCI.MS-PS2.A.1	2
12	MS-PS2-3, DCI.MS-PS2.B.1	2
13	MS-PS2-5, DCI.MS-PS2.B.3, SEP.MS.C.2	2
14	MS-PS2-4, DCI.MS-PS2.B.2, SEP.NOS.MS.B.1	3
15	MS-PS2-3, DCI.MS-PS2.B.1, SEP.MS.A.2	2
16	MS-PS2-3, DCI.MS-PS2.B.1, CCC.MS.B.2	2
17	MS-PS2-5, DCI.MS-PS2.B.3, CCC.MS.B.2	2
18	MS-PS2-1, DCI.MS-PS2.A.1	2
19	MS-PS2-1, DCI.MS-PS2.A.1, SEP.MS.F.4	2
20	MS-PS2-1, DCI.MS-PS2.A.1, CCC.MS.D.2	2
21	MS-PS2-1, DCI.MS-PS2.A.1	2
22	MS-PS2-2, DCI.MS-PS2.A.2, SEP.NOS.MS.B.1	3
23	MS-PS2-3, DCI.MS-PS2.B.1, CCC.MS.B.2	2
24	MS-PS2-1, DCI.MS-PS2.A.1, CCC.STSE.MS.B.2	2
25	MS-PS2-2, DCI.MS-PS2.A.2, SEP.MS.C.3	1
26	MS-PS2-2, DCI.MS-PS2.A.3	2
27	MS-PS2-2, DCI.MS-PS2.A.2	2
28	MS-PS2-2, DCI.MS-PS2.A.2, SEP.MS.C.3	2
29	MS-PS2-2, DCI.MS-PS2.A.2, SEP.NOS.MS.B.1	3
30	MS-PS2-4, DCI.MS-PS2.B.2, CCC.MS.D.2	2
31	MS-PS2-5, DCI.MS-PS2.B.3	2
32	MS-PS2-4, DCI.MS-PS2.B.2	3
33	MS-PS2-1, DCI.MS-PS2.A.1, SEP.MS.F.4	3
34	MS-PS2-4, DCI.MS-PS2.B.2, SEP.MS.G.1	3
35	MS-PS2-5, DCI.MS-PS2.B.3, CCC.MS.B.2	3
36	MS-PS2-1, DCI.MS-PS2.A.1, CCC.MS.D.2	3
37	MS-PS2-5, DCI.MS-PS2.B.3, SEP.MS.C.2	3

38	MS-PS2-4, DCI.MS-PS2.B.2, CCC.MS.D.2	3
39	MS-PS2-4, DCI.MS-PS2.B.2, SEP.MS.G.1	3
40	MS-PS2-4, DCI.MS-PS2.B.2, SEP.MS.G.1, CCC.MS.D.2	3

1. **1A.** *Sideways unbalanced force* is correct because an unbalanced force is required to move an object at rest.

   2F. *Newtons* is correct because it is the unit used to describe force according to the International System of Units (SI Units).

2. **A.** This is correct because the amount of batteries can easily be changed using resources available in the classroom by adding more batteries in the electromagnet. Also, this question would lead to a practical experiment, with an independent and dependent variable, testing the effect on the strength of the electromagnet, which fulfills the purpose stated.

   B. This is incorrect because it does not fulfill the purpose stated to test the magnitude of the force produced. The number of times the wire is wrapped around the nail does affect the strength of the force and it may be a question that needs to be asked while setting up the experiment relating to the purpose. However, it does not directly address a factor that could affect the magnitude of the force.

   C. This is incorrect because it is not possible to create an electromagnet that is strong enough to pick up large objects such as cars in the classroom. Since it cannot be tested with the resources available, it would not lead to a practical experiment. Also, the question does not reference a specific factor to be tested to represent the independent variable in the experiment.

   D. This is incorrect because it would not lead to a practical experiment and it does not address the purpose stated to test the magnitude of the force produced. While this is a question that should be asked while designing the experiment, it does not involve an independent and dependent variable in order to set up a practical experiment. Also, it relates to safety rather than determining what affects the magnitude of the force.

3. **A.** *Repel* is correct for the first diagram and *The magnets will...* because magnets can interact at a distance, and like poles repel.

   B. *Attract* is correct for the second diagram and *The magnets will...* because magnets can interact at a distance, and opposite poles attract.

   C. *Have no interaction* is not used because both sets of magnets shown will interact even though they are not touching because magnets can interact at a distance.

   D. *The magnets are not touching* is not used because while it is true that the magnets are not touching, this is not a reason why they do or do not interact.

   E. *A field exists between the magnets* is correct for the first and second diagrams and *because...* because forces that act at a distance can be explained by fields that extend through space. Both sets of magnets will interact even though they are not touching because a magnetic field exists between them.

   F. *Electricity exists between the magnets* is not used because while electric fields are also an example of forces that act at a distance, the examples given here are of magnetic fields.

4. The number list should be 3, 2, 4, 1. Gravitational attraction is proportional to mass, so as mass increases, the gravitational attraction increases. Object D shows the smallest gravitational attraction to the fifth object, so it must have the smallest mass. Objects B and A show the second and third largest gravitational attractions to the fifth object, so they must have the second and third largest masses, respectively. Object C shows the largest gravitational attraction to the fifth object, so it must have the largest mass of the four objects.

5. **A.** *False* is correct because the direction of the electric field is outward away from the positive charge and inward toward the negative charge.

   B. *True* is correct because the positive and negative charges are closest together at this point.

   C. *False* is correct because the charges are distributed around each ball, not just located along the sides facing each other. These charges are also attracted to each other, but the field is weaker as you move vertically away from the center because the charges are farther apart.

D. *False* is correct because the balls move toward each other and have opposite charges, so they are attracted to one another, not repelled.

E. *True* is correct because without an attractive force between the two balls, the strings would hang straight down rather than be tilted toward each other due to the forces exerted by gravity (gravitational) and the dowel rod (normal). The electric field exerts a force perpendicular to the normal and gravitational forces that cause the balls to move toward each other.

6. **1B.** *Incorrect* is correct because objects B and D will have the weakest gravitational attraction because they are the least massive objects in the table.

2E. *Increases as the total mass of the objects increases* is correct because gravitational attraction is directly dependent on the mass of both objects. The larger the objects' masses, the stronger the gravitational attraction between them.

7. The number list should be 2, 1, 3. The gravitational force between the center ball and the blue ball is the greatest, followed by the red ball and then the yellow ball. The magnitude of the gravitational attraction between two objects depends on their masses, so the larger the gravitational attraction, the more total mass must be present.

8. **A.** *The force of the electromagnet would increase* is correct for *Wrap the wire around the nail nine times instead of eight* because increasing the number of wraps of wire around the nail increases the magnitude of the magnetic strength delivered to the iron core. Since the size of the force depends on the magnitude of the magnetic strength, the force of the electromagnet increases with an increased number of turns of the wire around the core.

The force of the electromagnet would increase is also correct for *Replace the battery with one that generates more current in the wire* because the size of electromagnetic forces depends on the magnitude of the current involved. Increasing the amount of current generated increases the magnitude of the current through the wire.

B. *The force of the electromagnet would decrease* is correct for *Replace the nail with a plastic straw of the same size* because the size of electromagnetic forces depends on the magnitude of magnetic strength. By removing the iron core of the electromagnet, the magnetic strength decreases significantly, decreasing the electromagnetic force.

C. *The force of the electromagnet would stay the same* is not used because all scenarios described will result in a change in the force of the electromagnet.

9. Use the rubric below to evaluate total points earned for this item. *[max point: 2]*

DCI, SEP - 2 Points	
Claims	The student is able to: 1. describe that a larger force will cause a larger change in motion (DCI); and 2. identify the independent and dependent variables in an investigational design (SEP).
Evidence of Mastery of Disciplinary Core Ideas	1 point for correctly comparing the components of different scenarios in order to describe Newton's second law **Part 2:** One point is earned for comparing the two experiments and explaining that they can be used to prove that increasing the force on an object will cause an increased change in motion. The following response, or an equivalent, is acceptable. • In the first experiment, Anderson used a 20-gram mass to create a force. In the second experiment, he used a 40-gram mass, so the mass was increased. This means that the force of gravity on the mass will be larger for the 40-gram mass. Using this setup, Anderson could show that increasing the force on the cart would cause the cart to move faster.

Evidence of Mastery of Science and Engineering Practices	1 point for correctly identifying the independent and dependent variables in the investigation **Part 1:** One point is earned for identifying reasonable independent and dependent variables based on the investigation. The following responses, or an equivalent, are acceptable. • The force applied by the hanging mass is the independent variable because it is what Anderson is changing in the experiment. The acceleration of the cart is the dependent variable because it changes based on the force that's applied to the cart. • The mass of the hanging object is the independent variable because it is what Anderson is changing in the experiment. The acceleration of the cart is the dependent variable because it changes based on the mass of the hanging object. • The mass of the hanging object is the independent variable because it is what Anderson is changing in the experiment. The force on the cart from the mass is the dependent variable because it changes based on the mass of the hanging object.

10. Use the rubric below to evaluate total points earned for this item. *[max point: 2]*

	DCI Only - 1 Point
Claims	The student is able to show that the force exerted by one object on a second object is equal in strength to the force that the second object exerts on the first but in the opposite direction (DCI).
Evidence of Mastery of Disciplinary Core Ideas	1 point for correctly using Newton's third law to draw arrows in the "during the collision" image **Part 1:** One point is earned for drawing arrows of equal sizes pointing toward each other only during the collision. The following response, or an equivalent, is acceptable. **Before the Collision** 2 m/s 0 m/s **During the Collision** **After the Collision** 0 m/s 2 m/s

11. A. This is incorrect because the plan does not mention the speeds of the spacecraft or meteor, so their speed as they collide cannot be assumed. Additionally, Newton's third law does not mention the speed of objects.

B. This is incorrect because the plan does not mention the acceleration of the spacecraft or meteor, so it cannot be assumed. If there was acceleration after the collision, then it would depend upon the mass of each object, which cannot be assumed either. Additionally, Newton's third law does not mention the acceleration of objects.

C. This is incorrect because Newton's third law states that for any pair of interacting objects, the force exerted by the first object on the second object is opposite in direction. Therefore, the force of one object would not be exerted on a second object at a right angle.

D. This is correct because Newton's third law states that for any pair of interacting objects, the force exerted by the first object on the second object is equal in strength to the force that the second object exerts on the first, but in the opposite direction.

E. This is incorrect because Newton's third law states that for any pair of interacting objects, the force exerted by the first object on the second object is equal in strength to the force that the second object exerts on the first, but in the opposite direction. The forces would not be exerted in the same direction.

F. This is correct because Newton's third law states that for any pair of interacting objects, the force exerted by the first object on the second object is equal in strength to the force that the second object exerts on the first.

12. A. This is correct because the magnetic field generated by an electromagnet depends on the current in the electromagnet.

B. This is incorrect because static electricity is not created when the magnitude of the current increases.

C. This is incorrect because polarity does not change when the magnitude of the current increases.

D. This is incorrect because the iron nail will be more attracted to the electromagnet when the magnitude of the current increases.

13. A. *Longer string Y* is not used because the length of string Y has no impact on determining whether or not magnetic fields can act through metal or other materials or on how different types of magnets affect the ability of magnetic fields to act through aluminum. Although the length of string Y would affect the strength of the magnetic attraction between the magnet and the paper clip, Arianna is not testing that purpose with this experimental setup.

B. *Shorter string Y* is not used because the length of string Y has no impact on determining whether or not magnetic fields can act through metal or other materials or on how different types of magnets affect the ability of magnetic fields to act through aluminum. Although the length of string Y would affect the strength of the magnetic attraction between the magnet and the paper clip, Arianna is not testing that purpose with this experimental setup.

C. *Book between magnet and paper clip* is correct for *to determine whether a magnetic field can act through thin or thick materials* because materials of the same type but different thicknesses should be tested. The book is thick, whereas a paper napkin is thin.

D. *Aluminum foil instead of bar magnet* is not used because aluminum is not a magnetic metal. Replacing the bar magnet with aluminum foil would remove the source of the magnetic field in this experimental setup, preventing Arianna from testing the purposes listed in the table.

E. *Horseshoe magnet instead of bar magnet* is correct for *to determine whether a magnetic field can act through aluminum with different types of magnets* because the type of magnet should be changed in order to test this purpose.

F. *Paper napkin between magnet and paper clip* is correct for *to determine whether a magnetic field can act through thin or thick materials* because the same material with different thicknesses should be tested. The paper and the book are both made of paper but have different thicknesses, so they should be tested between the magnet and paper clip to see what effect, if any, they have on the magnetic field.

G. *Aluminum foil between magnet and paper clip* is correct for *to determine whether a magnetic field can act through different metals* because different types of nonmagnetic metals should be placed between the magnet and the paper clip. *Aluminum foil between magnet and paper clip* is also correct for *to determine whether a magnetic field can act through aluminum with different types of magnets* because the purpose involves testing by placing aluminum between the objects interacting in the magnetic field.

H. *Copper sheet between magnet and paper clip* is correct for *to determine whether a magnetic field can act through different metals* because different types of nonmagnetic metals should be placed between the paper clip and magnet to determine whether a magnetic field can act through metal.

14. Use the rubric below to evaluate total points earned for this item. *[max point: 3]*

<table>
<tr><th colspan="2">DCI, SEP - 3 Points</th></tr>
<tr><td>Claims</td><td>The student is able to:
1. compare masses using knowledge that the gravitational force between two objects is dependent on the masses of the objects (DCI); and
2. use data to formulate an explanation (SEP); and
3. make logical and conceptual connections between evidence and explanations to describe a phenomenon (SEP).</td></tr>
<tr><td>Evidence of Mastery of Disciplinary Core Ideas</td><td>1 point for correctly comparing the masses
Part 2: One point is earned for concluding that B must be more massive than C because the gravitational attraction between A and B is greater than the gravitational attraction between A and C. The following response, or an equivalent, is acceptable.
• The gravitational attraction between objects A and B is greater than the attraction between objects A and C. This means that object B must be more massive than object C.</td></tr>
<tr><td>Evidence of Mastery of Science and Engineering Practices</td><td>2 points for correctly explaining the differences in gravitational attractions
Part 1: One point is earned for using the data given to explain that the total masses of objects A and B must be different from that of objects A and C because the gravitational attractions differ even though they are the same distance apart. The following response, or an equivalent, is acceptable.
• Objects A and B have a larger gravitational attraction than objects A and C even though they are the same distance apart so the total masses must be different.
Part 3: One point is earned for explaining that gravitational force between C and D is greater than the gravitational force between A and C even though C and D are farther apart because of mass. The following response, or an equivalent, is acceptable.
• The gravitational force between C and D could be greater than the gravitational force between A and C if the total mass of C and D is greater than the total mass of A and C.</td></tr>
</table>

15. A. *Not relevant* is correct because it is the rod's rotation that generates the electric current, which is not dependent upon the length of the rod.

B. *Relevant* is correct because the greater the magnetic field is, the more electric current it can generate.

C. *Not relevant* is correct because the wire carries the electric current to the light bulb regardless of how close it is to the generator.

D. *Relevant* is correct because the speed of the rotation of the magnet field is what generates the electric current.

E. *Relevant* is correct because the more wire that is affected by the magnetic field, the more current will be generated in it.

16. A. This is correct because doubling the number of magnets increases the magnetic field, which increases the force on the wires that make up the rotor and causes the rotor to spin faster.

B. This is incorrect because if the magnetic field were reversed, the rotor would still spin, but it would spin in the opposite direction.

C. This is incorrect because the addition of a second magnet would not interrupt the flow of charged particles. If the current were interrupted, the rotor would stop.

D. This is incorrect because the number of magnets affects the strength of the magnetic field. A stronger magnetic field increases the force on the rotor, causing the rotor to spin faster.

17. Use the rubric below to evaluate total points earned for this item. *[max point: 3]*

DCI, CCC - 3 Points	
Claims	The student is able to: 1. the electric field between two sets of two charged objects (DCI); and 2. show how the charge of the objects determines the type of force (attract/repel) (CCC); and 3. show how distance between charged particles affects the shape of the field between two objects (CCC).
Evidence of Mastery of Disciplinary Core Ideas	1 point for correctly drawing electric field lines **Part 1:** One point is earned for drawing electric field lines that do not cross. The following response, or an equivalent, is acceptable.
Evidence of Mastery of Crosscutting Concepts	1 point for correctly showing how the distance between the charges affects the shape of the field between the two objects **Part 2:** One point is earned for showing that the field lines are continuous and move between the two charges from one charge to the other and that the particles farther apart will have field lines that are spaced farther apart. The following response, or an equivalent, is acceptable. 1 point for correctly showing how the charge of the objects determines the type of force (attract/repel) **Part 3**: One point is earned for drawing arrows pointing away from the positive charge and toward the negative charge. The following response, or an equivalent, is acceptable. 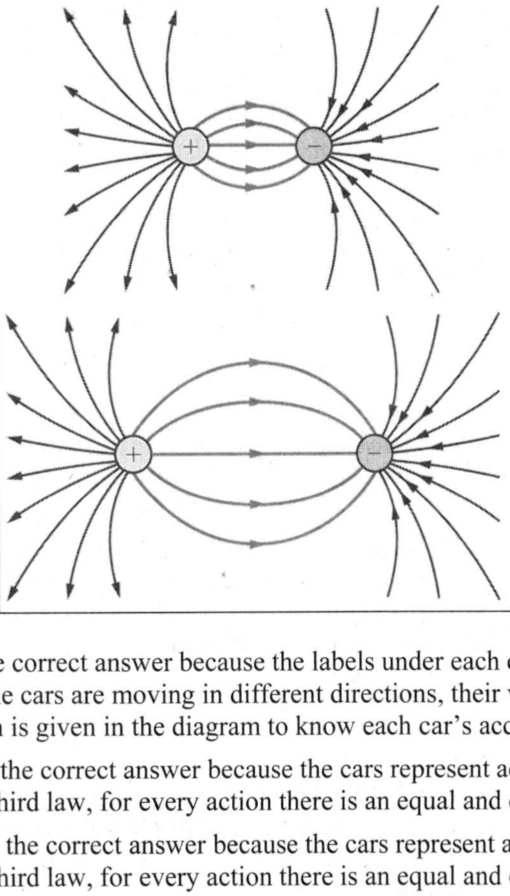 + − + −

18. 1B. *Speed* is the correct answer because the labels under each car indicate the same speed: 5 miles per hour (mph). If the cars are moving in different directions, their velocity cannot be the same. Not enough information is given in the diagram to know each car's acceleration rate.

2D. *Equal to* is the correct answer because the cars represent action and reaction forces. According to Newton's third law, for every action there is an equal and opposite reaction.

3H. *Opposite* is the correct answer because the cars represent action and reaction forces. According to Newton's third law, for every action there is an equal and opposite reaction.

4D. *Equal to* is the correct answer because an increase in the mass/size of car A will not change the fact that the forces of the two cars when they hit each other will be equal (and opposite), by Newton's third law.

19. A. This image *Does Not Illustrate Newton's Third Law* as it relates to collisions. Although it is true that there is an action-reaction force pair any time an object is on a surface (the girl pushes down on the ice, while the ice pushes up on the girl), the girl is not colliding with another object. This demonstration would not be effective at explaining Newton's third law.

B. This image *Illustrates Newton's Third Law* as it relates to collisions. When the girl hits the hockey puck, the hockey stick exerts a force upon the puck, while the puck exerts an equal force on the stick in the opposite direction. This collision of stick and puck clearly shows an action-reaction force pair.

C. This image *Does Not Illustrate Newton's Third Law* as it relates to collisions. Although it is true that there are a number of force pairs in the drawing, Lei's demonstrations are meant to show forces related to collisions. These skaters are simply moving side by side. They are not colliding with each other. This demonstration would be ineffective at explaining Newton's third law.

D. This image *Illustrates Newton's Third Law* as it relates to collisions. The hockey puck on the left exerts a force on the hockey puck on the right. The hockey puck on the right exerts an equal force in the opposite direction on the hockey puck on the left. This collision clearly shows an action-reaction force pair.

20. A. This is incorrect because, while it is true that cart A will be moving to the left after the collision, it will be moving at a speed greater than 0.5 m/s. Before the collision cart A is moving toward cart B, which means it is initially moving to the right at 0.5 m/s.

B. This is incorrect because this is the description for cart B with incorrect speeds. Before the collision, cart A is moving toward cart B, which means cart A is moving to the right at 0.5 m/s. The force from cart B pushing in the opposite direction will cause cart A to move backward. However, if cart A started out moving to the right, it should have ended up moving to the left at a speed greater than 0.5 m/s.

C. This is correct because cart A starts out moving toward cart B, so it starts out moving to the right 0.5 m/s. Newton's third law states that for any pair of interacting objects, the force exerted by the first object on the second object is equal in strength to the force that the second object exerts on the first, but in the opposite direction. When they collide, cart A exerts a force to the right, while cart B exerts a force to the left, but at a speed greater than 0.5 m/s. This force to the left causes cart A to move to the left at a speed greater than its speed before the collision.

D. This is incorrect because cart A should be moving to the left after the collision and at a speed greater than 0.5 m/s. While it is true that cart A moves to the right before the collision, it is moving at 0.5 m/s and cart B is moving to the left at 1.0 m/s. When the cars collide, they push on each other with equal but opposite forces. The force from cart B causes cart A to change direction and move backward, toward the left at a speed greater than its speed before the collision.

21. A. This statement is *False* because Newton's third law states that for any pair of interacting objects, the force exerted by the first object on the second object is equal in strength to the force that the second object exerts on the first but in the opposite direction. Therefore, the forces exerted by both the boy and the tree on each other are equal.

B. This statement is *True* because Newton's third law states that for any pair of interacting objects, the force exerted by the first object on the second object is equal in strength to the force that the second object exerts on the first but in the opposite direction. The tree is exerting a downward force against the ground, due to gravity, so the ground exerts an equal force upward against the tree.

C. This statement is *False* because Newton's third law states that for any pair of interacting objects, the force exerted by the first object on the second object is equal in strength to the force that the second object exerts on the first but in the opposite direction.

D. This statement is *False* because Newton's third law states that for any pair of interacting objects, the force exerted by the first object on the second object is equal in strength to the force that the second object exerts on the first but in the opposite direction. Therefore, the boy is exerting a force against the tree and the tree's force is felt in the opposite direction against the boy.

E. This statement is *True* because forces can be exerted by any type of object.

22. **A.** *Push the ball down a ramp* is incorrect because this will cause the ball to accelerate after it is pushed. The ball will roll farther in 1 second than the ball in the original investigation.

B. *Mark the distance after 2 seconds* is incorrect because in 2 seconds the ball will roll a greater distance than in the original investigation. Additionally, the desire is to cause a ball to roll a shorter distance in 1 second, so changing the amount of time would not provide the correct data.

C. *Use a 1 N force* is correct because this is a smaller force applied to the same mass as in the original investigation. For any given object, a larger force causes a larger change in motion; therefore, a smaller force causes a smaller change in motion, and the ball will roll a shorter distance in the same amount of time of 1 second.

D. *Use a 1 kg ball* is incorrect because this is a smaller mass with the same force applied as in the original investigation. The greater the mass of the object, the greater the force needed to achieve the same change in motion. Therefore, the original ball with a mass of 12 kg would require more force than a ball with a mass of 1 kg to achieve the same change in motion (roll the same distance in 1 second). Since the force will be the same in both investigations, the ball with the mass of 1 kg will have a greater change in motion (roll a greater distance in 1 second) than the ball in the original investigation.

E. *Use a 20 N force* is incorrect because this is a greater force applied to the same mass as in the original investigation. For any given object, a larger force causes a larger change in motion; therefore, the ball will roll a greater distance in the same amount of time of 1 second.

F. *Use a 20 kg ball* is correct because this is a greater mass with the same force applied as in the original investigation. The greater the mass of the object, the greater the force needed to achieve the same change in motion. Therefore, the original ball with a mass of 12 kg would require less force than a ball with a mass of 20 kg to achieve the same change in motion (roll the same distance in 1 second). Since the force will be the same in both investigations, the ball with the mass of 20 kg will have a smaller change in motion (roll a shorter distance in 1 second) than the ball in the original investigation.

23. Use the rubric below to evaluate total points earned for this item. *[max point: 3]*

DCI, CCC - 3 Points	
Claims	The student is able to: 1. identify attractive electric forces (DCI); and 2. explain how distance between interacting objects affects the strength of electric forces (DCI); and 3. predict phenomena in a designed system using the cause-and-effect relationship between distance and the strength of interaction of two charged objects (CCC).
Evidence of Mastery of Disciplinary Core Ideas	1 point for correctly identifying the type of electric forces **Part 1:** One point is earned for concluding that balloon B could have a positive charge because of the attraction shown by the two balloons. Any of the following responses, or an equivalent, is acceptable. • Balloon B could have a positive charge because it is attracted to balloon A. • Balloon B could have a neutral charge because it is attracted to balloon A. Objects with no net charge can be attracted to a charged object if their charges are free to move and reorient themselves. 1 point for correctly explaining how distance affects the strength of electric forces **Part 2:** One point is earned for explaining that distance will weaken the electric force between the two balloons. The following response, or an equivalent, is acceptable. • The electric force between the balloons will decrease because electric force decreases as distance between objects increases.

Evidence of Mastery of Crosscutting Concepts	1 point for correctly describing the behavior of the balloons **Part 2:** One point is earned for predicting that balloon B will no longer hang at an angle because distance will decrease the attraction between two oppositely charged objects. The following response, or an equivalent, is acceptable. • Balloon B will hang straight down from the ceiling because balloon A will be too far away to attract it, and that attraction is what pulled balloon B to the left.

24. 1A. *55 N* is correct. If a roller coaster traveling 50 km/h crashes into the stopping device with a force of 55 N, the stopping device will exert 55 N of force on the roller coaster. For each action force, there is an equal and opposite reaction force.

2D. *Equal* is correct. The safety harness will apply an equal force to the passenger. According to Newton's third law of motion, for each action force, there is an equal and opposite reaction force. The action of the passenger on the safety harness will produce an equal reaction force from the safety harness on the passenger.

3G. *Opposite* is correct. According to Newton's third law of motion, for each action force, there is an equal and opposite reaction force. If the passenger pushes forward on the safety harness, the safety harness will press backward with the same amount of force, which keeps the passenger in his or her seat.

25. A. This is incorrect because the type of surface is the variable being tested in this experiment. Using another type of surface would add to the variation of the independent variable, so it would not be a controlled variable.

B. This is incorrect because the type of surface is the variable being tested in this experiment, so the smooth floor would be the independent variable, not a controlled variable.

C. This is correct because the type of surface is the variable being tested in this experiment. The same marbles used in the original experiment should be used as a control so Riley and Jessie can compare their new data to their original data.

D. This is incorrect because Riley and Jessie should gather the same data they gathered in the original experiment. However, the time it takes for the marbles to reach a certain distance is a dependent variable, not a controlled variable.

26. A. This statement is true. The distances of 0/25/50 cm are the references for the motion of the object in both investigations.

B. This statement is true. $F = m \cdot a$ The mass was measured in grams, and the acceleration in $\frac{cm}{s^2}$.

C. This statement is false. The distances were constant, and the time taken to reach those distance points was varied.

D. This statement is false. The distances were constant, and the time taken to reach those distance points was varied.

E. This statement is true. The four forces on the marbles are gravity, normal force, the force from the roll, and friction. The direction of these forces given in the stem would result in the motion described in the passage.

27. A. This is correct because applying more force to the large marble would give it a greater acceleration and cause it to reach the 50 cm mark faster than before, so it will reach the 50 cm mark at the same time as the smaller marble.

B. This is correct because reducing the initial acceleration of the small marble will cause it to reach the 50 cm mark more slowly than before, so it will reach the 50 cm mark at the same time as the larger marble.

C. This is incorrect because given the same force, the large marble will have a lower acceleration than the small marble, due to its larger mass. This would cause the large marble to arrive at the 50 cm mark after the small marble, as shown in the data tables in the passage.

D. This is incorrect because given the same force, two marbles of different mass will have different accelerations. Even though the second marble is now larger than it was before, the two masses are different and the marbles would arrive at the 50 cm mark at different times.

E. This is correct because if both marbles have the same mass and they are rolled with the same force, they will both arrive at the 50 cm mark at the same time.

28. **1C.** *Force* is correct for the first blank. To double the acceleration, Riley and Jessie must double the force. The acceleration of an object is directly proportional to the magnitude of the net force applied to the object.

2A. *Acceleration* is correct for the second blank. In this investigation, the acceleration is a dependent variable. The acceleration is dependent on the amount of force applied. If the force changes, the acceleration will also change.

3C. *Force* is correct for the third blank. In this investigation, Riley and Jessie are changing the force in order to test its effect on the acceleration of the marble, so force is the independent variable.

4D. *Mass* is correct for the fourth blank. In this investigation, Riley and Jessie are changing the force applied to the same small marble to test the effect of force on the acceleration of the marble. Because they are using the same marble every time, the mass of the marble is a controlled variable.

5B. *Distance* is correct for the fifth or sixth blank. To test their idea, Riley and Jessie should repeat the experiment and measure the distance and time. To determine whether doubling the force did indeed double the acceleration, the acceleration will need to be calculated. The distance traveled over a specific time is needed to make this calculation.

6E. *Time* is correct for the fifth or sixth blank. To test their idea, Riley and Jessie should repeat the experiment and measure the distance and time. To determine whether doubling the force did indeed double the acceleration, the acceleration will need to be calculated. The distance traveled over a specific time is needed to make this calculation.

29. Use the rubric below to evaluate total points earned for this item. *[max point: 3]*

DCI, SEP - 3 Points	
Claims	The student is able to: 1. analyze components of a scenario to predict motion in terms of acceleration (DCI); and 2. explain the logical connection between the investigation in the passage and the investigation described (SEP); and 3. describe a logical connection between the data and the purpose of the investigation (SEP).
Evidence of Mastery of Disciplinary Core Ideas	1 point for correctly comparing the accelerations **Part 1:** One point is earned for predicting that the golf ball will have a smaller acceleration than the table tennis ball because it has more mass. The following response, or an equivalent, is acceptable. • The golf ball will have a smaller acceleration than the table tennis ball because the golf ball has a greater mass.

Evidence of Mastery of Science and Engineering Practices	1 point for correctly comparing the investigations and explaining differences **Part 2:** One point is earned for comparing the independent variables in the two investigations and constructing a logical explanation of differences. The following response, or an equivalent, is acceptable. • The independent variable in the investigation in the passage is the mass of the marble. While the independent variable in this investigation is also the mass of the ball, the size of the diameter of the ball is also an independent variable being tested. The purpose of both experiments was to test the effect of mass on acceleration. However, the purpose of this new experiment was also to show that it is not size that affects the acceleration. 1 point for correctly explaining why a table tennis ball and a golf ball were used **Part 3:** One point is earned for explaining that the large and small marbles would not have produced valid data based on the purpose of the experiment. The following response, or an equivalent, is acceptable. • The purpose of this new experiment was to show that mass, not size, affects the acceleration. The table tennis ball and golf ball have approximately the same size but different masses. The marbles have different masses, but they also have different sizes, so they would not be useful in ruling out the effect of size on acceleration.

30. A. *1 N* is correct for the second scale because it has the shortest spring. The length of the spring indicates that the mass it is holding is the lightest, so the smallest upward force is required to equal the gravitational force on the mass.

B. *3 N* is correct for the third scale because its spring length is intermediate to the other two springs. The upward force required to equal the gravitational force is proportional to the mass being held by the spring.

C. *9 N* is correct for the first scale because it has the longest spring. The length of the spring indicates that the mass it is holding is the heaviest, so the largest upward force is required to equal the gravitational force on the mass.

31. A. This is correct because diagram A shows that magnetic fields create attraction between the unlike poles of two magnets.

B. This is incorrect because diagram B shows that unlike fields create repulsion.

C. This is incorrect because diagram C shows magnetic fields crossing, and they do not cross. They create forces that repel or attract each other, but they do not cross over.

D. This is incorrect because diagram D shows no attraction between the unlike poles of two magnets.

32. A. *The objects' masses are relatively small* is correct for the *gravitational attraction between Pascal and René* because gravity depends on mass. The relatively small masses of Pascal and René mean that the gravitational attraction between them is so small that it cannot be felt.

B. *The objects are very close together* is not used because although distance between objects is a factor in determining the gravitational attraction between them, it does not explain why the gravitational attraction between Pascal and Earth can be felt but the gravitational attraction between Pascal and René cannot.

C. *The objects' masses are the same* is not used because two objects having the same mass does not determine the gravitational attraction between them but rather how large their masses are.

D. *One object has a mass that is very large* is correct for the *gravitational attraction between Pascal and Earth* because Earth's mass is large enough for Pascal to experience significant gravitational attraction toward it.

E. *No gravitational attraction exists between these objects* is not used because all matter, regardless of the magnitude of the mass, has gravitational attraction to other objects.

33. **A.** This is correct because the billiard balls have the same mass, so when they collide, they experience the same acceleration in opposite directions. Because the acceleration is equal in magnitude, it is easier to demonstrate that each ball experiences the same force.

B. This is incorrect because the toy truck would exert the same force on the toy car as the toy car exerts on the truck. The acceleration of the toy truck and the toy car would be different, but the forces upon impact are equal.

C. This is incorrect because although the billiard balls should be chosen to prove Newton's third law, the fact that the balls have the same diameter does not affect the acceleration or force that should be controlled in order to prove that the forces exerted on each object during the collision are equal.

D. This is incorrect because any of the objects could have been used to show Newton's third law. However, because the billiard balls have the same mass, a collision between the two makes it easier to visualize equal but opposite action-reaction force pairs.

34. Use the rubric below to evaluate total points earned for this item. *[max point: 3]*

	DCI, SEP - 3 Points
Claims	The student is able to: 1. identify which objects must have the smallest and largest masses based on gravitational attractions (DCI); and 2. construct a written explanation for the relationship between mass and gravitational attraction (SEP); and 3. support an explanation using data given in the table (SEP).
Evidence of Mastery of Disciplinary Core Ideas	1 point for correctly ordering the objects **Part 1:** One point is earned for ordering the objects in terms of mass. The following response, or an equivalent, is acceptable. • Object B has the largest mass and object D has the smallest mass. Object C has a larger mass than D but a smaller mass than A.
Evidence of Mastery of Science and Engineering Practices	1 point for correctly explaining the relationship **Part 2:** One point is earned for explaining that the gravitational attraction between objects depends on their masses. The following response, or an equivalent, is acceptable. • The more massive the objects are, the greater the gravitational attraction between them. 1 point for correctly justifying the ordering **Part 3:** One point is earned for justifying the ordering of the objects in terms of mass with evidence from the table. The following response, or an equivalent, is acceptable. • The gravitational attraction is the largest between objects A and B and objects B and C, so object B must have the largest mass. The smallest gravitational attraction is between objects A and D and objects C and D, so object D must have the smallest mass. The gravitational attraction between C and D is the smallest, so C must have the next smallest mass other than object D, which means object A has a mass between that of objects B and C.

35. Use the rubric below to evaluate total points earned for this item. *[max point: 3]*

	DCI, CCC - 3 Points
Claims	The student is able to: 1. explain forces that act at a distance using a field (DCI); and 2. describe the force that results due to the orientation of two magnets (CCC); and 3. explain the effect of orientation of two magnets on the magnetic field and forces (CCC).

Evidence of Mastery of Disciplinary Core Ideas	1 point for correctly drawing a conclusion and explaining reasoning **Part 3:** One point is earned for determining that the needle is a magnet as well because of the effect of the magnetic field on the needles in Sam's observations. The following response, or an equivalent, is acceptable. • The compass needle must be a magnet, too, because Sam's observations show that the north end of the needle is always turned in the direction of the magnetic field lines.
Evidence of Mastery of Crosscutting Concepts	1 point for correctly describing the behavior of the magnets **Part 1:** One point is earned for describing that the magnets will be attracted to one another when opposite poles are brought close. The following response, or an equivalent, is acceptable. • The two magnets will move toward one another. 1 point for correctly explaining the effect on the magnetic field lines and the forces **Part 2:** One point for explaining how the position of the poles affects the shape of the magnetic field between two magnets and how this affects the attractive and repulsive forces. The following response, or an equivalent, is acceptable. • When opposite poles are close to each other, the magnetic field lines go directly from one pole to the other and the opposite poles attract. When like poles are close to each other, the magnetic field lines move away from each other and like poles repel.

36. A. The picture of a left arrow is correct for the *direction of Cart 2 before collision* because the mine carts are moving toward each other. It is also correct for the *direction of Cart 1 after collision* because the force acting on Cart 1 during the collision is in the direction pointing to the left.

B. The picture of a right arrow is correct for the *direction of Cart 1 before collision* because the mine carts are moving toward each other. It is also correct for the *direction of Cart 2 after collision* because the force acting on Cart 2 during the collision is in the direction pointing to the right.

C. *No motion* is not used because both mine carts are in motion before the collision and a force is applied to both during the collision, causing the mine carts to be in motion before and after the collision.

D. *Equal to 2 m/s* is correct for the *speed of Cart 1 before collision* and the *speed of Cart 2 before collision* because the stem states that the mine carts are moving toward each other at a speed of 2 m/s.

E. *Less than 2 m/s* is correct for the *speed of Cart 2 after collision* because the same force is applied to Carts 1 and 2 during the collision but Cart 2 has more mass.

F. *Greater than 2 m/s* is correct for the *speed of Cart 1 after collision* because the same force is applied to Carts 1 and 2 during the collision but Cart 1 has less mass.

37. A. *Tie a magnet to the ruler so it hangs over the edge of the workbench* is correct for *Step 4* because the magnet needs to be suspended from an inanimate object so that its response is not influenced by human movement.

B. *Insert one end of a ruler underneath the bottom textbook* is correct for *Step 2* because the ruler needs to be anchored before the magnet can be tied to it. Alternatively, this is correct for *Step 3* if *Tie a string in the middle of a bar magnet* is matched with *Step 2.*

C. *Touch one pole of a second magnet to the north pole of the hanging magnet* is not used because then Denise would not be investigating how forces act over a distance.

D. *Tie a string in the middle of a bar magnet* is correct for *Step 3* because the string must be tied to the magnet before the magnet can be tied to the ruler. Alternatively, this is correct for *Step 2* if *Insert one end of a ruler underneath the bottom textbook* is matched to *Step 3.*

E. *Hold one pole of a second magnet near the north pole of the hanging magnet* is correct for *Step 5* because Denise is investigating how the magnets exert force on each other over a distance. She will observe that the magnet will turn until the opposite pole of the hanging magnet aligns with the pole of the held magnet.

F. *Touch the other pole of a second magnet to the north pole of the hanging magnet* is not used because then Denise would not be investigating how forces act over a distance but whether opposites attract or repel.

G. *Hold the other pole of a second magnet near the north pole of the hanging magnet* is correct for *Step 6* because Denise is investigating how the magnets exert force on each other over a distance. She will observe that the magnet will again turn until the opposite pole of the hanging magnet aligns with the pole of the held magnet.

H. *Place a piece of paper between the magnets* is not used because paper does not affect the magnetic field, and paper is not affected by the field.

38. Use the rubric below to evaluate total points earned for this item. *[max point: 4]*

	DCI, CCC - 4 Points
Claims	Student is able to: 1. predict the outcome of the investigation using knowledge of gravitational attraction (DCI); and 2. explain the relationship between mass and gravitational attraction (DCI); and 3. use the weights as a model to represent the interaction of two masses on the gravity of the system (CCC); and 4. identify the data that need to be collected to demonstrate the relationship between mass and gravitational force (CCC).
Evidence of Mastery of Disciplinary Core Ideas	1 point for correctly predicting the outcome of the investigation **Part 3:** One point is earned for predicting that the bungee cord will stretch the most due to the heaviest mass. The following response, or an equivalent, is acceptable. • The heaviest mass will cause the bungee cord to stretch more than the lighter masses. 1 point for correctly explaining how the prediction demonstrates the relationship **Part 4:** One point is earned for explaining that the heaviest mass will stretch the bungee cord more because heavier objects have a greater gravitational attraction to Earth, and the gravitational attraction is proportional to mass so as the mass increases, so does the gravitational attraction. The following response, or an equivalent, is acceptable. • The prediction demonstrates the relationship between mass and gravitational attraction because gravitational attraction increases as mass increases.
Evidence of Mastery of Crosscutting Concepts	1 point for correctly designing the investigation **Part 1:** One point is earned for designing an investigation that would model the relationship between mass and gravitational force. The amount the bungee cord stretches can be related to the gravitational attraction between each mass and Earth. The following response, or an equivalent, is acceptable. • The students should tie a loop in the end of the bungee cord, if needed. Then they could hang each mass from the loop to see how much it stretches from gravity. 1 point for correctly identifying the data **Part 2:** One point is earned for identifying the data that need to be collected to demonstrate the relationship between mass and gravitational force. The following response, or an equivalent, is acceptable. • The length of the bungee cord should be measured and recorded with each mass attached it.

39. A. This is incorrect because Planet Y has more mass than Planet X because the mass of the students would not change and a greater gravitational attraction indicates greater mass of the planet. Therefore, the higher gravitational attraction of Planet Y on each student means that the mass of Planet Y is greater.

B. This is incorrect because gravitational attraction increases as the net mass of two objects increases. The mass of the students does not change, so the increase in gravitational attraction between the students and Planet Y compared with that between the students and Planet X must mean that Planet Y is more massive than Planet X.

C. This is correct because the data show the gravitational attraction between students and Planet Y is greater than that between the students and Planet X. Because the mass of the students would not change, the increase in gravitational attraction can be explained only if Planet Y is more massive than Planet X.

D. This is incorrect because the distance between Planet X and Planet Y is irrelevant. However, students may choose this answer because they know that gravitational attraction is dependent on the distance between two objects as well as the mass.

40. Use the rubric below to evaluate total points earned for this item. *[max point: 5]*

DCI, SEP, CCC - 5 points	
Claims	The student is able to: 1. explain the lengths of the spring using the relationship between gravitational attractions and mass (DCI); and 2. justify an argument supported by the evidence to support an explanation (SEP); and 3. explain how the experimental setup relates to mass and gravitational attraction (CCC).
Evidence of Mastery of Disciplinary Core Ideas	1 point for correctly explaining the differences in length **Part 1:** One point is earned for explaining that the length of the spring depends on the object's mass. The greater the object's mass, the greater the attractive force, which causes the spring to stretch farther. The following response, or an equivalent, is acceptable. • The springs stretch farther with greater mass because of gravity.
Evidence of Mastery of Science and Engineering Practices	2 points for correctly justifying and explaining the order using data **Part 3:** One point is earned for justifying the students' order for the objects. The following response, or an equivalent, is acceptable. • The students have correctly ordered the objects from heaviest to lightest. **Part 3:** One point is earned for using the data to support the reasoning behind the order. The following response, or an equivalent, is acceptable. • The data support their reasoning because the bag of plastic blocks stretches the spring the most, so it must have the greatest mass. The pack of index cards stretches the spring second most, so it must be less massive than the bag of plastic blocks but more massive than the deck of playing cards. The toy car stretches the spring the least, so it must be the least massive.
Evidence of Mastery of Crosscutting Concepts	2 points for correctly explaining how the experimental setup relates mass to gravitational attraction **Part 2:** One point is earned for explaining that the gravitational attraction is directly proportional to the object's mass. The following response, or an equivalent, is acceptable. • Each of the objects is attracted to Earth due to gravity so objects with more mass have more gravitational attraction. **Part 2:** One point is earned for explaining how gravitational attraction relates to the differences in the length of the spring. The following response, or an equivalent, is acceptable. • The stronger the gravitational attraction, the more the spring stretches.

End-of-Module Test B – Forces, Motion, & Fields

Item Analysis		
Item #	**Standards**	**DOK**
1	MS-PS2-2, DCI.MS-PS2.A.3	1
2	MS-PS2-3, DCI.MS-PS2.B.1, SEP.MS.A.2	1
3	MS-PS2-5, DCI.MS-PS2.B.3	1

4	MS-PS2-4, DCI.MS-PS2.B.2	2
5	MS-PS2-5, DCI.MS-PS2.B.3	2
6	MS-PS2-4, DCI.MS-PS2.B.2, SEP.MS.G.1	2
7	MS-PS2-4, DCI.MS-PS2.B.2	2
8	MS-PS2-3, DCI.MS-PS2.B.1	2
9	MS-PS2-2, DCI.MS-PS2.A.2, SEP.MS.C.3	2
10	MS-PS2-1, DCI.MS-PS2.A.1, SEP.MS.F.4	2
11	MS-PS2-1, DCI.MS-PS2.A.1	2
12	MS-PS2-3, DCI.MS-PS2.B.1	2
13	MS-PS2-5, DCI.MS-PS2.B.3, SEP.MS.C.2	2
14	MS-PS2-4, DCI.MS-PS2.B.2, SEP.NOS.MS.B.1	3
15	MS-PS2-3, DCI.MS-PS2.B.1, SEP.MS.A.2	2
16	MS-PS2-3, DCI.MS-PS2.B.1, CCC.MS.B.2	2
17	MS-PS2-5, DCI.MS-PS2.B.3, CCC.MS.B.2	2
18	MS-PS2-1, DCI.MS-PS2.A.1	2
19	MS-PS2-1, DCI.MS-PS2.A.1, SEP.MS.F.4	2
20	MS-PS2-1, DCI.MS-PS2.A.1, CCC.MS.D.2	2
21	MS-PS2-1, DCI.MS-PS2.A.1	2
22	MS-PS2-2, DCI.MS-PS2.A.2, SEP.NOS.MS.B.1	3
23	MS-PS2-3, DCI.MS-PS2.B.1, CCC.MS.B.2	2
24	MS-PS2-1, DCI.MS-PS2.A.1, CCC.STSE.MS.B.2	2
25	MS-PS2-2, DCI.MS-PS2.A.2, SEP.MS.C.3	1
26	MS-PS2-2, DCI.MS-PS2.A.3	2
27	MS-PS2-2, DCI.MS-PS2.A.2	2
28	MS-PS2-2, DCI.MS-PS2.A.2, SEP.MS.C.3	2
29	MS-PS2-2, DCI.MS-PS2.A.2, SEP.NOS.MS.B.1	3
30	MS-PS2-4, DCI.MS-PS2.B.2, CCC.MS.D.2	2
31	MS-PS2-5, DCI.MS-PS2.B.3	2
32	MS-PS2-4, DCI.MS-PS2.B.2	3
33	MS-PS2-1, DCI.MS-PS2.A.1, SEP.MS.F.4	3
34	MS-PS2-4, DCI.MS-PS2.B.2, SEP.MS.G.1	3
35	MS-PS2-5, DCI.MS-PS2.B.3, CCC.MS.B.2	3
36	MS-PS2-1, DCI.MS-PS2.A.1, CCC.MS.D.2	3
37	MS-PS2-5, DCI.MS-PS2.B.3, SEP.MS.C.2	3
38	MS-PS2-4, DCI.MS-PS2.B.2, CCC.MS.D.2	3
39	MS-PS2-4, DCI.MS-PS2.B.2, SEP.MS.G.1	3
40	MS-PS2-4, DCI.MS-PS2.B.2, SEP.MS.G.1, CCC.MS.D.2	3

1. **1A.** *Sideways unbalanced force* is correct because an unbalanced force is required to move an object at rest.

2D. *Newtons* is correct because it is the unit used to describe force according to the International System of Units (SI Units).

2. A. This is correct because this question would lead to a practical experiment, with an independent and dependent variable, testing the effect on the strength of the electromagnet, which fulfills the purpose stated.

B. This is incorrect because it does not fulfill the purpose stated to test the magnitude of the force produced. The number of times the wire is wrapped around the nail does affect the strength of the force and it may be a question that needs to be asked while setting up the experiment relating to the purpose. However, it does not directly address a factor that could affect the magnitude of the force.

C. This is incorrect because it would not lead to a practical experiment and it does not address the purpose stated to test the magnitude of the force produced. While this is a question that should be asked while designing the experiment, it does not involve an independent and dependent variable in order to set up a practical experiment. Also, it relates to safety rather than determining what affects the magnitude of the force.

3. A. *Repel* is correct for the first diagram and *The magnets will...* because magnets can interact at a distance, and like poles repel.

B. *Attract* is correct for the second diagram and *The magnets will...* because magnets can interact at a distance, and opposite poles attract.

C. *A field exists between the magnets* is correct for the first and second diagrams and *because...* because forces that act at a distance can be explained by fields that extend through space. Both sets of magnets will interact even though they are not touching because a magnetic field exists between them.

D. *Electricity exists between the magnets* is not used because while electric fields are also an example of forces that act at a distance, the examples given here are of magnetic fields.

4. The order should be from top to bottom D, B, A, C because gravitational attraction is proportional to mass, so as mass increases, the gravitational attraction increases. Object D shows the smallest gravitational attraction to the fifth object, so it must have the smallest mass. Objects B and A show the second and third largest gravitational attractions to the fifth object, so they must have the second and third largest masses, respectively. Object C shows the largest gravitational attraction to the fifth object, so it must have the largest mass of the four objects.

5. A. *False* is correct because the direction of the electric field is outward away from the positive charge and inward toward the negative charge.

B. *True* is correct because the positive and negative charges are closest together at this point.

C. *False* is correct because the balls move toward each other and have opposite charges, so they are attracted to one another, not repelled.

6. 1B. *Incorrect* is correct because objects B and D will have the weakest gravitational attraction because they are the least massive objects in the table.

2D. *Increases as the total mass of the objects increases* is correct because gravitational attraction is directly dependent on the mass of both objects. The larger the objects' masses, the stronger the gravitational attraction between them.

7. The number list should be 2, 1, 3. The gravitational force between the center ball and the blue ball is the greatest, followed by the red ball and then the yellow ball. The magnitude of the gravitational attraction between two objects depends on their masses, so the larger the gravitational attraction, the more total mass must be present.

8. **A.** *The force of the electromagnet would increase* is correct for *Wrap the wire around the nail nine times instead of eight* because increasing the number of wraps of wire around the nail increases the magnitude of the magnetic strength delivered to the iron core. Since the size of the force depends on the magnitude of the magnetic strength, the force of the electromagnet increases with an increased number of turns of the wire around the core.

   B. *The force of the electromagnet would decrease* is correct for *Replace the nail with a plastic straw of the same size* because the size of electromagnetic forces depends on the magnitude of magnetic strength. By removing the iron core of the electromagnet, the magnetic strength decreases significantly, decreasing the electromagnetic force.

   C. *The force of the electromagnet would stay the same* is not used because both scenarios described will result in a change in the force of the electromagnet.

9. Use the rubric below to evaluate total points earned for this item. *[max point: 2]*

DCI, SEP - 2 Points	
Claims	The student is able to: 1. describe that a larger force will cause a larger change in motion (DCI); and 2. identify the independent and dependent variables in an investigational design (SEP).
Evidence of Mastery of Disciplinary Core Ideas	1 point for correctly describing Newton's second law **Part 2:** One point is earned for describing that the setup shows that increasing the force on an object will cause an increased change in motion. The following response, or an equivalent, is acceptable. • This setup could show that increasing the force on the cart would cause the cart to move faster.
Evidence of Mastery of Science and Engineering Practices	1 point for correctly identifying the independent and dependent variables in the investigation **Part 1:** One point is earned for identifying reasonable independent and dependent variables based on the investigation. One of the following responses, or an equivalent, is acceptable. • The force applied by the hanging mass is the independent variable because it is what Anderson is changing in the experiment. The acceleration of the cart is the dependent variable because it changes based on the force that's applied to the cart. • The mass of the hanging object is the independent variable because it is what Anderson is changing in the experiment. The acceleration of the cart is the dependent variable because it changes based on the mass of the hanging object. • The mass of the hanging object is the independent variable because it is what Anderson is changing in the experiment. The force on the cart from the mass is the dependent variable because it changes based on the mass of the hanging object.

10. Use the rubric below to evaluate total points earned for this item. *[max point: 1]*

DCI Only - 1 Point	
Claims	The student is able to show that the force exerted by one object on a second object is equal in strength to the force that the second object exerts on the first but in the opposite direction (DCI).
Evidence of Mastery of Disciplinary Core Ideas	1 point for correctly using Newton's third law to draw arrows in the "during the collision" image **Part 1:** One point is earned for drawing arrows of equal sizes pointing toward each other only during the collision. The following response, or an equivalent, is acceptable. **Before the Collision** 2 m/s 0 m/s **During the Collision** **After the Collision** 0 m/s 2 m/s

11. A. This is incorrect because the plan does not mention the acceleration of the spacecraft or meteor, so it cannot be assumed. If there was acceleration after the collision, then it would depend upon the mass of each object, which cannot be assumed either. Additionally, Newton's third law does not mention the acceleration of objects.

B. This is correct because Newton's third law states that for any pair of interacting objects, the force exerted by the first object on the second object is equal in strength to the force that the second object exerts on the first, but in the opposite direction.

C. This is incorrect because Newton's third law states that for any pair of interacting objects, the force exerted by the first object on the second object is equal in strength to the force that the second object exerts on the first, but in the opposite direction. The forces would not be exerted in the same direction.

D. This is correct because Newton's third law states that for any pair of interacting objects, the force exerted by the first object on the second object is equal in strength to the force that the second object exerts on the first.

12. A. This is correct because the magnetic field generated by an electromagnet depends on the current in the electromagnet.

B. This is incorrect because static electricity is not created when the magnitude of the current increases.

C. This is incorrect because polarity does not change when the magnitude of the current increases.

13. **A.** *Book between magnet and paper clip* is correct for *to determine whether a magnetic field can act through thin or thick materials* because materials of the same type but different thicknesses should be tested. The book is thick, whereas a paper napkin is thin.

B. *Aluminum foil between magnet and paper clip* is correct for *to determine whether a magnetic field can act through different metals* because different types of nonmagnetic metals should be placed between the magnet and the paper clip. *Aluminum foil between magnet and paper clip* is also correct for *to determine whether a magnetic field can act through aluminum with different types of magnets* because the purpose involves testing by placing aluminum between the objects interacting in the magnetic field.

C. *Copper sheet between magnet and paper clip* is correct for *to determine whether a magnetic field can act through different metals* because different types of nonmagnetic metals should be placed between the paper clip and magnet to determine whether a magnetic field can act through metal.

14. Use the rubric below to evaluate total points earned for this item. *[max point: 3]*

DCI, SEP - 3 Points	
Claims	The student is able to: 1. compare masses using knowledge that the gravitational force between two objects is dependent on the masses of the objects (DCI); and 2. make logical and conceptual connections between evidence and explanations (SEP).
Evidence of Mastery of Disciplinary Core Ideas	1 point for correctly comparing the masses **Part 2:** One point is earned for concluding that B must be more massive than C because the gravitational attraction between A and B is greater than the gravitational attraction between A and C. The following response, or an equivalent, is acceptable. • The gravitational attraction between objects A and B is greater than the attraction between objects A and C. This means that object B must be more massive than object C.
Evidence of Mastery of Science and Engineering Practices	2 points for correctly explaining the difference in gravitational attraction **Part 1:** Two points are earned for using the data given to explain that the total masses of objects A and B must be different from that of objects A and C because the gravitational attractions differ even though they are the same distance apart. The following response, or an equivalent, is acceptable. • Objects A and B have a larger gravitational attraction than objects A and C even though they are the same distance apart so the total masses must be different.

15. **A.** *Not relevant* is correct because it is the rod's rotation that generates the electric current, which is not dependent upon the length of the rod.

B. *Relevant* is correct because the greater the magnetic field is, the more electric current it can generate.

C. *Not relevant* is correct because the wire carries the electric current to the light bulb regardless of how close it is to the generator.

16. **A.** This is correct because doubling the number of magnets increases the magnetic field, which increases the force on the wires that make up the rotor and causes the rotor to spin faster.

B. This is incorrect because if the magnetic field were reversed, the rotor would still spin, but it would spin in the opposite direction.

C. This is incorrect because the number of magnets affects the strength of the magnetic field. A stronger magnetic field increases the force on the rotor, causing the rotor to spin faster.

17. Use the rubric below to evaluate total points earned for this item. *[max point: 3]*

<table>
<tr><th colspan="2">DCI, CCC - 3 Points</th></tr>
<tr><td>Claims</td><td>The student is able to:
1. draw the electric field between two sets of two charged objects (DCI); and
2. show how the charge of the objects determines the type of force (attract/repel) (CCC); and
3. show how distance between charged particles affects the shape of the field between two objects (CCC).</td></tr>
<tr><td>Evidence of Mastery of Disciplinary Core Ideas</td><td>1 point for correctly drawing electric field lines
Part 1: One point is earned for drawing electric field lines that do not cross. The following response, or an equivalent, is acceptable.</td></tr>
<tr><td>Evidence of Mastery of Crosscutting Concepts</td><td>1 point for correctly showing how the distance between the charges affects the shape of the field between the two objects
Part 2: One point is earned for showing that the field lines are continuous and move between the two charges from one charge to the other and that the particles farther apart will have field lines that are spaced farther apart. The following response, or an equivalent, is acceptable.
1 point for correctly showing how the charge of the objects determines the type of force (attract/repel)
Part 3: One point is earned for drawing arrows pointing away from the positive charge and toward the negative charge. The following response, or an equivalent, is acceptable. 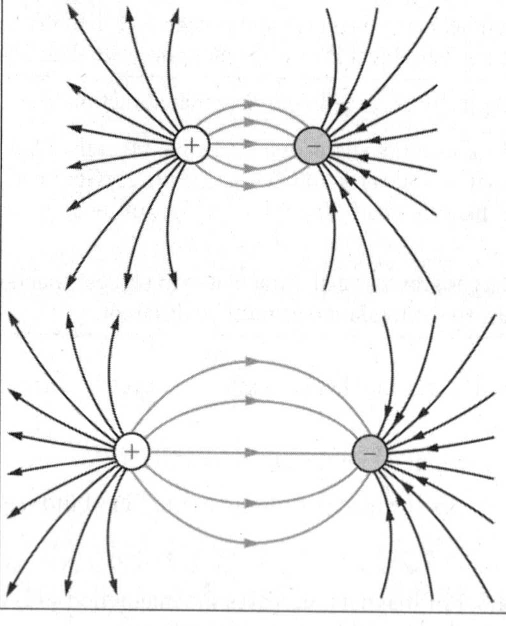
+ −
+ −</td></tr>
</table>

18. 1B. *Speed* is the correct answer because the labels under each car indicate the same speed: 2 miles per hour (mph). Not enough information is given in the diagram to know each car's acceleration rate.

2C. *Equal to* is the correct answer because the cars represent action and reaction forces. According to Newton's third law, for every action there is an equal and opposite reaction.

3E. *Opposite* is the correct answer because the cars represent action and reaction forces. According to Newton's third law, for every action there is an equal and opposite reaction.

4C. *Equal to* is the correct answer because an increase in the mass/size of car A will not change the fact that the forces of the two cars when they hit each other will be equal (and opposite), by Newton's third law.

19. A. This image *Does Not Illustrate Newton's Third Law* as it relates to collisions. Although it is true that there is an action-reaction force pair any time an object is on a surface (the girl pushes down on the ice, while the ice pushes up on the girl), the girl is not colliding with another object. This demonstration would not be effective at explaining Newton's third law.

B. This image *Illustrates Newton's Third Law* as it relates to collisions. The hockey puck on the left exerts a force on the hockey puck on the right. The hockey puck on the right exerts an equal force in the opposite direction on the hockey puck on the left. This collision clearly shows an action-reaction force pair.

20. A. This is incorrect because this is the description for cart B with incorrect speeds. Before the collision, cart A is moving toward cart B, which means cart A is moving to the right at 0.5 m/s. The force from cart B pushing in the opposite direction will cause cart A to move backward. However, if cart A started out moving to the right, it should have ended up moving to the left at a speed greater than 0.5 m/s.

B. This is correct because cart A starts out moving toward cart B, so it starts out moving to the right 0.5 m/s. Newton's third law states that for any pair of interacting objects, the force exerted by the first object on the second object is equal in strength to the force that the second object exerts on the first, but in the opposite direction. When they collide, cart A exerts a force to the right, while cart B exerts a force to the left, but at a speed greater than 0.5 m/s. This force to the left causes cart A to move to the left at a speed greater than its speed before the collision.

C. This is incorrect because cart A should be moving to the left after the collision and at a speed greater than 0.5 m/s. While it is true that cart A moves to the right before the collision, it is moving at 0.5 m/s and cart B is moving to the left at 1.0 m/s. When the cars collide, they push on each other with equal but opposite forces. The force from cart B causes cart A to change direction and move backward, toward the left at a speed greater than its speed before the collision.

21. A. This statement is *True* because Newton's third law states that for any pair of interacting objects, the force exerted by the first object on the second object is equal in strength to the force that the second object exerts on the first but in the opposite direction. The tree is exerting a downward force against the ground, due to gravity, so the ground exerts an equal force upward against the tree.

B. This statement is *False* because Newton's third law states that for any pair of interacting objects, the force exerted by the first object on the second object is equal in strength to the force that the second object exerts on the first but in the opposite direction.

C. This statement is *False* because Newton's third law states that for any pair of interacting objects, the force exerted by the first object on the second object is equal in strength to the force that the second object exerts on the first but in the opposite direction. Therefore, the boy is exerting a force against the tree and the tree's force is felt in the opposite direction against the boy.

22. A. *Use a 1 N force* is correct because this is a smaller force applied to the same mass as in the original investigation. For any given object, a larger force causes a larger change in motion; therefore, a smaller force causes a smaller change in motion, and the ball will roll a shorter distance in the same amount of time of 1 second.

B. *Use a 1 kg ball* is incorrect because this is a smaller mass with the same force applied as in the original investigation. The greater the mass of the object, the greater the force needed to achieve the same change in motion. Therefore, the original ball with a mass of 12 kg would require more force than a ball with a mass of 1 kg to achieve the same change in motion (roll the same distance in 1 second). Since the force will be the same in both investigations, the ball with the mass of 1 kg will have a greater change in motion (roll a greater distance in 1 second) than the ball in the original investigation.

C. *Use a 20 N force* is incorrect because this is a greater force applied to the same mass as in the original investigation. For any given object, a larger force causes a larger change in motion; therefore, the ball will roll a greater distance in the same amount of time of 1 second.

D. *Use a 20 kg ball* is correct because this is a greater mass with the same force applied as in the original investigation. The greater the mass of the object, the greater the force needed to achieve the same change in motion. Therefore, the original ball with a mass of 12 kg would require less force than a ball with a mass of 20 kg to achieve the same change in motion (roll the same distance in 1 second). Since the force will be the same in both investigations, the ball with the mass of 20 kg will have a smaller change in motion (roll a shorter distance in 1 second) than the ball in the original investigation.

23. Use the rubric below to evaluate total points earned for this item. *[max point: 3]*

DCI, CCC - 3 Points	
Claims	The student is able to: 1. identify attractive electric forces (DCI); and 2. predict phenomena in a designed system using the cause-and-effect relationship between distance and the strength of interaction of two charged objects (CCC).
Evidence of Mastery of Disciplinary Core Ideas	2 points for correctly identifying the type of electric forces **Part 1:** Two points are earned for concluding that balloon B could have a positive charge because of the attraction shown by the two balloons. The following response, or an equivalent, is acceptable. • Balloon B could have a positive charge because it is attracted to balloon A. • Balloon B could have a neutral charge because it is attracted to balloon A. Objects with no net charge can be attracted to a charged object if their charges are free to move and reorient themselves
Evidence of Mastery of Crosscutting Concepts	1 point for correctly describing the behavior of the balloons **Part 2:** One point is earned for predicting that balloon B will no longer hang at an angle because distance will decrease the attraction between two oppositely charged objects. The following response, or an equivalent, is acceptable. • Balloon B will hang straight down from the ceiling because balloon A will be too far away to attract it, and that attraction is what pulled balloon B to the left.

24. 1A. *55 N* is correct. If a roller coaster traveling 50 km/h crashes into the stopping device with a force of 55 N, the stopping device will exert 55 N of force on the roller coaster. For each action force, there is an equal and opposite reaction force.

2C. *Equal* is correct. The safety harness will apply an equal force to the passenger. According to Newton's third law of motion, for each action force, there is an equal and opposite reaction force. The action of the passenger on the safety harness will produce an equal reaction force from the safety harness on the passenger.

3F. *Opposite* is correct. According to Newton's third law of motion, for each action force, there is an equal and opposite reaction force. If the passenger pushes forward on the safety harness, the safety harness will press backward with the same amount of force, which keeps the passenger in his or her seat.

25. A. This is incorrect because the type of surface is the variable being tested in this experiment. Using another type of surface would add to the variation of the independent variable, so it would not be a controlled variable.

B. This is incorrect because the type of surface is the variable being tested in this experiment, so the smooth floor would be the independent variable, not a controlled variable.

C. This is correct because the type of surface is the variable being tested in this experiment. The same marbles used in the original experiment should be used as a control so Riley and Jessie can compare their new data to their original data.

26. A. This statement is true. The distances of 0/25/50 cm are the references for the motion of the object in both investigations.

B. This statement is true. $F = m \cdot a$ The mass was measured in grams, and the acceleration in acceleration in $\frac{cm}{s^2}$.

C. This statement is false. The distances were constant, and the time taken to reach those distance points was varied.

D. This statement is true. The four forces on the marbles are gravity, normal force, the force from the roll, and friction. The direction of these forces given in the stem would result in the motion described in the passage.

27. A. This is correct because applying more force to the large marble would give it a greater acceleration and cause it to reach the 50 cm mark faster than before, so it will reach the 50 cm mark at the same time as the smaller marble.

B. This is correct because reducing the initial acceleration of the small marble will cause it to reach the 50 cm mark more slowly than before, so it will reach the 50 cm mark at the same time as the larger marble.

C. This is incorrect because given the same force, the large marble will have a lower acceleration than the small marble, due to its larger mass. This would cause the large marble to arrive at the 50 cm mark after the small marble, as shown in the data tables in the passage.

D. This is correct because if both marbles have the same mass and they are rolled with the same force, they will both arrive at the 50 cm mark at the same time.

28. 1C. *Force* is correct for the first blank. To double the acceleration, Riley and Jessie must double the force. The acceleration of an object is directly proportional to the magnitude of the net force applied to the object.

2A. *Acceleration* is correct for the second blank. In this investigation, the acceleration is a dependent variable. The acceleration is dependent on the amount of force applied. If the force changes, the acceleration will also change.

3C. *Force* is correct for the third blank. In this investigation, Riley and Jessie are changing the force in order to test its effect on the acceleration of the marble, so force is the independent variable.

4D. *Mass* is correct for the fourth blank. In this investigation, Riley and Jessie are changing the force applied to the same small marble to test the effect of force on the acceleration of the marble. Because they are using the same marble every time, the mass of the marble is a controlled variable.

5B. *Distance* is correct for the fifth blank. To test their idea, Riley and Jessie should repeat the experiment and measure the distance and time. To determine whether doubling the force did indeed double the acceleration, the acceleration will need to be calculated. The distance traveled over a specific time is needed to make this calculation.

29. Use the rubric below to evaluate total points earned for this item. *[max point: 3]*

DCI, SEP - 3 Points	
Claims	The student is able to: 1. analyze components of a scenario to predict motion in terms of acceleration (DCI); and 2. explain the logical connection between the investigation in the passage and the investigation described (SEP).
Evidence of Mastery of Disciplinary Core Ideas	1 point for correctly comparing the accelerations **Part 1:** One point is earned for predicting that the golf ball will have a smaller acceleration than the table tennis ball because it has more mass. The following response, or an equivalent, is acceptable. • The golf ball will have a smaller acceleration than the table tennis ball because the golf ball has a greater mass.

Evidence of Mastery of Science and Engineering Practices	2 points for correctly comparing the investigations and explaining differences **Part 2:** Two points are earned for comparing the independent variables in the two investigations and constructing a logical explanation of differences. The following response, or an equivalent, is acceptable. • The independent variable in the investigation in the passage is the mass of the marble. While the independent variable in this investigation is also the mass of the ball, the size of the diameter of the ball is also an independent variable being tested. The purpose of both experiments was to test the effect of mass on acceleration. However, the purpose of this new experiment was also to show that it is not size that affects the acceleration.

30. A. *1 N* is correct for the second scale because it has the shortest spring. The length of the spring indicates that the mass it is holding is the lightest, so the smallest upward force is required to equal the gravitational force on the mass.

B. *3 N* is correct for the third scale because its spring length is intermediate to the other two springs. The upward force required to equal the gravitational force is proportional to the mass being held by the spring.

C. *9 N* is correct for the first scale because it has the longest spring. The length of the spring indicates that the mass it is holding is the heaviest, so the largest upward force is required to equal the gravitational force on the mass.

31. A. This is correct because diagram A shows that magnetic fields create attraction between the unlike poles of two magnets.

B. This is incorrect because diagram B shows that unlike fields create repulsion.

C. This is incorrect because diagram C shows magnetic fields crossing, and they do not cross. They create forces that repel or attract each other, but they do not cross over.

32. A. *The objects' masses are relatively small* is correct for the *gravitational attraction between Pascal and René* because gravity depends on mass. The relatively small masses of Pascal and René mean that the gravitational attraction between them is so small that it cannot be felt.

B. *The objects are very close together* is not used because although distance between objects is a factor in determining the gravitational attraction between them, it does not explain why the gravitational attraction between Pascal and Earth can be felt but the gravitational attraction between Pascal and René cannot.

C. *One object has a mass that is very large* is correct for the *gravitational attraction between Pascal and Earth* because Earth's mass is large enough for Pascal to experience significant gravitational attraction toward it.

D. *No gravitational attraction exists between these objects* is not used because all matter, regardless of the magnitude of the mass, has gravitational attraction to other objects.

33. A. This is correct because the billiard balls have the same mass, so when they collide, they experience the same acceleration in opposite directions. Because the acceleration is equal in magnitude, it is easier to demonstrate that each ball experiences the same force.

B. This is incorrect because the toy truck would exert the same force on the toy car as the toy car exerts on the truck. The acceleration of the toy truck and the toy car would be different, but the forces upon impact are equal.

C. This is incorrect because although the billiard balls should be chosen to prove Newton's third law, the fact that the balls have the same diameter does not affect the acceleration or force that should be controlled in order to prove that the forces exerted on each object during the collision are equal.

34. Use the rubric below to evaluate total points earned for this item. *[max point: 3]*

DCI, SEP - 3 Points	
Claims	The student is able to: 1. identify which objects must have the smallest and largest masses based on gravitational attractions (DCI); and 2. construct a written explanation for the relationship between mass and gravitational supported by the data given in the table (SEP).
Evidence of Mastery of Disciplinary Core Ideas	1 point for correctly ordering the objects **Part 1:** Onc point is carned for ordering the objects in terms of mass. The following response, or an equivalent, is acceptable. • Object B has the largest mass and object D has the smallest mass. Object C has a larger mass than D but a smaller mass than A.
Evidence of Mastery of Science and Engineering Practices	2 points for correctly justifying the order using the relationship **Part 2:** Two points are earned for explaining the relationship between mass and gravitational attraction and connecting this to the data in the table. The following response, or an equivalent, is acceptable. • The gravitational attraction between objects depends on their masses. The more massive the objects are, the greater the gravitational attraction between them. In the table, the larger the gravitational attractions must have more massive objects involved.

35. Use the rubric below to evaluate total points earned for this item. *[max point: 3]*

DCI, CCC - 3 Points	
Claims	The student is able to: 1. explain forces that act at a distance using a field (DCI); and 2. explain the effect of orientation of two magnets on the magnetic field and forces (CCC).
Evidence of Mastery of Disciplinary Core Ideas	2 points for correctly drawing a conclusion and explaining reasoning **Part 2:** Two points are earned for determining that the needle is a magnet as well because of the effect of the magnetic field on the needles in Sam's observations. The following response, or an equivalent, is acceptable. • The compass needle must be a magnet, too, because Sam's observations show that the north end of the needle is always turned in the direction of the magnetic field lines.
Evidence of Mastery of Crosscutting Concepts	1 point for correctly describing the behavior of the magnets **Part 1:** One point is earned for describing that the magnets will be attracted to one another when opposite poles are brought close. The following response, or an equivalent, is acceptable. • The two magnets will move toward one another.

36. A. The picture of a left arrow is correct for the *direction of Cart 2 before collision* because the mine carts are moving toward each other. It is also correct for the *direction of Cart 1 after collision* because the force acting on Cart 1 during the collision is in the direction pointing to the left.

B. The picture of a right arrow is correct for the *direction of Cart 1 before collision* because the mine carts are moving toward each other. It is also correct for the *direction of Cart 2 after collision* because the force acting on Cart 2 during the collision is in the direction pointing to the right.

C. *Equal to 2 m/s* is correct for the *speed of Cart 1 before collision* and the *speed of Cart 2 before collision* because the stem states that the mine carts are moving toward each other at a speed of 2 m/s.

D. *Less than 2 m/s* is correct for the *speed of Cart 2 after collision* because the same force is applied to Carts 1 and 2 during the collision but Cart 2 has more mass.

E. *Greater than 2 m/s* is correct for the *speed of Cart 1 after collision* because the same force is applied to Carts 1 and 2 during the collision but Cart 1 has less mass.

37. A. *Tie a magnet to the ruler so it hangs over the edge of the workbench* is correct for *Step 3* because the magnet needs to be suspended from an inanimate object so that its response is not influenced by human movement.

B. *Insert one end of a ruler underneath the bottom textbook* is correct for *Step 2* because the ruler needs to be anchored before the magnet can be tied to it.

C. *Touch one pole of a second magnet to the north pole of the hanging magnet* is not used because then Denise would not be investigating how forces act over a distance.

D. *Hold one pole of a second magnet near the north pole of the hanging magnet* is correct for *Step 4* because Denise is investigating how the magnets exert force on each other over a distance. She will observe that the magnet will turn until the opposite pole of the hanging magnet aligns with the pole of the held magnet.

E. *Touch the other pole of a second magnet to the north pole of the hanging magnet* is not used because then Denise would not be investigating how forces act over a distance but whether opposites attract or repel.

F. *Hold the other pole of a second magnet near the north pole of the hanging magnet* is correct for *Step 5* because Denise is investigating how the magnets exert force on each other over a distance. She will observe that the magnet will again turn until the opposite pole of the hanging magnet aligns with the pole of the held magnet.

38. Use the rubric below to evaluate total points earned for this item. *[max point: 4]*

DCI, CCC - 4 Points	
Claims	Student is able to: 1. explain the relationship between mass and gravitational attraction (DCI); and 2. use the weights as a model to represent the interaction of two masses on the gravity of the system (CCC).
Evidence of Mastery of Disciplinary Core Ideas	2 points for correctly explaining how this demonstrates the relationship between mass and gravitational attraction **Part 2:** Two points are earned for explaining that the heaviest mass will stretch the bungee cord more because heavier objects have a greater gravitational attraction to Earth, and the gravitational attraction is proportional to mass so as the mass increases, so does the gravitational attraction. The following response, or an equivalent, is acceptable. • The heaviest mass will stretch the bungee cord more because heavier objects have a greater gravitational attraction. Gravitational attraction increases as mass increases.
Evidence of Mastery of Crosscutting Concepts	2 points for correctly identifying the data that need to be collected **Part 1:** Two points are earned for identifying the data that need to be collected to demonstrate the relationship between mass and gravitational force. The following response, or an equivalent, is acceptable. • The length of the bungee cord should be measured and recorded with each mass attached it.

39. A. This is incorrect because Planet Y has more mass than Planet X because the mass of the students would not change and a greater gravitational attraction indicates greater mass of the planet. Therefore, the higher gravitational attraction of Planet Y on each student means that the mass of Planet Y is greater.

B. This is correct because the data show the gravitational attraction between students and Planet Y is greater than that between the students and Planet X. Because the mass of the students would not change, the increase in gravitational attraction can be explained only if Planet Y is more massive than Planet X.

C. This is incorrect because the distance between Planet X and Planet Y is irrelevant. However, students may choose this answer because they know that gravitational attraction is dependent on the distance between two objects as well as the mass.

40. Use the rubric below to evaluate total points earned for this item. *[max point: 5]*

DCI, SEP, CCC - 5 points	
Claims	The student is able to: 1. explain the lengths of the spring using the relationship between gravitational attractions and mass (DCI); and 2. justify an argument supported by the evidence to support an explanation (SEP); and 3. describe how the experimental setup relates to mass and gravitational attraction (CCC).
Evidence of Mastery of Disciplinary Core Ideas	1 point for correctly explaining the differences in length **Part 1:** One point is earned for explaining that the length of the spring depends on the object's mass. The greater the object's mass, the greater the attractive force, which causes the spring to stretch farther. The following response, or an equivalent, is acceptable. • The springs stretch farther with greater mass because of gravity.
Evidence of Mastery of Science and Engineering Practices	2 points for correctly justifying a claim using data **Part 3:** Two points are earned for justifying the students' order for the objects using the data. The following response, or an equivalent, is acceptable. • The students have ordered the objects from largest to smallest mass because it is the same as the order of the objects from the largest to the smallest number in the table.
Evidence of Mastery of Crosscutting Concepts	2 points for correctly describing the relationship **Part 2:** Two points earned for describing that the gravitational attraction and length of the spring is directly proportional to the object's mass. The following response, or an equivalent, is acceptable. • Objects that stretch the spring farther have more mass and more gravitational attraction.